1806 1807 1808 1809 1810 1811 1812 1813 1814 1815 181

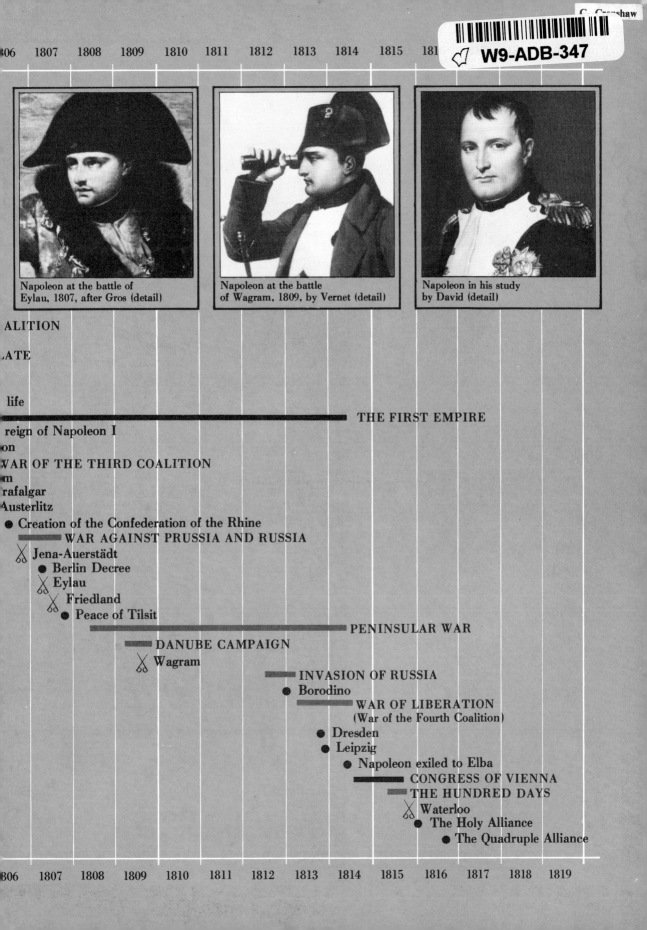

Napoleon at the battle of
Eylau, 1807, after Gros (detail)

Napoleon at the battle
of Wagram, 1809, by Vernet (detail)

Napoleon in his study
by David (detail)

ALITION

ATE

life

━━━━━━━━━━━━━━━━━━━━━━ THE FIRST EMPIRE

reign of Napoleon I

on

WAR OF THE THIRD COALITION

m

rafalgar

Austerlitz

● Creation of the Confederation of the Rhine

▬▬▬ WAR AGAINST PRUSSIA AND RUSSIA

✕ Jena-Auerstädt

● Berlin Decree

✕ Eylau

✕ Friedland

● Peace of Tilsit

▬▬▬▬▬▬▬ PENINSULAR WAR

▬▬▬ DANUBE CAMPAIGN

✕ Wagram

▬▬▬ INVASION OF RUSSIA

● Borodino

▬▬▬ WAR OF LIBERATION
(War of the Fourth Coalition)

● Dresden

● Leipzig

● Napoleon exiled to Elba

▬▬▬ CONGRESS OF VIENNA

▬▬ THE HUNDRED DAYS

✕ Waterloo

● The Holy Alliance

● The Quadruple Alliance

1806 1807 1808 1809 1810 1811 1812 1813 1814 1815 1816 1817 1818 1819

NAPOLEON
Master of Europe
1805-1807

OVERLEAF
The Napoleonic device, from the cover
of a book, in red and gold

NAPOLEON
Master of Europe
1805-1807

Alistair Horne

WILLIAM MORROW
AND COMPANY, INC.
New York 1979

To Christopher Sandeman
In affectionate memory

Previous books by the author

Back into Power
The Land is Bright
Canada and the Canadians

The Fall of Paris – The Siege and the Commune 1870–1871
The Price of Glory – Verdun 1916
To Lose a Battle – France 1940

The Terrible Year – The Paris Commune, 1871
Death of a Generation
Small Earthquake in Chile
A Savage War of Peace – Algeria 1954–1962

Library of Congress Catalog Card Number 79–1981
ISBN 0–688–03500–0

Typeset in Monophoto Ehrhardt
Printed in Great Britain by
Butler and Tanner Limited
Frome and London

Contents

List of Maps

Author's Acknowledgments

I OWE A SPECIAL DEBT OF GRATITUDE to David Chandler for casting the eye of the expert over the work of an intruder; any errors that remain are mine alone. My thanks are also gratefully due to Miranda Ferguson, who so industriously delved among vast collections of pictorial material as well as editing the text, and to Mrs Marcella Cox for typing the manuscript. My gratitude also to the art editor Tim Higgins, the designer Sheila Sherwen, and the cartographer Peter White whose help has been invaluable. Among libraries and museums, I am particularly appreciative of the friendly helpfulness accorded me – not for the first time – by the *Musée de l'Armée* in Paris. Finally, I am beholden to my daughter, Zaza, for checking various points of Russian translation.

Foreword

My argument is that War makes rattling good history; but Peace is poor reading.
So I back Bonaparte for the reason that he will give pleasure to posterity.

'Spirit Sinister' from *The Dynasts* by Thomas Hardy, Act II Scene V

WE LIVE IN AN AGE of the debunker and the revisionist. From Florence Nightingale and General Gordon, to Montgomery and Churchill, few landmarks of the British past have survived recent years with their stature unimpaired. In America J. F. Kennedy, General MacArthur and even immortals like George Washington and Alexander Hamilton have taken a beating. Compared to the Athenian enlightenment of such modern states as Amin's Uganda and the Dergue's Ethiopia, the British Empire is now revealed to have been a ramshackle affair, based on cruelty and corruption. By the elevated standards of present-day Britain, those founders and administrators of Empire could clearly not have run a municipal council with competence, or honesty. On reading the works of our moguls of modern history, who have doubtless spent their lifetimes poring over the records with dedicated detachment from the seclusion of their ivory towers, one is sometimes left wondering how any history could ever have been made at all by the tiny, inadequate hands of those about whom they write. Thus no reputation is now entirely safe – even Napoleon's has recently come under attack, on almost every score.

Under extreme aggravation from his Anglo-Saxon Allies, in the First World War Marshal Foch once remarked: 'Now that I know about Coalitions, I respect Napoleon rather less!' Undoubtedly the Coalition leaders who confronted Napoleon were not always marked with the highest distinction. Also, as the Israelis have learned to their cost since 1967, it is easier to win wars than peace; unfortunately for France, Napoleon's military genius was in no way matched by his political and diplomatic sensitivity. Nonetheless, the fact remains – and is unlikely to be disputed by even the most dedicated revisionist – that in a remarkably short space of time Napoleon chalked up a career of military conquests almost unparalleled in the modern world. His physical empire may have proved hardly less ephemeral than Hitler's, but the legacy of his works was considerably less so, and generally rather more beneficial. Few institutions or monuments in modern France do not bear some correlation to his name. Thus this book humbly does not presume to offer any fresh analysis or criticism, but is simply an attempt to portray Napoleon at the peak of his success, and to record how he got there.

As an additional excuse for adding yet another title to the three hundred thousand already existing, there is always Thomas Hardy's remark in *The Dynasts* about war making 'rattling good history', and what more than that very Napoleonic saga with which *The Dynasts* deals? Apart from the perennial fascination that persists in Napoleon's military campaigns, there is

LEFT Napoleon as First Consul at Malmaison
in 1804 by François Gérard. He was made Consul
for life in August 1802.

9

about them a constant relevance, particularly with regard to his notions of space and movement. One tends to forget over what a vast geographical canvas the Napoleonic wars were waged; from the West Indies to Egypt and Syria, from Scandinavia to Sicily, from Lisbon to Moscow. Even India and the Far East were not outside the schemes of Grand Strategy, and it would have been perhaps more appropriate to label those two decades culminating in Waterloo the 'First World War', than to so name the briefer struggle of a hundred years later. In the course of that century following Napoleon, weaponry may have progressed considerably more than previously, but the style of warfare showed relatively little advance until the 'mass' battle *à la* Leipzig reached its apotheosis in the hideous stalemate bloodbaths of Flanders, the Somme and Verdun. The battles of the American Civil War owed much to the lessons inherited from the Napoleonic campaigns; while in terms of mobility, and what Liddell-Hart dubbed 'the indirect approach', they (and notably those of 1805–7) bear an even closer affinity to the mechanized techniques of 1939–45 and to the subsequent Israeli wars, than to the trench warfare of 1914–18. Finally, the elements of guerrilla and irregular warfare encountered by Napoleon in Spain and the Wars of National Liberation, which he provoked to burst on him in his latter years, have an even more modern ring about them today.

What date should one select as representing the summit of Napoleon's military success? Should it be 1802 when revolutionary France had finally been relieved of any external threat to her natural frontiers, and when, at the Peace of Amiens, Napoleon had a fair chance of agreement with the arch-enemy, England? Or should it be taken at the moment of the personal consolidation of his power – his coronation in 1804? Or in 1805, after the supreme battlefield triumph of Austerlitz? Or 1811, before the débâcle of Moscow and the year when England was most feeling the economic pinch as a result of her exclusion from Europe? But from the Peace of Tilsit in 1807, Napoleon – like Hitler from 1943 onwards – found himself militarily on the defensive in order to hold on to the vast territories he had already subjugated. It was also during the two years preceding Tilsit that the *Grande Armée* reached its apogee of excellence, winning its most brilliant succession of victories. Austerlitz, which had been called 'the first great battle of modern history', the brightest gem of them all in Napoleon's martial diadem, was also his first 'big' battle. Then followed the campaigns of Jena (1806) and Eylau-Friedland. Jena showed Napoleon, in his speed of concentration and pursuit, at his best as a strategist – though it lacked the tactical perfection seen at Austerlitz; while the terrible winter slogging match of Eylau was to foreshadow the worst of what Napoleon's uncontainable ambition was to bring him. Both campaigns, however, are of outstanding importance to students of military history, who may well criticize the present author for compressing the account of them, by comparison with the space devoted to Ulm and Austerlitz. His excuse is that, vital milestones as were Jena and Eylau-Friedland on Napoleon's road to success, the way had already been charted by the supreme triumph of Austerlitz in 1805. There was of course the small matter of Trafalgar in 1805, which was to cost him forever any hope of control of the seas. Nevertheless, it was the peace treaty dictated after the 1805–7 campaigns that seemed to come closest to granting Napoleon unchallenged, and unchallengeable, dominion on the mainland of Europe. After Tilsit he looked, at least temporarily, unbeatable.

PART ONE

Adventurer in Ascent

Young General Bonaparte at the Battle of Arcola.

1

The Road to Tilsit

... it were better not to have lived at all than to leave no trace of one's existence behind.

Napoleon

THROUGHOUT THE DAY of 24 June 1807, the hammers of the *Grande Armée* had clattered frantically to complete a large raft on the River Niemen in faraway East Prussia. The little town of Tilsit had been ransacked for all the richest materials it could provide, to furnish an elegant pavilion of striped canvas aboard the raft. At opposing ends the pavilion was surmounted by the Imperial eagles of Russia and France. Napoleon was determined that no pomp should be missing at this meeting of the two most powerful rulers on earth, which had been proposed earlier that day by Tsar Alexander I, his armies recently humbled on the battlefield of Friedland. For Napoleon, the Corsican adventurer receiving on terms almost of condescension rather than equality the Emperor of All the Russias, this first encounter was to represent the pinnacle of glory in a career of already meteoric achievement.

Completed, the raft was anchored exactly midway between the shores of the river, on which were encamped the rival forces that only ten days previously had been at each other's throats. Simultaneously, with superb military timing, at one o'clock on 25 June, boats carrying the two potentates set off from either bank. With Napoleon came his brother-in-law, the dashing cavalryman, Murat; Marshals Bessières and Berthier, the ever-faithful chief-of-staff, newly dignified Prince of Neuchâtel; generals Caulaincourt, Grand-Equerry, future Foreign Minister and chronicler, and Duroc, Grand-Marshal of the Empire. Tsar Alexander was accompanied by, among others, the Grand-Duke Constantine with his unpleasing countenance, and General Bennigsen, whose army it was that had just received such a drubbing at Friedland. Perhaps because he disposed of the more efficient oarsmen, Napoleon arrived first at the raft – thus acquiring for himself the air of host on this freshly declared neutral territory. Nevertheless, the first act of the rival emperors on boarding was to embrace each other warmly. The Niemen at that point was no wider than the Seine, consequently the gesture was clearly visible in both camps and wildly applauded. It seemed as if lasting peace was already a reality.

The two emperors then withdrew into the privacy of the pavilion. 'Why are we at war?' they asked each other (so Adolphe Thiers[1] tells us) with Alexander following up: 'I hate the English as much as you do!' To which Napoleon exclaimed 'In that case peace is made!' Alexander expressed his grievance at the false promises with which the absent perfidious ones had lured Russia into a disastrous war on their behalf, then abandoning her to fight it single-handed. That first 'summit talk' lasted an hour-and-a-half; after it, Napoleon confided in a letter to

LEFT Napoleon, Alexander I, Queen Louise and
King Frederick William III of Prussia at Tilsit, 1807.
Detail of a painting by Gosse.

Empress Josephine his delight with the former adversary: 'He is a truly handsome, good and youthful emperor; he has a better mind than is commonly supposed. . . .'

For a fortnight the intimate talks, the courtesies, and the fêting continued. Napoleon praised Bennigsen and the Grand-Duke Constantine, whom he had first encountered at the head of the élite Russian Imperial Guard at Austerlitz; Alexander praised the martial prowess of Murat and Berthier. Alexander was invited to inspect the French Imperial Guard; Napoleon was shown Alexander's fierce Cossack and Kalmuck warriors. They went for long rides together along the banks of the Niemen, while Napoleon unfolded the various new projects his restless mind was already conceiving. Day by day a cordiality, almost an affection, seemed to grow between the two men. On one occasion (according to Baron Méneval[2]) when Napoleon had pressed the Tsar to remain in his camp for dinner, he offered his guest the use of his own gold toilet-case with which to change. How much further could fraternity be taken! But, behind all this, much hard bargaining was going on. While Napoleon spared no effort in his endeavours to charm the apparently impressionable young Tsar, not quite the same degree of camaraderie between equals was reserved for the latter's unhappy ally, Frederick William, King of Prussia. His armies having been vanquished and his dominions overrun the previous year, in the utmost humiliation that Napoleon had inflicted upon any of his foes, the heir to Frederick the Great was made to wait, like a poor relation, in the rain on the Russian bank, only to be admitted to the councils of his fellow rulers after their cordiality *à deux* had already been established. 'Sad, dignified and stiff' (according to Thiers) Frederick William was easily bullied by Napoleon. It was left to his attractive queen, Louise, to turn on the charm. 'She is full of *coquetterie* toward me,' Napoleon wrote to Josephine, but was able to assure her (in this case with conviction): '. . . do not be jealous, I am an oilcloth off which all that sort of thing runs. It would cost me too dear to play the *galant.*'

On 7 July, Napoleon signed a formal peace treaty with Alexander at Tilsit. Pointedly, a similar settlement with broken Prussia was not signed and ratified until several days later. In the public treaty between Napoleon and Alexander, much play was made of their newly discovered fraternal feelings for each other and their hopes for active cooperation in the future. More to the point, under the secret articles attached, the Tsar was to abandon any romantic crusading notions about liberating Europe from the revolutionary French; instead, at the expense of Napoleon's ally, Turkey, he was encouraged to pursue expansion along the traditional Russian route – towards the south-east. As a penalty to the Swedes for their rashness in joining the Coalition Wars against Napoleon, Swedish Finland was to be ceded to Russia. But it was, of course, against the still-unvanquished and physically almost untouchable distant arch-enemy, England, that Napoleon's ire was chiefly directed. She was to be excluded totally from Europe, with Russia joining the Continental System if by November Britain had not acquiesced to Napoleon's terms.

If the terms granted Russia were flatteringly and calculatedly benevolent, those for Prussia were correspondingly harsh. Despite the *coquetteries* of Queen Louise, Prussia was to be shorn of half her territories. Those west of the Elbe would be transmuted into a new Kingdom of Westphalia for the benefit of Napoleon's brother Jérome. To the East, Prussia's Polish provinces were to be handed over to create a new Grand Duchy of Warsaw (in itself a source of some

The Imperial Embrace on the Raft or
Boney's New Drop. A British cartoonist's view of
Tilsit, published in 1807. The cartoon emphasises
the plight of the King of Prussia.

disappointment to Napoleon's recently acquired mistress, the patriotic Marie Walewska, who, in giving herself, had hoped for nothing less than restored nationhood for her proud but oppressed people). Crushing war indemnities were imposed upon King Frederick William, plus a permanent French military occupation, and, to ensure that Prussia would henceforth never aspire to be more than a second-rate German power, the remainder of the German states had been organized into a puppet Confederation of the Rhine.

On 9 July, Napoleon took leave of his new friend (who was tactfully wearing the *Légion d'Honneur* for the occasion), bestowing on him one last warm embrace, and watching until Alexander disappeared out of sight on his bank of the Niemen. Earlier Napoleon had written to his Minister of the Interior, Fouché, instructing him:

See to it that no more abuse of Russia takes place, directly or indirectly. Everything points to our policy being brought into line with that of this Power on a permanent basis.

News of Tilsit reached London only in the third week in July, during a summer of heat so stifling that haymakers were fainting in the fields of Buckinghamshire. No intimation of the secret clauses had been received from her former allies, but it was abundantly clear that, at

LEFT Alexander I introduces his ferocious Cossacks to Napoleon. A detail of a painting by Bergeret.

BELOW Napoleon bids farewell to his new friend, a painting by Serangeli. His marshals look on sceptically.

Tilsit, the two emperors had effectively divided the continent between them into two spheres of influence in which England was to be permitted no part. From Gibraltar to the Vistula and beyond, Napoleon now ruled either directly or through princes who were his creations (over the previous two years he had given out more crowns than the Holy Roman Emperors had in a thousand), or his dependants. Before Austerlitz Napoleon had been an object of fear, after Tilsit he held Europe spellbound with terror. He was its undisputed master. 'One of the culminating points of modern history,' a starry-eyed supporter declared of Tilsit; '... the waters of the Niemen reflected the image of Napoleon at the height of his glory.'[3]

How, IN SO SHORT A SPACE OF TIME, had Napoleon managed to acquire these trappings of mastery which Tilsit now seemed to vest in him? One needs, rapidly, to turn back the clock some twenty years. At Tilsit he was still only thirty-seven, and – because of his youth at the conclusion of his most famous run of victories – one tends to forget that he was born under the reign of Louis XV and started his military career under Louis XVI. If he was a child of the *Ancien Régime*, he was also very much a product of that event dubbed by Thomas Carlyle 'the Death-Birth of a World', and was steeped in the French Revolutionary heritage, without which he would surely never have got as far as Tilsit. Commissioned as a second lieutenant in 1785 at the age of sixteen, this scion of the lesser Corsican nobility made his first real mark on military affairs some eight years later, at the Siege of Toulon. The key naval base was then held by an English fleet under the command of Admiral Hood; Napoleon, as a twenty-four-year-old artillery captain, was brought in to advise the not very distinguished commander of the French revolutionary forces besieging it. With his genius for the swift *coup d'œil* which was later to stand him in such good stead, he gave the brilliant appreciation that if the Le Caire promontory overlooking Toulon harbour could be seized, guns sited there would make the harbour untenable for Hood's ships. The strategy succeeded, and the British were driven out; wounded in the thigh, Napoleon became a hero in the ranks of the incompetent revolutionary army (though still unknown outside it), was promoted to the dizzy rank of *général de brigade* when he was still only twenty-four, and made artillery commander to the Army of Italy.

After a brief, fallow period of considerable frustration his next opportunity came when, by chance, he happened to be in Paris on sick leave during the autumn of 1795. A revolt was pending against the Convention and Napoleon was called in by his friend and protector, Paul Barras, to forestall it. He positioned a few guns (brought up at the gallop by a young cavalry captain called Murat) on the key streets leading to the Tuileries Palace. Three years previously he had witnessed the mob storm the same palace, and the weakness of the King on that occasion had made a lasting impression on him. 'If Louis XVI had shown himself on horseback, he would have won the day,' Napoleon wrote to his brother Joseph. He was determined not to repeat the same error and showed no hesitation in giving the order to fire. Discharged at point-blank range, the historic 'whiff-of-grapeshot' of the *Treizième Vendémiaire* put the mob convincingly to flight. For the first time since 1789 the Paris 'street' which had called the tune throughout the Revolution had found a new master whom it would not lightly shrug off. Barras, grateful but also nervous at having Napoleon too near the centre of power, now appointed him – at the age of twenty-seven – Commander-in-Chief of the French Army of Italy.

ABOVE *The Battle of the Pyramids*, 21 July 1798, by François Watteau.
Napoleon was victorious on land in Egypt, but the French fleet
was defeated at sea.

LEFT A romanticized portrayal of a young Napoleon at the Battle of
Rivoli in January 1796. Detail of a painting by Philippoteaux.

Ever since 1792, France had been at war with the First Coalition of her enemies who were
bent upon reversing the revolutionary tide that seemed to threaten all Europe, and restoring
the *status quo ante* in France. As Thomas Carlyle saw it, the guillotining of Louis XVI '... has
divided all friends; and abroad it has united all enemies ...'; on the other hand, in the view
of Friedrich Engels and others, had it not been for the stimulating effect of foreign intervention,
the Revolution might quietly have choked on its own vomit. It was a question of the chicken
or the egg. The fortunes of war had swung back and forth; lack of adequate preparation and
incompetence among the new leaders of the revolutionary French forces had been matched
by differences of interest and lethargy among the Allies; the stiff forms of eighteenth-century

warfare, unaltered since the days of Frederick the Great, had encountered a new revolutionary fervour, but was lamentably supported with guns and equipment. Marching into France, the Duke of Brunswick and his Prussians were halted and turned about, surprisingly, by the cannonade at Valmy in September 1792, first harbinger of a new form of warfare.[4]

In 1793 the French forces, resurgent under the organizational genius of Lazare Carnot (whom even Napoleon was to rate 'the organizer of victory'), and fired by their first victories to carry the Revolution to all the 'oppressed nations' of Europe, swept into Belgium and threatened Holland. During the bitter winter of 1794–5, one of France's few naval victories was achieved when French cavalry captured the Dutch fleet by riding across the frozen Texel. By June 1794, Jourdan had chased the last Coalition soldier across the French frontier. The British bungled a landing at Quiberon Bay, while – defeated, and invaded in its turn – Prussia abandoned the First Coalition the following year. But, over-extended, under-equipped and unhelped by the dithering and corrupt rule of the Directory, France's new 'Army of the Sambre-and-Meuse' now experienced a series of defeats across the Rhine at the hands of the Austrians.

It was at this point that, called in by Barras, Napoleon was sent to Italy to wrest the initiative from the Austrians. He found the army unpaid, hungry, poorly equipped and on the verge of mutiny. Stendhal cites the example[4] of three officers who owned but one pair of shoes, one pair of breeches and three shirts between them; elsewhere in *The Charterhouse of Parma*, he relates how, at Napoleon's legendary action on the 'Bridge at Lodi', another French officer had the soles of his shoes 'made out of fragments of soldiers' caps also picked up on the field of battle'. By his extraordinary capacity to inspire, Napoleon totally transformed the forces under him within a matter of days, and over the next eighteen months caused them – with minimal resources – to win a series of victories. These ended with the Battle of Rivoli, as impressive a battle as any the world had yet seen. By October 1797, he had defeated seven armies, captured 160,000 prisoners and over 2,000 cannon, and chased the Austrians to within a hundred miles of Vienna. Here, for the first but not the last time, he forced the beaten Austrians to sign peace with France, thus marking a definitive end to the wars of the First Coalition.

Napoleon now became the idol of France, his star irresistibly in the ascendant as he returned in triumph to Paris. 'From that moment,' he wrote after the first Italian campaign, 'I foresaw what I might be. Already I felt the earth flee from beneath me, as if I were being carried into the sky.'

At the Treaty of Campoformio (17 October 1797), France was ceded Belgium and control of the left bank of the Rhine. In return for Venice and its territories, Austria recognized France's establishment of an Italian satellite state, the Cisalpine Republic – from which seed, eventually, was to germinate the modern united nation of Italy. Of her foes of the First Coalition, only England remained at war with France, but with no weapon to strike at her across the Channel; so she contented herself by extending her Empire at the expense of both enemy and allies. After Campoformio, however, in exchange for a durable peace, she too declared herself ready to accept France's 'natural frontiers' and even to hand back colonies captured during the past hostilities. At last, revolutionary France was offered the security for which she had fought so passionately for the previous five years; it looked like a good time to make peace with England.

Nothing, however, succeeds like success, and it now went to the weak head of the Directory.

Back in 1790, the Constituent Assembly had declared the noble ideal: 'The French nation renounces the undertaking of any war with a view to making conquests, and it will never use its forces against the liberty of any people.' But, not unlike the heirs to Lenin in the twentieth century, the Directory, inflated by Napoleon's achievements now let itself be enticed into graduating from a basically defensive war, with an aim of saving the Revolution and securing France's frontiers, to one of expansion and enrichment. It is instructive that France's wars of aggrandizement began, not under the Consulate or the Empire, but under the revolutionary movement.

In France, the new hero was put in command – briefly – of the Army of England, charged with carrying the war across the Channel. The previous year, 1797, General Hoche with 14,000 troops and 16 ships of the line had made an abortive descent on Ireland, which had been disrupted by storms. After an inspection in January 1798 of the 120,000 troops mustered between Étaples and Walcheren for an invasion attempt, Napoleon abandoned the idea as 'too chancy to risk *la Belle France* on the throw of a dice'. Instead, he placed in the mind of the Directory the idea of striking at British sea-power by a campaign in Egypt, and in the Eastern Mediterranean – the key to England's empire and trade in the Orient.

With England's Pitt still under the misapprehension that Napoleon was heading for Ireland, he sailed for Egypt and what was to prove, militarily, his most disastrous campaign to date. Ensuing operations followed the familiar course, with Napoleon winning round after round on land (for example, the Battle of the Pyramids) and with Nelson sweeping the seas (Aboukir Bay and the Nile). The fighting moved up into Palestine and the Levant, and in his massacre of prisoners at Jaffa Napoleon revealed himself at his most ruthless and cruel. His own forces were decimated by plague (to which Napoleon himself seemed miraculously immune), with the Revolutionary General Kléber growling that he was 'the kind of general who needed a monthly income of ten thousand men'. Meanwhile, encouraged by British naval successes, before the end of 1798 a Second Coalition comprising England, Naples, Austria, Russia and Turkey had come into being, and had begun to threaten the French position in both northern Italy and the Netherlands. Abandoning his battered army in the Middle East and dodging Nelson's patrols, Napoleon hastened back to France, landing secretly at Fréjus on 9 October 1799. In Paris, he found the Directory tottering. On 9 November – *18 Brumaire* in the Revolutionary Calendar – Napoleon effected a *coup d'état* which ended the rule of the Directory, then established himself as First Consul, with a tenure of ten years and dictatorial powers greater than those of Louis XIV at the height of his glory. Both within France and beyond, this was heralded as signifying the end of the Revolution. In Russia, the mad Tsar Paul – already at odds with his Austrian ally over Italy – withdrew from the Coalition; in France, even the critical Madame de Stael was delighted, though her father, the banker Necker, cautioned: 'Your nerves are overwrought.... Unfortunately, everything rests on the life of one man.'

But the war still continued. Consolidated in power politically, Napoleon set off once more to chastise the Austrians. By an astonishing feat of transporting an army of 50,000 secretly over the eight-thousand-foot Great St Bernard Pass, still covered in snow in the May of 1800, Napoleon struck the unwary Austrians from the rear. June brought him his stunning victory at Marengo, north of Genoa. It was a copy-book classic of manoeuvre; though, as was characteristic of Napoleon, the panegyrical bulletin he issued afterwards (aimed in part at further terrifying a demoralized foe) made it sound rather more a calculated, according-to-plan result than was actually the case, and disallowed the element of opportunism that had played an integral part in the victory, as it so often did with his other triumphs.[5] The *coup de grace* to Austrian arms was administered by Moreau's victory at Hohenlinden in Bavaria on 3 December. It was a small consolation that, the following summer, General Abercromby's British expeditionary force was to defeat Napoleon's abandoned Army of the Orient and expel the last Frenchman from Egypt; for the Second Coalition had now collapsed in ruins.

The resulting Peace of Lunéville in 1801 with the Austrians, which forced them out of most of northern Italy, was followed by the Peace of Amiens with England in March 1802. Under its provisions a smarting England agreed to part with most of her recent colonial acquisitions, including Malta, while Napoleon was left – for the time being – in unchallenged military supremacy, and a grateful France confirmed him Consul for life. On the other hand, Nelson at Copenhagen (2 April 1801) had once again demonstrated to Napoleon the impotence of his attempts to gain control of the seas. Neither side was particularly happy with the peace terms; England deeply concerned by Napoleon's hegemony over Europe and resentful at her territorial deprivations; France soon finding England in default for not withdrawing her forces from Malta. Nevertheless, for the first time in a decade, a glimmer of lasting peace flickered over the battered European nations, and, once again, it looked like as good a time as any for bringing the sequence of wars to a definitive end. But peace was to prove illusory. As Napoleon had written prophetically to his lieutenant and potential rival, Moreau, during the more ecstatic moments of 1800: 'Greatness has its beauties, but only in retrospect and in the imagination.'

Notes to chapter 1
1 *The Consulate and Empire*, Vol. VII, pp. 337–8.
2 From *Napoleon et Marie Louise: Souvenirs Historiques de Baron de Ménéval*, Vol. 1, p. 186 (Paris, 1844).
3 M. de Bourienne, *Memoirs of Napoleon Bonaparte*, Vol. II, p. 18 (London, 1836).
4 From *The Charterhouse of Parma*, p. 21.
5 In *Vie de Napoleon*.

2

The Peace Machine

He always applied all his means, all his faculties, all his attention to the action or discussion of the moment. Into everything he put passion. Hence the enormous advantage he had over his adversaries, for few people are entirely absorbed by one thought or one action at one moment.

Caulaincourt

AFTER AMIENS, what the English uncharitably dubbed 'the peace which passeth all understanding' heralded both for France and Napoleon a halcyon period. But it was brief. During the thirteen months it lasted, English tourists, the curious and the spendthrift, poured across the Channel in their tens of thousands; the tide of the mid-1970s in reverse. French goldsmiths, jewellers and makers of fancy-goods worked night and day to provide wares to satisfy their greedy visitors. In September 1802, many were drawn to the great industrial exhibition mounted to celebrate the revolutionary 'Year X' at which Richard Lenoir, the cotton-spinner, alone took 400,000 francs worth of orders. The gallants found their fancies much stimulated by the manifest seductiveness of the ladies of Parisian society, in their high-waisted, see-through gowns inherited from the Directory. Those foreigners privileged to be invited to the First Consul's birthday celebrations were agreeably surprised by the gracious *bonhomie* with which the great man greeted them. With the utmost regard for the sensibilities of his English visitors, he displayed, on either side of his chimney piece, busts of Fox and Nelson. The court around him exuded a certain brilliance – 'a newly-born government,' he told his secretary, 'must dazzle and astonish' – but, in contrast to the glitter of the generals and Mameluke orderlies that accompanied him on military parades, Napoleon's own uniform was striking by its simplicity, reminding the visitors more of an English sea captain in undress. Could this really be the monster who, so recently, had terrorized all Europe? At home he was undoubtedly at a peak of popularity that year, and success seemed to imbue him with a new aura of security. At first sight, the English visitors had to admit themselves favourably impressed by appearances of life under the new régime.

It was during this fleeting period of peace that Napoleon, acting with the same speed and remarkable concentration of energy which characterized all his military operations, established the majority of the civil reforms that were to provide France with a new constitution, set her finances in order, and comprise – *inter alia* – the *Code Napoleon*: his most durable achievements. If he had never fought a battle, these would surely still leave him one of the world's great constructive rulers.

In no way did he succeed more triumphantly than in the ambition he had declared in 1798 to '...make Paris not only the loveliest city that is, or that ever had been, but the loveliest

A watercolour of the Exhibition of the products of industry in the Louvre 1802, in which the contrasting *directoire* dresses of the women, the revolutionary uniforms of the soldiers, and the top-hats of what are probably English visitors, can be clearly seen. On the left is a display of Empire furniture.

that ever could be.' Sparked by the catastrophic floods of the previous winter, which had partly inundated the Champs Elysées, Napoleon began by reorganizing the quays of the Seine; he decreed, in 1802, the construction of the Quai d'Orsay which he eventually extended all the way to the École Militaire. Grandiose plans for canals and reservoirs were laid down, providing Paris with her modern water supply; streets were renumbered on a basis that survives to the present day. Christened the Musée Napoléon, the Louvre was completed in 1803 to house the Italian art treasures shamelessly looted in his recent campaigns. Inevitably there would come the grandiose architecture dedicated to military conquests; the charming Arc du Carrousel and the Vendôme Column (both to commemorate the Austerlitz triumph of 1805), and the Arc de Triomphe itself (not to be completed until the reign of Louis Philippe). There were also works of purely economic significance, like the Bourse (the foundation stone of which was laid in 1808, although the idea was conceived by Napoleon much earlier), and the vast Halle des Vins – designed to make Paris the foremost trading centre for wine in northern Europe.

The list of works initiated is an imposing one, especially considering the short amount of time Napoleon was able to spend on the home front: the Rue de Rivoli, Rue de Castiglione, Rue Napoléon (renamed Rue de la Paix), the Conseil d'État and the Cour des Comptes, four new bridges, the Madeleine transmogrified into a Temple of Victory with, facing it across the Concorde, the portico of the Palais Bourbon remodelled in Roman style to match. Everywhere new fountains and parks were constructed, and – not least – churches which had been vandalized during the Revolution were to be restored over the next twelve years at a cost of some £4m.

In this last endeavour, Napoleon was not influenced entirely by architectural values. The withering-away of the Revolution had been accompanied in the last years of the old century by a marked religious revival, hand in hand with the new Romantic movement, as exemplified by Chateaubriand's work, *Le Génie du Christianisme*, published in 1802. Returning to France in 1800 after seven years' self-exile, Chateaubriand had been deeply shocked at the ravages still left by the Revolution, particularly in its excesses of atheism: '... the ruinous castles, the belfries empty of bells, the graveyards with never a cross and the headless statues of saints.'

Immediately sensitive to the prevailing mood however, Napoleon, with one stroke of consummate skill, had healed the wounds that still divided France by his *Concordat* with Pope Pius VII. Ratified in 1802, the *Concordat* re-established the Roman Catholic Church as 'the religion of the greater majority of Frenchmen'; but at the same time it clearly demarcated its spiritual and temporal powers. The settlement was to last over a century, until the Church was disestablished in France. Meanwhile it removed the main grievances that had kept civil war smouldering in the Vendée, and helped gain for Napoleon the sympathies of Catholics in France as well as in the subject, or about-to-be subject, nations. Although rejected by Louis XVIII's government in exile, the *Concordat* was supported by most of the returning emigrés, including Chateaubriand who found a Paris where '... the emigré was returning and talking peaceably with the murderers of his nearest and dearest....'

Largely a tactical device, however, the *Concordat* did not imply any religious fervour in Napoleon himself. Under his régime, notes one writer[1]:

Congregations were treated to extracts taken from the Bulletins of the *Grande Armée*, and informed that the paths of conscription, as much as of holiness, led to Heaven.

Though the churches were to be repaired, there was no suggestion of returning the actual properties sequestrated by the Revolution.

Before 1782, education had been left largely in the hands of village priests and religious orders like the Jesuits. In 1795 a new secular system had been introduced by the Revolution onto which stem Napoleon now grafted, in 1802, one of the most famous and enduring of all his reforms – the *lycées*, or state secondary schools. Like so many of his reforms, the system was designed, at least in part, to serve his own aims by providing a steady flow of military and administrative cadres essential to the Napoleonic machine. At the same time he transformed the high-grade *École Polytechnique*, founded by the Convention in 1794, into a military college for gunners and engineers. He also set his seal on the *École Normale Supérieure*, equally initiated by the Convention and still today the breeding ground of a particular *genre* of French intellectual leadership. Typical of the fervent intervention in cultural matters that went *pari passu* with military campaigning was the 'living encyclopedia' of scientists, orientalists, and zoologists – including Monge the great mathematician and Champollion the Egyptologist – whom Napoleon had taken to Egypt with him. He had lost the war in Egypt, but discovered the Rosetta Stone.

Though the Directory had done much to improve France's political structure, between 1799 and 1804 the Constitution was extensively remodelled by Napoleon; of course greatly to the increment of his own personal power. As it did in his military technique, rationalization also lay at the heart of all Napoleon's civil reforms. In February 1800, the various departments were placed under the charge of Prefects; the following year the metric system was introduced, and in 1802 a new national police force was raised. France was to become more tightly centralized than ever it had been under the *Roi Soleil*. Prior to Napoleon, France had been bedevilled by the existence of 360 separate local *codes*; he now set about the immense task of unifying them into one set. By 1804 the *Code Civil* (later, and better, known as the *Code Napoléon*) was voted through the legislature. Though comprising over 2,000 articles, it took only four years to complete and is still largely operative. Typical both of his energy and personal interest in the work of administrative reform, Napoleon managed, almost incredibly, to attend no less than 57 of the 109 meetings devoted to the *Code Civil*. Regulating virtually every function of life, *inter alia* the *Code* insisted on the equal division of property among sons, thereby in fact doing more than the Revolution had done to fragment the big estates. Much emphasis was laid on the authority of the male, removing many of the contractual rights women had enjoyed under the *ancien régime*; this reflected his own, very Corsican disbelief in feminine equality.

Indispensable to Napoleon in all these endeavours at civil reform was the person of Jean Jacques Régis de Cambacérès, aged forty-five when he became Second Consul in 1799. Cambacérès was a known homosexual and pretentious gourmet, but also an outstanding jurist administrator and manipulator in the corridors of power. With a capacity for work rivalling even Napoleon's, as President of the Senate, of the Council of Ministers, the *Conseil d'État*, the *Conseil du Sceau des Titres* and the Privy Council, there was scarcely any aspect of Napoleon's 'Peace Machine' that lay outside his ken. Incapable of decision himself, over the five years that Napoleon was absent from Paris during his fourteen-and-a-half in power, Cambacérès faithfully drafted him a daily report. Unlike Fouché and Talleyrand, he was to remain totally loyal to his master, being created a Prince of the Empire and Duke of Parma for his pains.

The shaky French economic and financial system also received the full benefit of the two Consuls' attention, accompanied with often draconian measures. The Banque de France was established in 1800, and granted total control over the national debt and the issue of paper money. Industrial prosperity was stimulated by ubiquitous government intervention, and various innovations of social welfare encouraged – though along largely paternalistic lines. However, trade unions were ruthlessly stamped on as 'Jacobin' institutions, or as diseases exported by the insidious British. Unemployment was kept at a low level, but labour was hard and the hours long. In summer, builders worked from 6 a.m. to 7 p.m.; the life expectancy of bakers was under fifty, and up until 1813 children under ten were still employed in the mines. From 1803 onwards every working man had to carry a registration book stamped by his employer, without which he was treated as a vagabond, and when it came to litigation it was the employer's word that was always accepted. In rural France, the life of the average peasant – though improved by the Revolutionary land settlement – was not much affected by either the Consulate or the Empire. The great roads built by Napoleon radiated out towards frontiers with distinct military purposes, and did little to bring the countryside into contact with the modern world.

In general, however, both peasant and urban working classes seem to have been better fed than they were either before 1789 or after 1815 – partly because of strict government controls placed on corn exports and price levels – and they came to regard the Napoleonic era as one of relative prosperity. Napoleon claims to have gained the allegiance of the working classes by 'bread and circuses', and certainly the appeal to native jingoism of great victories such as Marengo went far to mitigate discontent for any loss of civil or political liberties. At the other end of the social scale, there were also great (and often scandalous) opportunities for self-enrichment; Talleyrand, the negotiator of the Peace of Lunéville, made a fortune by buying up Austrian bonds issued in Belgium, through knowing that one of the stipulations of the Treaty was that these bonds were to be honoured. Meanwhile, by 1804 the bourgeoisie owned approximately twice as much land in parts of northern France as it had done in 1789.

With perhaps just a passing similarity to the Soviet Union at the peak of its imperial power in the late 1970s, one class that was less than impressed by the compensation of 'bread and circuses' for an authoritarian régime was the intelligentsia. Not agreeing with Goethe's ecstatic view that Napoleon epitomized '... all that was reasonable, legitimate, and European in the revolutionary movement ...' a disenchanted Madame de Stael found that her France had become 'a garrison where military discipline and boredom rule'.

Culturally, the decorative arts probably thrived most under Napoleon: the Lyons silk industry was revitalized to satisfy the copious demands of the Bonaparte family, and by 1807 Jacob-Desmalter, Napoleon's favourite furniture-maker, was employing no less than 350 craftsmen. Everywhere the influence of the soldier left its impact on the austere built-to-last neo-classicism of Empire style;[2] the pharaonic motifs and fiery poppy shades brought back from the Egyptian campaign; the Winged Victories symbolizing military triumph; and the mythology and artifacts of Rome borrowed later to lend flavour to the new imperial mystique. At Malmaison, the love-nest Napoleon set up with Josephine, the council chamber was fitted up with striped canvas to resemble a campaign bivouac, inside of ten days after Marengo. On moving into the Tuileries Palace as First Consul, Napoleon promptly ordered the erasure of red republican caps, symbols

Napoleon's Council
Chamber at
Malmaison was
designed in the form
of a military bivouac
after the Battle
of Marengo.
RIGHT A design with
sketches of the
details of the room,
and (below) the
Chamber as it
is today.

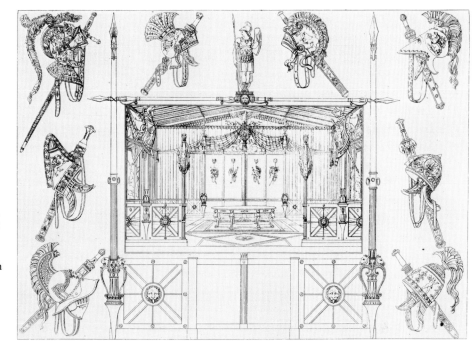

of liberty, that were painted on the walls: 'I don't like to see such rubbish.' These were replaced by busts of Alexander and Frederick the Great, along with Brutus and Demosthenes. Exemplifying the Roman 'high-seriousness' of the Empire was the painter David, who had abandoned the eighteenth-century frivolity of his uncle, Boucher ('It is pure, it is great, it is beautiful as antiquity,' he once said of Napoleon's head), and the great tragedian, Talma.

But the theatre fared less well under the heavy hand of Napoleon. By 1806, Fouché's Ministry of Police had acquired the right to censor all plays, and by the following year the list of theatres receiving government support had been reduced to eight. Already by 1803, Napoleon had ordered all new books to be submitted to the censor; when he came to power there had been over seventy newspapers in Paris, within a year these had been reduced to thirteen, all under strict censorship. Among other things, no caricatures of the ruler or his policies were permitted; which accounted for the serious dearth in the cartoonist's art of the times. (When the British Opposition leader, Charles James Fox, visited Napoleon in the autumn of peace of 1802, and rashly remarked that no one in England minded being abused in the press, his host shouted 'It is another thing here!' and strode away.)[3] Neither the Revolution nor the Empire was to produce any great music, leaving it to Beethoven to rhapsodize the feats of Napoleon. Apart from Chateaubriand and Madame de Stael, notable novelists were few. Perhaps more than from direct political persecution, artists suffered[4]

... from the restrictive, stifling atmosphere produced by fear, flattery and censorship. There was something distinctly 'second-hand' about much of the art of the period....

It was in this stifling atmosphere that Madame de Stael, her salon having become a focus of the opposition, was forced into exile in Switzerland by 1803. It was also this atmosphere and its essential lack of liberties which, once their gaze had penetrated the shiny surface of Napoleonic France, gradually disenchanted the liberal visitors from England, making them think themselves perhaps better off after all in their own backward but libertarian society.

By means of his civil initiative, Napoleon had contrived to gain successively the loyalties of most elements of French life: the Catholics, the bureaucracy, the peasantry and the bourgeoisie. With the old aristocracy his policy of reconciliation had been less successful, and it had continued to keep a mistrustful distance. So Napoleon decided to create an élite of his own, faithful to himself as the fountain-head of rewards, and in May 1802, he created the institution of the *Légion d'Honneur*.

By the end of the following year, Napoleon's authoritarian rule seemed to be totally established, with virtually all wires in the nation leading back to his one pair of hands. But one lynchpin in the whole structure was missing; the continuity of succession. Already in December 1800, the fact that the First Consul might be less than immortal had been suggested when, on his way to the opera, he had narrowly escaped the explosion of a powerful mine which killed several bystanders. The Jacobins were implicated (although Fouché held the Royalists responsible), and severe penalties were meted out. On being made Consul for life in August 1802, Napoleon was granted powers to nominate a successor, but his ambitions lay further. At the beginning of 1804, two further plots were uncovered; one led by a Vendée Royalist called Georges Cadoudal, the other by two generals, Pichegru and Moreau. Cadoudal (in whose

A sketch of the Coronation, 2 December 1804, by Jacques Louis David.
Napoleon removes the Imperial crown from the Pope's hands to
place it on his own head.

conspiracy the Addington government had rashly connived but which had been adroitly turned by that master-spy, Fouché) was executed, as were a dozen others in one of the few mass guillo-tinings of the Napoleonic era; Pichegru died in prison under dubious circumstances, while Moreau as the popular hero of Hohenlinden was permitted to disappear into exile, thereby removing one of the few potential rivals to Napoleon.[5] The Cadoudal plot provided Napoleon with just the excuse he needed to give himself an imperial crown and ensure the hereditary succession of the Bonaparte dynasty; but it was also to lead to his most deplorable blunder, the murder of the Duc d'Enghien.

Acting with a grandeur that was indicative of the vast power that he had already acquired in Europe, Napoleon summoned the Pope to Paris to officiate, on 2 December 1804, at Nôtre Dame while he himself placed the Imperial Crown on his own head – and Josephine's. The whole façade of the cathedral had been clad with a mock Gothic exterior for the occasion, provok-ing the comment from a wit that 'so much work has been done that God Himself would lose his bearings!' As he ascended the steps to the immense throne, Napoleon is said to have murmured to his brother: 'Joseph, if only our father could see us now!'

There were moments of dissonance that day; between the altar and the throne, a slight alterca-tion broke out between Josephine and her jealous sisters-in-law carrying her train, with the result that she was momentarily pinioned in her procession. Chagrined by receiving only two tickets for the coronation, David the court painter sought revenge by painting himself into the ponderous formal tableau; while in Vienna Beethoven, disillusioned by the worldly arrogance of his hero, cancelled his dedication of the 'Eroica'. In a state of *post coitum triste*, the new Emperor gloomed to his secretary, Decrès, the day following the great ceremony: 'I have come too late; men are too enlightened; there is nothing great left to do ...' This was not, however, a view widely shared by the denizens of the new Empire, bemused by the 'bread-and-circuses' feat *par excellence* of free feasting and fireworks which had accompanied the dazzling occasion. It merely seemed as if Napoleon had ascended to yet another pinnacle of glory, and of these there still promised to be no end.

At this moment when he had vested himself in the pomp-and-circumstance of power com-parable only to that of the Roman Caesars, of Charlemagne and of the Holy Roman Emperors, the man like his fortune stood at his zenith both physically and intellectually. Now still only thirty-five, *Le Petit Caporal* or *Le Tondu*, as the army called him affectionately, was beginning to show just a few signs of thickening; his cheeks were fuller, the waistband of his breeches tighter, his complexion sallower. Already he had been *cocu* by Josephine (and vice versa). Some of his less intimate officers thought possibly his gaze was a trifle duller, and they would reflect apprehensively among themselves that it was now over four years since he had won that last great military victory, at Marengo; could it be that 'perhaps the crown has squashed his brains?' But they would soon be proved wrong.

Millions of words have been written about Napoleon's complex personality, re-examining its mysteries and paradoxes (and sometimes, even, manufacturing new ones!). He hunted, not because he enjoyed it or was even particularly good on a horse, but because he deemed it part of the regal appanage. He espoused pageantry, insofar as it was a function of the courtly life designed to bedazzle the impressionable, but in fact was happier himself amid the almost martial

simplicity which Josephine had created for him at Malmaison. He was also no gourmet. He derided ambition in others, remarking disdainfully of his own creation, the *Légion d'Honneur*, 'it is by such baubles that men are governed', yet was boundless in his own ambition. He was bred on the egalitarian ideals of the Revolution, but was to found a new aristocracy and a new despotism of his own.[6] He condemned sexual love as 'harmful to society and to the individual happiness of men', yet was incapable himself of avoiding both its entanglements and torments of jealousy. He leaned towards mathematics and sciences of the reason, while mistrusting anything to do with human passions; yet he could never quite escape from being a child of the Romantic Movement himself.[7] He was (wrote George Rudé):

... a man of action and rapid decision, yet a poet and dreamer of world conquest; a supreme political realist, yet a vulgar adventurer who gambled for high stakes....

About certain facets of Napoleon's character there has been little argument. One was the extraordinary impact he has on people. 'The terror he inspires is inconceivable,' wrote Madame de Stael: 'One has the impression of an impetuous wind blowing about one's ears when one is near that man.'

As for his relationships with his soldiers, perhaps the single most remarkable feature was the total dedication he was able to exact; the *grognards* would march to Moscow and back for him – and then, once again, pick up their muskets during the Hundred Days. Another incontrovertible asset of Napoleon's was his almost superhuman reserve of energy. It was this energy which enabled him to be, so his admirer Goethe thought, '... in a permanent state of enlightenment, which is why his fate was more brilliant than the world has ever seen or is likely to see after him ...' He could concentrate eighteen hours a day without his mind clouding. 'I work the whole time,' he once explained to Count Roederer; 'It is not a *génie* that reveals to me suddenly what I have to say or to do in a circumstance which may surprise others, it's my reflection, it's meditation.'

By the beginning of 1805, that capacity for work was certainly undiminished. So too was the retentiveness of that remarkable, questing, restless mind and his genius for total concentration. As Caulaincourt, his trusted aide, explained:

He always applied all his means, all his faculties, all his attention to the action or discussion of the moment. Into everything he put passion. Hence the enormous advantage he had over his adversaries, for few people are entirely absorbed by one thought or one action at one moment.

'An infinite capacity for taking pains ...' '... an intuitive sense ...', '... an indomitable will to power ...', '... a firmness of aim ...'; these are some of the many qualities attributed to Napoleon. Perhaps above all he was a man of reflexive action, as opposed to meditation. A remark made in his youth revealed clearly his extrovert inclinations;

... when a man asks himself 'Why do I exist?' – then in my opinion, he is the most wretched of all. His machine breaks down, his heart loses the energy that is proper to men.

Even if it did not lead to happiness, he thought action was better than introspection, which inevitably showed the way to wretchedness. Insofar as he (a Voltairean sceptic) had any, this also applied to his religious beliefs. Such beliefs were perfectly acceptable for others (and

LEFT This portrait of the Empress Josephine at Malmaison, by François Gérard, conveys the wistful solitariness of an already fading beauty. The bouquet on the sofa symbolizes her dedication to the roses of Malmaison.

particularly women), but where he was concerned 'I am glad I have no religion,' he confided to his intimate, Bertrand: 'It is a great consolation I have no imaginary fears. I do not fear the future.'

His mistrust of intellectualism perhaps lay at the root of his aversion for Madame de Stael and her fellow ideologues; 'They talk, talk, talk,' he complained to his brother, Lucien. Occasionally it also led him into faulty conclusions, as when he rejected a blue-print by the American genius, Robert Fulton, for the invention of a submarine: 'All these inventors, all these project mongers are either schemers or visionaries. Don't mention him again.'

'Men are moved by two levers only: fear and self-interest,' he once declared. To some extent he approved of Robespierre's Terror, regarding it – like the actions of a late twentieth-century terrorist – as 'one of the inevitable phases' of revolution, a process that 'can be neither made nor stopped'. In no way ashamed of his own relentless looting of treasures in Italy, he regarded the acquisition of the booty of war by his subordinates as just one of the elements comprising the lever of 'self-interest'.

If it was his addiction to action that placed him on a treadmill leading, ineluctably, from one conquest to another, in terms of both strategy and tactics he did, however, also possess the rare capacity to bide his time, waiting for the *moment juste*. It was, he admitted, a characteristic to which the 'Gallic temperament' was ill-suited: '... yet it is solely in virtue of this that I have succeeded in everything that I have done.'

In all his personal relations, self-interest stood foremost. 'I have always been the victim of my attachment to him,' declared Jean Lannes, and there was no one more devoted among all Napoleon's marshals; 'He only loves you by fits and starts, that is, when he has need of you.' This same rather unattractive quality manifested itself in Napoleon's associations with women which played so important a part in his life. 'Fortune,' he declared to Marmont, 'is a woman, and the more she does for me the more I will demand from her.' His philosophy was very much that of the eternal Mediterranean male; the function of women should be confined to bed, family and Church. The aim of education must be 'not that girls should think, but that they should believe'. He complained:

We Westerners have spoilt everything by treating women too well. We are quite wrong to make them almost our equals. The Eastern peoples have been much more sensible.

As with his essential disinterest in *la bonne table*, he endeavoured to keep his amorous affairs on a matter-of-fact basis.

He was, however, by no means immune himself to passion in all its facets; there was the famous occasion when he collapsed senseless from excess in bed with Mademoiselle George, the famous actress (who, prefatory to their liaison, had provoked an explosion of applause in the theatre by reciting, just as Napoleon entered his box, the line '*Si j'ai séduit Cinna, j'en seduirai bien d'autres!*'). He could also be relentless when rebuffed; as with the virtuous Madame Recamier, who preserved her virginity – it was alleged – even with her boring banker husband. Nor, much as he may have affected to despise women, could he ever entirely restrain his passions from spilling over into his professional life, notably, of course, where Josephine was concerned.

A portrait of Napoleon with Murat's children,
by Ducis. This is a rare view of Napoleon,
as the frustrated father-figure.

It is always something of a mystery as to how Napoleon and the Creole, conveniently widowed at the age of thirty-one by Robespierre, ever became destined for each other. There was no cogent reason for Barras, master of the Directory, to hand over a perfectly good mistress to a relatively insignificant young general (although he appears to have retained certain rights for a few years afterwards); or for Josephine to marry an impecunious and relatively insignificant young officer. Napoleon deluded himself that she was wealthy enough to pay his debts and to provide him with heirs, on both of which counts he was disappointed.[8] (She also lied to him about her age.) Wildly extravagant, Josephine in fact increased his indebtedness, purchasing Malmaison for the astronomic sum of 325,000F, which she had no means of paying, while Napoleon was away in Egypt. The match began inauspiciously, with the future Emperor being bitten on the leg by Josephine's pug while making love to her on their wedding night, and little time elapsed before she was flagrantly unfaithful to him. Although he once declaimed haughtily, on the subject of separate bedrooms: 'Crimes only divide the husband from the wife ... only

RIGHT A love-letter from Napoleon to Josephine, written in August 1796, during the First Italian Campaign: 'I have arrived, my adorable friend; my first thought is to write to you. Your health and your face have not left my memory for one second during the whole journey.
I shall not be at peace until I have received letters from you. I await them with impatience.... If the deepest and the tenderest love could make you happy, then you should be so. I am overwhelmed with work. Adieu, my sweet Josephine, love me, behave yourself and think of me often, often.'

LEFT David's study of the Empress Josephine drawn from life and 'given to my son, Eugène'.

one for me and Madame Bonaparte', *male* fidelity was not rated quite so highly in the Corsican scale of things. In Egypt, Napoleon in his separation was solaced by a lady called *la Bellilote* who concealed a well-rounded pair of buttocks in tight officer's breeches, and there were a series of ladies like Mademoiselle George (whom an enraged Josephine once flushed *in flagrante* from the Imperial bedchamber).

But for most of his life it was Josephine who held some special magic for Napoleon; 'Sweet and matchless Josephine ... How strangely you work upon my heart!' he wrote in one of his many, deeply-moving letters to her, letters that all too often brought no reply. Abandoned many months by herself, creating the garden at Malmaison, growing her beautiful roses there and commissioning Redouté to paint them, was not enough to keep the hot-blooded Creole occupied. Napoleon knew this and while campaigning in distant lands she was constantly in his mind, driving him on and plaguing him with doubts:

I have not spent a day without loving you; I have not spent a night without embracing you; I have not so much as drunk a single cup of tea without cursing the pride and ambition which force me to

ARMÉE d'ITALIE

LIBERTÉ, ÉGALITÉ

RÉPUBLIQUE FRANÇAISE

Au Quartier-Général de Brescia le 13 fructidor

le an 4.me de la République Française.

BONAPARTE

Général en Chef de l'Armée d'Italie.

a Josephine

j'arrive ma adorable amie ma première pensée est de
t'écrire ta santé et ton image n'ont pas été un
instant de ma mémoire pendant toute la route je ne serai tranquille
que lorsque j'aurai reçu des lettres de toi j'en attends avec impatience
il n'est pas possible que tu te peignes mon inquiétude
je t'ai laissée triste, chagrine et demi-malade
si l'amour le plus profond et le plus tendre pouvait te
rendre heureuse tu devrais l'être ... je suis accablé
d'affaires

adieu ma douce Joséphine aime-moi porte-
toi bien et pense souvent souvent à moi

B

remain separated from the moving spirit of my life. In the midst of my duties, whether I am at the head of my army or inspecting the camps, my beloved Josephine stands alone in my heart, occupies my mind, fills my thoughts....

Then there would come the inevitable note on professional matters:

PS. The war this year has changed beyond recognition. I have had meat, bread and fodder distributed. ... My soldiers are showing inexpressible confidence in me; you alone are a source of chagrin to me; you alone are the joy and torment of my life....

A year later he was writing, from Verona:

I love you no longer; on the contrary, I detest you. You are a wretch, truly perverse.... You never write to me at all, you do not love your husband.... What business is so vital that it robs you of the time to write to your faithful lover?

and, a few days afterwards:

I have defeated the enemy ... I am dead with exhaustion. I beg you leave with all speed for Verona; I need you....

He had few illusions: 'She wanted everything,' he once complained. Late in life he admitted to Bertrand in what seems like more than passing honesty: 'I really did love her ... but I had no respect for her ... She had the prettiest little ———— imaginable.' Whatever it may have been, it was for many years to wield a most powerful influence over the most powerful man in Europe, in peace as in war.

Notes to chapter 2

1 Gwynne Lewis, *Life in Revolutionary France* (London, 1972).
2 'Simplify. This is for the Emperor,' Napoleon scrawled across the sketch for a candelabrum submitted by his architect, Percier.
3 Though he showed an almost morbid fascination with the grossly savage British cartoons about himself.
4 According to Gwynne Lewis, op. cit., p. 182.
5 Moreau eventually returned to Europe to fight for the Russians against Napoleon, and was mortally wounded at the Battle of Dresden.
6 As he once remarked revealingly to Benjamin Constant: '*Je ne hais point la liberté. Je l'ai écarté, lorsqu'elle obstruait ma route; mais je la comprends, j'ai été nourri dans ses pensées.*'
7 A measure of his suppressed romanticism is revealed in his own little-read novel, *Clisson et Eugénie*, written in purple prose during the fallow summer of 1795, and in which the hero, an aspiring young soldier, seeks a hero's death in battle on discovering that his wife, Eugénie, has fallen in love with his friend.
8 Although Josephine had two children, Eugène and Hortense, by de Beauharnais, and both Marie Walewska and Marie-Louise proved Napoleon's potency, one might well speculate on the causes of Josephine's later barrenness on examining the villainous douching devices, resembling brass garden syringes, that are laid out for the edification of tourists at Malmaison.

3

Uneasy Allies

Here, on our native soil, we breathe once more.
.... Oft have I looked round
With joy in Kent's green vales; but never found
Myself so satisfied in heart before.
Europe is yet in bonds; but let that pass
Thought for another moment. Thou art free,
My country! and 'tis joy enough and pride
For one hour's perfect bliss, to tread the grass
Of England once again. . . .

Wordsworth, 'Sonnets dedicated to Liberty', 1802

ALAS FOR Napoleon's imperial grand design – and alas for Europe – in the words of Winston Churchill[1] 'the tourist season was short'. The peace which followed the Treaties of Lunéville and Amiens was to turn out to be something like the Ribbentrop–Molotov Non-Aggression Pact of 1939; a brief unnatural truce which both sides sought to vitiate, while laying the blame on the other. What has been called the 'experimental peace'[2] (the terms of which were in fact more preferential to France than to England) was based on premises that were altogether too insubstantial.

It was not just the fact of the undiminished alarm which Napoleon's dynamism continued to arouse among his neighbours, but what he had inherited. The Great Revolution had so fundamentally shaken the whole European system that it was being excessively optimistic to presume that equilibrium could be restored by the exchange of an island here and a province there. If, in France, Napoleon was most intrinsically both product of it and heir to it, then beyond her frontiers there was also barely a nation whose institutions had not been profoundly affected by the Revolution and its consequences. In Poland, Kosciuszko, sparked by what he had experienced in America and observed in France, launched an abortive insurrection against the Russian oppressor in 1794. In Prussia, where intellectuals like Kant and Hegel, Goethe and Schiller were sharply divided by the Revolution, Silesian peasants in 1792 had declined to pay their tithes to their Junker landlords; in Piedmont, Italian peasants had rioted for land reform. In England radical agitation had spread through Thomas Hardy's[3] 'Corresponding Society', although perhaps a more influential phenomenon was the religious revival (especially within the Nonconformist churches) provoked by outrage at the excesses of French atheism. And in Austria, where the reigning Habsburg had been forced to watch impotently while his sister had been first humiliated, then guillotined, there were also those dynastic considerations not lightly to be papered over. Moreover, in the words of Pitt at the time: 'the dreadful sentence which they have executed on their unfortunate monarch applies to every sovereign now existing'.

Not unlike other periods that precede great upheavals (such as Europe on the eve of 1914), the years leading up to the French Revolution had been a time of growing commercial prosperity for almost the whole continent, including Russia. Yet, by the time of his coronation and in comparison with the powerful, modern apparatus, both civil and military, which he was forging in France, Napoleon could with some justice regard his European rivals as looking conspicuously archaic, indeed almost fragile. They also seemed paralysed by endless division, both internally and among themselves. We will speak of purely military matters later, but in Austria, Maria Theresa's successor, Joseph II, had made earnest endeavours towards civil reform before his death in 1790. He abolished torture and serfdom, and dissolved seven hundred monasteries to help finance education and poor relief. But too often his reforms represented more a private Utopia rather than what his subjects specifically wanted at any given time. Like Louis Napoleon, a century later, he might well have been dubbed 'the well-intentioned', and he too had a knack of going about things the wrong way. He offended the Bohemians by imposing German officials on them, and most of his reforms were wrecked by the church and nobility whom he had alienated. He longed to prove himself a great military leader and expand his already unwieldy Empire, but a series of silly wars only left Austria at odds with her neighbours; and outraged Bavaria was particularly to prove a thorn in Austria's side throughout the Napoleonic campaigns. His wanton share in the partition of Poland resulted in Austria's permanent enmeshment with both Prussia and Russia. He died six months before the storming of the Bastille, leaving an embittered epitaph:

> Here lies Joseph II, who failed in everything he undertook.

His more level-headed successor, Leopold II, managed to shore up the tottering throne and showed every promise of succeeding where his brother had failed. Yet even his endeavours as peacemaker in the Netherlands only had the effect of upsetting both England and Holland, with further disastrous consequences for Austrian policy in the early wars against Revolutionary France. Then, after a bare two years' reign, Leopold was dead of dysentery. His successor, Francis I, aged thirty-six when he succeeded to the throne in 1804, immediately found himself plunged into war with France.

It was under the benevolent influence of Maria Theresa and her two sons that Vienna became the musical centre of gravity of Europe, drawing to it Gluck, Mozart, Hadyn and eventually Beethoven. But, as Arthur Bryant observes, Austria's highly civilized denizens also continued – in the gentlemanly eighteenth-century manner – to view war rather '... as a professional activity to be performed, like music, according to clearly recognized rules and conventions....' For military success has never been Austria's highest distinction. And there was also the eternal disadvantage of the hotch-potch of *Mitteleuropa* nationalities which, in varying degrees of resentfulness, comprised the Empire, and which were to cause its final break-up a century later. As for Francis' allies in the various coalitions, the only interest shared with Austria was the negative factor of opposition to revolutionary and Napoleonic France. Fortunate for Francis was his own endowment with the Habsburg talent for survival, developed to the highest degree.

The social institutions of her north German neighbour, Prussia, were yet more archaic than those of Austria. If anything, since the death of Frederick the Great, serfdom had received

RIGHT The Emperor in all his Imperial glory
by Jean Auguste Dominique Ingres.

Francis I of Austria (1768–1835) and, as Francis II, the last of the Holy Roman Emperors, on an outing with the Empress Karoline Auguste. An absolutist who detested the French Revolution, which had guillotined his aunt, Marie-Antoinette, Francis despised Napoleon; yet – for reasons of state – he permitted his daughter, Marie-Louise, to marry Napoleon in 1810.

further impulsion as peasants were bullied by landlords to increase grain output to exploit boom export markets. In East Prussia they were sometimes committed to five or six days' work a week for their Junker; it was not therefore surprising that, as previously noted, they had reacted in sympathy with the principles of the French Revolution. In terms of military efficiency, Prussia since Frederick had also declined in inverse ratio to the age of its commanders. Having received a drubbing in the Revolutionary wars, she was reluctant to risk her neck against Napoleon's France and would prove to be little more than a posthumous entrant in the next round.

As in contemporary Prussia, in the late eighteenth-century Russia of Catherine the Great and her son, mad Paul I, serfdom had actually increased its hold. Like the Austrians, Catherine abolished torture and she also talked about agrarian reform, but most of her radical ideas were cured by the immense alarm which the Pugachev Rebellion provoked. Thus, in effect, serfdom spread to embrace a still wider class of Russians, and to the Ukraine as well; while bonds between the landowners and the ruler became even closer. Autocracy took another turn under the dark, brief reign of Paul, who closed down most of Russia's printing presses not banned by his mother, and – in a manner familiar to modern times – outlawed all western books. He gave away as personal 'presents' some 600,000 serfs, while at the same time introducing a decree (which was entirely unenforceable) limiting serfdom to only three days a week. Stepping to the throne over the strangled body of his father in 1801, young Alexander I initiated the steady move towards emancipation of the serfs; although the number receiving their freedom was the merest drop in the ocean, and it is recorded that, by the time of Napoleon's invasion of Russia, some fifty-eight per cent of all Russians were still not free men. To escape from the deprivations of serfdom Russians flocked to join the army, where Catherine had benevolently reduced the terms of service from life to a leisurely twenty-five years. 'God, how sad our Russia is!' sighed Pushkin on reading *Dead Souls*, Gogol's powerful indictment of serfdom. But no Russian serf blamed the Tsar for his troubles. The Tsar was purely ill-advised, and when called to do so they would fight for him to the last breath in their bodies.

Alexander was prompt to introduce numerous other timely reforms – in education, in censorship, in recasting governmental administration (thereby incorporating some lessons learnt from Napoleon), and in reordering Russia's finances, while at the same time he was also to reverse Paul's inconsistent foreign policy which had ended by coming down on the side of Napoleon. Much of Catherine's boundless energy had been channelled into south-easterly conquests, at the expense of the Ottoman Turks and greatly to the alarm of England. Such alarms were by no means diminished by a crazy scheme concerted between Paul and Napoleon to invade India with a force of Don Cossacks, and Nelson was actually on his way to take punitive action in the Baltic when Paul was assassinated.

Brought up in a frugal and virtuous atmosphere which owed something to the principles of Jean-Jacques Rousseau, Alexander was still a virgin when married (at sixteen). He was only twenty-four when he succeeded to the throne, but it was soon apparent that the new Tsar came out of a totally different mould to either his father or grandmother. Napoleon remarked of him patronizingly, that 'to be very able, he lacks only decision', yet he was to prove a most tenacious adversary. The fact remained, however, that Alexander's Russia was no more a natural ally of England's – or, for that matter, of Napoleon's other enemies – than Catherine's Russia had been. Therein lay a constant advantage to France, with her strategically central position and internal lines of communication placed astride Europe.

Although, in the years 1805–7, on dry land the actual killing of Frenchmen and the dying was to be accomplished by Austrians, Russians and Prussians,[4] behind the whole scheme of things hovered the shadow of England; enigmatic, aloof, but immensely powerful. And, inestimably rich! She had made a remarkable recovery from the crippling costs,[5] and the humiliation, of the American War of Independence, which had ended with a pious hope of 'a Christian, universal, and perpetual peace'. It was only a bare decade later, however, that the French Revolutionary wars exploded. The twenty years and more of conflict that were to ensue would cause the shelving of much urgently needed social reform; yet Wordsworth was not being totally smug, when, on returning from France in the summer of 1802, he could write:

> ... *Oft have I looked round*
> *With joy in Kent's green vales; but never found*
> *Myself so satisfied in heart before.*
> ... *Thou art free,*
> *My country! and 'tis joy enough and pride*
> *For one hour's perfect bliss, to tread the grass*
> *Of England once again. ...*

More than anything else, it was this sense of personal freedom that distinguished England from her continental allies. Prussians and Russians would later fight with maximum ferocity when their sovereignty had been trampled underfoot, or the war carried deep into their own homeland; but the dogged determination of the English stemmed from being the only European people who could in any way term themselves 'free men'. They alone had a monarchy subject to parliamentary democracy; society and its privileges were becoming as open to wealth as to birth, in this nation of shopkeepers where the merchant was now as 'respectable' as the aristocrat. Though she remained largely an agricultural economy, industrially she still headed the world by a long lead. But the true prosperity of England lay in her mercantile marine – incomparably the world's greatest – which in turn depended upon the protective supremacy of the Royal Navy. Between 1793 and Waterloo, English coffers were able to pay out £52 million in subsidies to the Allies alone. At the prevailing value of the pound (approximately ten times its rate today), it was indicative of the amazing extent of British prosperity.

With English merchants, profiteers, landlords and farmers getting inflated prices for their produce during the war, it was France who was to suffer more from the boycott of the 'Continental System'. But this was a prosperity that was, however, far from universal in England. Reforms that were as badly needed, here as elsewhere, were adjourned (for instance, virtually the only major reform passed was Wilberforce's prohibition of slavery in 1807). 'While desires increase,' George III wrote gloomily to the younger Pitt in 1787, 'the means of satisfying the people have been much diminished.' It could have been said of many other pre-revolutionary times in history. In 1795, a year of terrible weather which ruined crops, killed lambs by the intense cold and sent the price of food soaring, mass demonstrations in London had shouted 'No war, no Pitt, no King!' The king's coach was stoned by hungry subjects, and Pitt began to have serious fears of the Revolution crossing the Channel. In Ireland conditions were grimmer than usual, not helped by the ingenuity of Government forces who, at this time, invented a device called 'pitch-capping' whereby the forefathers of the IRA had their heads smeared with pitch and gunpowder and set alight. In 1798 there was a brief rebellion, dangerously fanned by France.

Throughout the Napoleonic Wars conditions were harsh for the poor, and poverty spread. Because of the blockade, wheat trebled in price between 1792 and 1812. In the country, bread and cheese became the staple diet of the labourer, washed down with tea or beer; meat – let alone John Bull's traditional joint of beef – was seldom seen. In a nation that listed two hundred capital offences on its statute books, the laws were savagely tilted against the hunger-driven poacher. Things were worse in the grubby, overcrowded[6] cities to which the underpaid and underemployed countrymen had flocked, unable to bring with them the compensatory joys of rural life. Badly-built slums innocent of sanitation sprawled, uncontrolled by any kind of planning. Factory and mine workers existed forgotten, without social welfare, distractions or hope – except that provided from Nonconformist pulpits. Their children were required to labour cruel hours; women, forced out of decayed 'cottage industries' made city nights hideous with 'the harlot's cry from street to street'; and it was the age of the Luddite.

Yet it could in no way be said that, overall, England was unhappy, or the mood of the country unhealthy. By comparison with other nations, and even (or perhaps especially) by today's standards, there were many aspects of English life at the turn of the century that seem to have been wistfully good. The country cried for reform, but not for revolution; it had a strong sense of fair play and was law-abiding, though still without a police force. As Arthur Bryant remarks, if a man was knifed in the street, passers-by did not hurry on, and Southey reckoned that contemporary Britons would put out an insurrection as they would a fire. From top to bottom, England had never been more dedicated (until, perhaps, the 1960s) to the pursuit of pleasures, some healthier than others. Fornication was regarded as an essential proof of virility; as an indication of the scale of the industry the splendidly outrageous diarist, Harriet Wilson (who later smuggled her memoirs out of Paris via the diplomatic bag) and both her sisters, were all 'kept ladies'. The example was set by the frivolity of the Prince of Wales, married secretly to Mrs Fitzherbert in 1785, and his world. It was during the height of the Napoleonic Wars that dandyism, coupled with the name of 'Beau' Brummel, reached a peak of extravagance. With its nightly balls and masquerades, London society was seen by Wordsworth (rather censoriously) as 'glittering like a brook in the open sunshine':

> *The wealthiest man among us is the best:*
> *. . . Rapine, avarice, expense,*
> *This idolatry; and these we adore:*
> *Plain living and high thinking are no more.*

With the improvement of the fowling-piece, the *Sportsman's Directory* could declare in 1792: 'The rage for shooting was never at a higher pitch than at present . . . the art of shooting flying [i.e. birds on the wing] is arrived at tolerable perfection. . . .' Duelling flourished, and in further pursuit of the stimulus of danger, the upper classes had become hunting mad; in 1790 steeplechasing was introduced, and in 1801 the Duke of Richmond laid out a racecourse at Goodwood.

Pleasure, however, was by no means only the prerogative of 'the wealthiest man'. On horse or on foot, people would travel almost any distance to attend a prize-fight and reports of such sporting events would often eclipse news from the battle-front. Because of popular pressure a bill to end bull-baiting failed in 1802, and the hardly less cruel sport of cock-fighting continued to thrive under the patronage of 'Prinnie'. For all the hardships, there was also much wholesome joy to be found in humbler rustic life, as the childhood memories of Wordsworth and Cobbett record. 'The beauty of field and wood and hedge, the immemorial customs of rural life,' writes G. M. Trevelyan:[7]

. . . the village green and its games, the harvest-home, the tithe feast, the May Day rites, the field sports – had supplied a humane background and an age-long tradition to temper poverty.

Rural England and its picturesque market towns would never again be so unspoilt, and this was also the great age of Constable, Turner and Morland. Poetry, too, was on a high plateau – reflecting, perhaps, as Wordsworth noted, a

> *. . . central peace subsisting at the heart*
> *Of endless agitation. . . .*

It has often been commented on how the novels of that great contemporary chronicler, Jane Austen, barely mention the wars raging beyond the Channel. American visitors were also usually

The Turbelent M.ͬ Fight-all   The Hon.ᵇˡᵉ M.ͬ Tax-all   The Worshipfull M.ͬ Take-all

Drawn by M.ͬ West.

THREE PLAGUES OF EUROPE.

Pub'd by Roberts Caricature Warehouse 9.ᵗ Middle row Holborn

Two British cartoonists' views of the Napoleonic Wars depict:
ABOVE Pitt's popularity rating as being on a par with Napoleon and the Devil,
because of his high taxation policy; and (right) Napoleon, frequently belittled as
a Lilliputian figure, being 'studied' by a gross, Brobdingnagian George III.

struck by the absence of any signs of war. There were no fortifications, and few soldiers to be seen on the streets (the explanation was simple, of course – England had few soldiers). Even 'those far-off ships' of which Mahan wrote and which alone stood between England and French conquest were, for most of the time, as unseen to English eyes as they were to Napoleon's. The fact is that, because of the many distractions at home, Englishmen found little time to think about the war. High among such distractions was, of course, the perennial spectacle – as diverting as a good prize-fight – of the politicians, Pitt, Sheridan, Fox and Addington mauling each other, mostly on domestic matters. If the war came home to Englishmen it was generally through the heavy taxes levied to finance it (there was no end to Pitt's inventiveness, past and present; taxes on windows, on horses, and even ladies' hats; or via the vituperation of the cartoonists. Headed by Gillray, Rowlandson and many others, the Napoleonic Wars fuelled one of the greatest periods of English political caricature. Immensely skilful, and boundlessly

The KING of BROBDINGNAG, and GULLIVER.

_Vide Swift's Gulliver Voyage to Brobdingnag.

imaginative, the cartoons were often of a viciousness barely exceeded in Goebbels' Germany, and usually of an unrestrained coarseness. The Royal Family, and even the king, were by no means sacrosanct; while Napoleon generally appears as a contemptible little figure, a Tom Thumb, or a Lilliputian Gulliver being chastised (or sometimes copiously excreted upon) by a robust, Brobdingnagian John Bull.[8] The cartoonists undoubtedly succeeded in whipping up patriotic emotions against Napoleon, but they also did a grave disservice by causing the British public vastly to underrate him. At the same time, by depicting – with almost equal savagery – the British political scene as one of total anarchy, they contributed materially to leading Napoleon to commit the same errors about England.

Anarchic, frivolous, venal, greedy, slothful, disloyal, disorganized, untrustworthy and un-warlike; this was how Napoleon saw *Perfide Albion*. He was later to attribute the staunchness of the British infantry line purely to the benefits of flogging. He was quite incapable of compre-hending the basic ruggedness that lay behind the unattractive and unimpressive façade; or, more important, that deep attachment to Freedom that united, and would continue to unite, Englishmen of all walks of life whenever they felt menaced by his system. When invasion loomed, Wordsworth echoed the jingoism of his compatriots with his 'We must be free or die ...' and

We are all with you now from shore to shore:
Ye men of Kent, 'tis victory or death!

It was a fundamental misappraisal that was to lead Napoleon into the same kind of faulty speculation and disaster as it would, later, the Kaiser and Hitler. On his journey round the West Country during the 1802 peace, Nelson, in his quiet understatement, judged the mood better than

... I have not the slightest doubt, from the result of my observations during this tour, that the native, the inbred spirit of Britons, whilst it continues as firmly united as at present, is fully adequate.

SOMETHING REMAINS TO BE SAID, briefly, about the new-born giant across the Atlantic – the United States of America – although she was to play no active role in the campaigns of 1805–7, but also just for that reason. Already American naval presence on the high seas could make itself felt (as Britain was to discover in 1812), and possible US involvement in the war was a factor not lightly to be dismissed. Politically the 'American example', reinforced by the involve-ment of Lafayette and Tom Paine, had had a powerful influence on the origins of the French Revolution. When, in 1793, revolutionary France decreed a 'war of all peoples against all kings', the recent rebels were swept with almost hysterical enthusiasm. It waned somewhat on the news that she had guillotined the good friend of the 'embattled farmers', Louis XVI. Though Jefferson still regarded France's 'the most sacred cause that ever man was engaged in', he and Washington opted for a benevolent neutrality. Then France sent as an envoy Citizen Genet, well described by Samuel Eliot Morison[9] as the 'quaintest of many curious diplomats sent by European governments to the United States'. Genet's instructions were to exploit the US as a privateering base, which was bad enough, but he went further by proceeding to inaugurate Jacobin Clubs wherever he set foot on his travels. It was as if today a Soviet ambassador toured

RIGHT A cartoon entitled *The British Butcher* by Thomas Rowlandson. Austerity in Britain during the Revolutionary Wars meant that an unpopular Pitt was blamed for the average Briton's inability to afford his traditional roast beef.

The BRITISH-BUTCHER,
Supplying JOHN-BULL with a Substitute for BREAD. Vide. Message to Lord Mayor.

BILLY the BUTCHER'S advice to JOHN BULL.

Since Bread is so dear, (and you say you must Eat,)
For to save the Expence, you must live upon Meat;
And as Twelve Pence the Quartern you can't pay for Bread
Get a Crown's worth of Meat, — it will serve in its stead.

the country implanting Communist cells; and America reacted comparably. Recalled in disgrace, Citizen Genet saved his head by marrying an American heiress and settling down in New York.

Together with a certain disenchantment with France, America's infant commerce now realized its need for British capital. Then, in September 1797, came Washington's famous Farewell Address, establishing the corner-stone of US foreign policy for many years to come:

Europe has a set of primary interests which to us have none, or a very remote relation. Hence she must be engaged in frequent controversies, the causes of which are essentially foreign to our concerns ... Our detached and distant situation invites us to pursue a different course ... 'Tis our true policy to steer clear of permanent alliances, with any portion of the foreign world ...

There now ensued an uncertain period with the US navy defensively involved in a quasi-war against French privateers (in which USS *Constellation* acquitted herself with distinction), followed by comparable clashes with Britain at sea, and a Teddy Roosevelt-style sideshow (perhaps not in accord with the strictest interpretation of the Farewell Address) against the pirates of Tripoli. Meanwhile, Napoleon had come to power and grandiosely declared his intent to make France paramount in the New World as well, once he had finished in Europe. In 1800, by secret treaty with Spain, France took over the vast (and largely virgin territory) of 'Louisiana' as a substitute for those lost *'quelques arpentes de neige'* (as Voltaire had scathingly termed them) in Canada. At the same time a French expeditionary force was dispatched to seize Toussaint l'Ouverture's negro republic of freed slaves in Hispaniola (Haiti). Castro's installation of Soviet rockets in Cuba was hardly more disturbing to American tranquillity. 'The day that France takes possession of New Orleans,' President Jefferson wrote to his minister in Paris in April 1802, 'we must marry ourselves to the British fleet and nation.' The following year he sent James Monroe as envoy extraordinary to treat with Napoleon.

Although it was to turn out to be the best bargain in American history, Monroe's opening bid was excessively modest, with a fall-back offer of $7·5 million just for New Orleans. But, if this failed, his instructions were to break off and seek 'a closer connection with Great Britain'. His negotiating partner was the astute Talleyrand, who, as a royalist exile, had spent two years in America.[10] At the Philadelphia bookshop of Saint Mery (who, as a sideline to books, had introduced contraceptives to the grateful Americans), Talleyrand had mixed with a curious group of expatriate aristocrats, who had fought for liberty in America while opposing it in their own country. He allegedly shocked Philadelphians by consorting publicly with a coloured lady. Nevertheless, during his time in the US he had ingested the clear lesson that the country was still, at heart, more English than not, and that its 'utility' to England would '... increase in proportion as the English Government gives up its present haughtiness of demeanour in all its relations with America.'[11] Therefore, on the eve of renewed war with England, France would have to lean over backwards to prevent America falling into the English camp.

Meanwhile, his forces decimated by yellow fever in Hispaniola and his restless eyes already focusing elsewhere, Napoleon had lost interest in the New World. On 11 April 1803 (by which time Anglo-French relations were once more on the brink of rupture), Talleyrand staggered the American negotiators by offering to sell them the entire 'Louisiana' Territory, as big in

LEFT A portrait of the young Napoleon by David.

area as the whole of the existing United States. Three weeks later the Louisiana Purchase was signed, at a price of $12 million – or only $4·5 million more than Monroe had been briefed to offer for New Orleans alone – and this regardless of Napoleon's promise to Spain never to sell to a third power.

'You will fight England again,' Napoleon remarked hopefully as he shook hands on the deal with the Americans. But at least the US would remain strictly neutral in the now imminent War of the Third Coalition; and on 7 November, as Napoleon was closing in on Vienna, Jefferson's army explorers, Lewis and Clark, were to reach the Pacific, thereby blazing the trail for America's 'Manifest Destiny' from burning sea to burning sea while the rest of the world, distracted, grappled in the heart of Europe. "*from sea to shining sea*."

Thus to Napoleon all the omens could not help but look favourable to getting what he wanted – hegemony over Europe – and preferably by peaceful means. The United States had opted for neutrality, and his former enemies in Europe seemed reluctant to face war again. With twenty-seven million[12] to England's fifteen, Prussia's six, and Austria's twenty million, France had the largest population from which to draw fresh soldiers – except for Mother Russia's thirty-nine million – and the efficiency of her existing forces showed that she could beat any combination that might attack her. The potential coalition powers had, as previously noted, no common interest to bind them together, except opposition to France, and England and Russia looked as if they might easily come to blows over conflicting interests in the Near East and the island of Malta; while, internally, England herself seemed anarchic, led by a weak and aimless government under 'Doctor' Addington, and with no land forces worth mentioning.[13] The only four remaining factors of menace were the Royal Navy, the manpower resources of the Russian Army, the plottings of the Bourbons and 'Pitt's gold', the British funds capable of mounting a fresh coalition. However – especially with Pitt ailing and safely out of power – these factors showed no serious sign of combining against him, and by the beginning of 1803, Napoleon's voice had taken on a more strident note. He annexed Piedmont (although his guarantee of the integrity of the Italian states had been a *quid pro quo* for England's surrender of Malta), and sent Marshal Ney to invade Switzerland, which enraged even 'Doctor' Addington.

On her side, England by 1803 was becoming increasingly alarmed at France's naval activity, which included large numbers of flat-bottomed invasion barges. Her fears were not without reason; Napoleon intended to use the years of peace to construct twenty-five ships-of-the-line annually which, within six or seven years, would make him (at least theoretically) unbeatable at sea. Addington infuriated Napoleon by refusing to withdraw from the key naval bastion of Malta. What Fox called 'reciprocal Billingsgate' mounted in the press of both countries, and with it national feeling. In March, Napoleon had lost his temper at a public *levée*, shaking his cane at the English ambassador, Lord Whitworth, to the point where Whitworth expected to be struck, and exclaiming: 'Now you mean to force me to fight for fifteen more years!'

After another month of terse negotiations, Whitworth received what amounted to a final ultimatum to pass on to Napoleon; England would recognize the Italian annexations, in exchange for Napoleon's evacuating Holland and Switzerland and accepting a ten-year English tenure of Malta. Enraged that anybody should present *him* with an ultimatum, at the same time taking it no more seriously than Hitler was to take Chamberlain's 1939 guarantee to the Poles, Napoleon

LEFT Talleyrand, former Bishop of Autun, Prince of Benevento, wit and libertine, and Napoleon's Foreign Secretary. He later defected to Tsar Alexander and served under the Restoration as France's adroit representative at the Congress of Vienna (1814–15), ending his career as King Louis-Philippe's ambassador to England. The painter, Pierre Paul Prud'hon, had tactfully concealed his deformed foot.

Mort de Monseigneur le Duc D'ENGHIEN.

The execution of the Duc d'Enghien, which Talleyrand
described as being 'worse than a crime, it was a blunder'.
A contemporary woodcut by an unknown Frenchman.

rejected the British terms. It was the first big mistake of his career. Instead of the years of peace he had hoped for, in which he could have made his power virtually unassailable, on 18 May 1803 France found herself again at war with England. The following day the blockading ships of Admiral Cornwallis were once more in position outside Brest.

Then, nearly a year later, Napoleon followed up this error with an even greater one. Shaken by the Cadoudal conspiracy against him, he decided upon an act of sheer terror that would deter his royalist foes once and for all. The thirty-two-year-old Duc d'Enghien was (says Duff Cooper[14]):

... not only the least blameworthy but the most admirable of the Bourbon princes.... Young, handsome and chivalrous he resembled more a hero of romance than a prince of the nineteenth century.

While prepared to fight for his family rights with the *Armée des Emigrés*, he alone had steadfastly refused to have any dealings with the conspirators against Napoleon, and lived quietly – following the pursuit of love – in the independent German state of Baden. On the night of 14 March 1804, he was kidnapped by a French cavalry detachment sent by Napoleon, and spirited off to the sinister Château de Vincennes. A week later, after a perfunctory court martial which produced no evidence against him, he was executed by firing squad, with his inseparable dog, and buried in a grave which had been dug well in advance. All Europe was outraged by the killing; in Russia, Tsar Alexander, the blood of whose own murdered father was barely dry,[15] felt personally affronted, ordered court mourning, and despatched a protest to France. It was Napoleon's blackest deed, but also, in the immortal phrase of Talleyrand, 'worse than a crime, it was a blunder'. Chateaubriand resigned as Napoleon's envoy in Switzerland, declaring later that the murder of d'Enghien changed the course of his life, 'as it did Napoleon's'. Indeed, for Napoleon it was to become the Ghost of Banquo, haunting him throughout his life; but, more immediately, it was to provide one of the principal causes of the renewal of coalitionary war against him.

Only a few weeks before the murder, George III had caught a chill while inspecting Volunteers and had gone off his head again,[16] having to be restrained from addressing Parliament with the words 'My Lords and Peacocks!' This made inevitable the departure of his feeble and unpopular favourite Addington, and the return of Pitt. On 19 May 1804, the reins of power were taken up again by the bellicose Pitt, bent – as always – on confrontation with Napoleon. It was the same day that, in Paris, a *Senatus Consultum* declared Napoleon Emperor of the French.

Notes to chapter 3

1 *A History of the English-Speaking Peoples*, Vol. III, p. 240.
2 By Carola Oman, *Lord Nelson* (London, 1947).
3 Not to be confused with the novelist.
4 The British army never put more than 40,000 men into action at any one time; the whole Peninsular War cost less than 40,000 British dead.
5 The war alone cost her £100 million.
6 London at this time already numbered 865,000 in population, compared with Paris's 650,000 and Vienna's 200,000.
7 *English Social History* (London 1944).
8 With comparable inaccuracy, Gillray portrays Josephine as a mountainous, blowsy tart.
9 *The Oxford History of the American People* (New York, 1965).
10 On the eve of his departure from England, he had asked an American general, who chanced to be staying in the same inn, for letters of introduction. The general replied sadly: 'I am perhaps the only American who cannot give you letters for his own country.' His name was Benedict Arnold.
11 Letter to Lord Shelburne.
12 Over the century following Napoleon, France's population grew remarkably slowly, to reach only 39·6 million by 1914; partly, in itself, a delayed consequence of the losses suffered during the Napoleonic wars.
13 Addington, the natural pacifist, had actually halved the army, disbanded the militia 'Volunteers' and discharged 40,000 sailors in order to abolish Pitt's income tax.
14 *Talleyrand*, p. 139.
15 Although some hold Alexander himself to have been not wholly innocent of the murder.
16 George's madness is now thought to have been Porphyria's Disease rather than real insanity.

4

Jumping the Ditch

They want us to jump the ditch, and we *will* jump it!   Napoleon

PITT IS TO Addington, As London is to Paddington,' wrote George Canning at a time
when Paddington was an undistinguished outer suburb.[1] To every English schoolboy
Pitt the Younger has long come to embody the spirit of warlike resistance to Napoleon;
probably his more successful contribution lay in times of peace rather than of war.
As a successful war leader, he had certainly not proved himself to be in the same league as
his father, great Chatham; on the other hand it was a very different France he had to face.
During the first Revolutionary Wars he had erred by frittering away his forces on minor expedi-
tions – for instance, to the West Indies, where disease (such as Napoleon was to encounter
in Hispaniola) had been victor[2] – instead of concentrating all on Europe. Like his father, however, Pitt was totally uncompromising in his determination to break the power of France. 'He
possessed perserverance and courage and never flinched from criticism,' remarks Winston
Churchill,[3] and indeed it was with Churchillian oratory that Pitt could turn upon his
opponents. Fox, he once declared:

... defies me to state, in one sentence, what is the object of the war. I know not whether I can do
it in one sentence, but in one word I can tell him that it is 'security'; security against a danger, the
greatest that ever threatened the world. It is security against a danger which never existed in any past
period of society ...

(How remote, perhaps even exaggerated, that danger may seem after the passage of nearly two
centuries and other, greater dangers!)

A cold and lonely personality who never married, proud and unlovable, if there was one thing
Pitt hated almost as much as France it was fecklessness. He disciplined himself with an icy
self-control (he had once had a painful tumour removed from his cheek without flinching).
His constant need to raise taxes in order to prosecute the wars was not destined to endear him
to the good-living merchants of England, and it was Pitt's added misfortune to have lived at
that time of peak viciousness in political satire, where his extenuated, angular figure proved
a godsend to the cartoonists. It was only towards the end of his days, and afterwards, that he
achieved anything resembling universal popularity.

With the war going badly again, in 1800 Pitt had found himself more unloved than ever
before and the following year he resigned over the issue of emancipation for the Irish Catholics,
after seventeen years in office. His successor, Addington, ('that mass of conciliation and clem-
ency' as his enemies called him), had promptly opened peace negotiations with Napoleon.
Out of power, but appointed Warden of the Cinque Ports,[4] Pitt passed his time riding, sailing

RIGHT Pitt, out of office, as 'Colonel Commandant
of the Cinque Port Volunteers'; his residence as
Warden – Walmer Castle – is in the background.

and partridge shooting, planting fruit-trees and growing wheat at Walmer Castle, his official residence, or gazing out over the Kentish cliffs, in deepest concern, at Napoleonic France. As 'Addington's peace' looked less and less appealing, so Pitt's allure was rekindled. At a party to celebrate his birthday on 28 May 1802, (from which Pitt was absent), a thousand guests rose to toast Pitt's health and sing the doggerel composed by George Canning:

And O! if again the rude whirlwind should rise,
The dawning of peace should fresh darkness deform,
The regrets of the good and the fears of the wise
Shall turn to the pilot that weathered the storm.

Returning to the Commons on the outbreak of war the following May, Pitt made one of the greatest orations ever heard there: 'and all for war, and for war without end,' noted Creevey the diarist.

Having started his prime ministerial career at the absurdly early age of twenty-four, Pitt was still not quite forty-four when recalled to power in 1804. Yet already he was a very sick man; often in pain, he had difficulty sleeping at night. Never physically robust, at the time of his resignation Pitt had been warned by his doctor that, unless he took a proper holiday and a 'cure', he would not survive the next parliamentary session. His chronic gout was not improved by excessive port-drinking, and in 1802 friends were deeply shocked by his bloated face and shaking hands. But, whatever the state of his health, nothing would in any way deflect him from pursuing the war against Napoleon with the utmost resolve.

The heroic view of Pitt is, of course, not entirely shared on the Continent:

Their *ploughshare was the sword in hireling hands,*
Their *fields manured by gore of other lands ...*

so noted even England's Byron of his nation's farmers, enriched by the war. To continental eyes, indeed, Pitt more often appears as the paymaster, 'buying' others to fight England's battles for her, at *their* expense in blood, while she aggrandized herself with fresh colonies. If Pitt had been less dedicated to the destruction of Napoleon, could not a compromise settlement have been achieved, thereby saving Europe – and France – untold misery? Yet it is doubtful whether, by 1804, with Napoleon firmly set on his imperial path of unlimited ambition, confrontation could long have been avoided. One thing was certain; as long as Pitt and Napoleon faced each other, no negotiated peace would be possible.

On returning to office, Pitt set himself two immediate objectives: to woo the Tsar, still outraged by the murder of the Duc d'Enghien, and to restore the effectiveness of the Royal Navy. The threat of Napoleon's naval construction programme, and the more immediate one of the growing flotilla of invasion barges, was very real in British eyes. When war with France had broken out in 1793, the navy had been in a bad state; four years later, not without cause, the mutinies at Spithead and the Nore broke out. Nevertheless, by the following year Nelson was able to wipe out the French fleet off Egypt. It was a reverse from which perhaps Napoleon's navy – already shaken by the havoc wreaked by the Revolution's purges of the officer corps – never properly recovered professionally. As Napoleon himself wrote of that abortive campaign:

'If it had not been for the English I should have been emperor of the East, but wherever there is water to float a ship, we are sure to find [them] in our way.'

The problem, for England, was to provide enough of those ships, and keep them there. Much of Pitt's restless energy was dedicated to reform and ship-building. Conditions gradually improved, and yet they were still appalling and it was, by modern standards, inconceivable that any human-being should have tolerated them. There was the brutality: the press-gangs on shore, and the floggings on board ship – a dozen lashes, the normal penalty for petty theft (double that for drunkenness), sufficed to rip the skin off a man's back. At sea the crews experienced months in disgustingly cramped quarters, rats eating the bandsmen's bagpipes, weevils in the hard-tack, scurvy and the boredom of prolonged blockade duty. Then, when the few minutes of battle at last came there were the horrible scenes of carnage, the dreadful wounds caused by cannon ball and jagged splinters of oak inadequately tended in the surgeons' hopelessly ill-equipped cockpit, the badly wounded dumped overboard together with the dead. Nevertheless, the one quality the British sailors never lacked was enthusiasm and the stimulus did not lie just in the greedy lure of prize money.

The contrast between their grievances and their indiscipline on the one hand and their splendid spirit in action and on the blockade service may seem unaccountable ...

writes G. M. Trevelyan,[5] continuing (perhaps a trifle eulogistically):

The explanation lay in this: the men before the mast knew that, for all the ill treatment they received, the nation regarded them as its bulwark and glory; that at the sight of one of Nelson's men with his tarry pigtail, the landsman's eye kindled with affection and pride. The country that used them so ill looked to them confidently to protect her, and they knew it.

At the time of the renewed outbreak of war in 1803, however, the Royal Navy was also a highly professional force. It was (in contrast to the Army) in the hands of the educated sons of gentlemen of modest means, like Nelson. Relations between officers and men were, particularly under Nelson, generally excellent. At the top Pitt had appointed as First Lord, Admiral Sir John Jervis, who had taken his new title of St Vincent from the battle which had saved England in 1797. An unflappable figure, it was he who, during the 1803 invasion scare, had declared challengingly: 'I don't say the French can't come. I say they can't come by sea.'

Body and soul, he stood for the all-out, offensive blockade of Napoleon's ports. At the same time, under pressure from Addington, he had instituted certain ill-chosen economies which undoubtedly handicapped the Navy when war came again. He was replaced, briefly, by Lord Melville, who was in turn to be succeeded in April by Lord Barham. Very much Pitt's appointee, Barham (previously Admiral Sir Charles Middleton) had been the great administrator who had resurrected the Navy after the war with America. Although aged seventy-eight, he was still full of vigour, and knew more about reactivating ships than anybody in the business. In the short time that was to elapse before the ultimate showdown at Trafalgar, Barham was to prove – in Arthur Bryant's view – 'the greatest naval administrator since Samuel Pepys'.

Just below came a galaxy of brilliant sea commanders: 'Billy-go-tight' Cornwallis, the sixty-year-old Commander-in-Chief of the Channel Fleet; Collingwood, who had served so long at sea it was said his children scarcely knew him; Cotton, Calder, Cochrane and Pellew – and, above, the genius of the frail but fearless Nelson. It was they who maintained the super standards boasted by the navy of that day. Ships-of-the-line, though minute by twentieth-century measurements, then represented (again quoting Arthur Bryant) 'the highest masterpieces of the constructional skill and capacity of their age'. After decades of hard training, the British handling of these exquisite, yet primitive, pieces of equipment was unsurpassable, and so was the tactical seamanship of the commanders. When it came to the crucial factor of gunnery, nobody could concert a broadside with such deadly efficacy; it was something that Napoleon's navy, for all its enthusiasm, could never emulate.

Yet, on the outbreak of war in 1803, England could count no more than 55 capital ships against France's 42; though because Addington's declaration had taken Napoleon by surprise, only 13 of these latter were ready for immediate service. Nevertheless, the margin was still uncomfortably slim by the critical spring of 1805 when – with Spain and Holland aligned against her as well – Barham had only 83 battleships in commission, and many of those badly in need of repair. But the spirit made up for much; putting to sea in May 1803, Nelson wrote to Emma Hamilton: 'I have no fears', and the following year (to his friend, Alexander Davison):

... I am expecting the French to put to sea – every day, hour and moment; and you may rely that, if it is within the power of man to get at them, it shall be done; and I am sure that all my brethren look forward to that day as the finish of our laborious cruise.

Of 1803–5 it could be said with truth that *only* the Royal Navy of St Vincent, Barham and Nelson stood between Napoleon and world domination. Certainly had it proved unable to prevent Napoleon landing a substantial force in England, her prospects would have been dim, for the British Army came out of a very different mould to the Navy. It was, according to one contemporary description:

... lax in its discipline, entirely without system, and very weak in numbers. Each colonel of a regiment managed it according to his own notions, or neglected it altogether; professional pride was rare; professional knowledge even more so. Never was a kingdom less prepared for a stern and arduous conflict.

Officers (including the future Duke of Wellington) had to buy their way in, and upwards; advancement by merit alone was rare. The system produced some brave and capable officers, but in essence they remained amateurs, regarding war more as a sport than a profession. As for the rank-and-file, even Wellington once declared (admittedly in a fit of anger) that they 'all enlisted for drink!' Corporal punishment, even more brutal than in the senior service, endeavoured to maintain discipline.

Administration at the top in the Army was chaotic; throughout the war, with Parliament fearful of the odium conscription might bring, voluntary enlistment was the only means of obtaining troops. Under Addington's peace economies, the Army had actually been reduced to under 150,000 – barely enough to garrison Ireland and the Empire and less than Napoleon would later be able to throw into just one of his big battles. To make up the deficit, a body of militiamen, or Volunteers, had been formed; a horde of untrained, unarmed, undisciplined but eager amateurs, they could only have further confused the Regular Army's task had an invasion ever materialized. There was a long way to go before General Bell could boast of the

Peninsular Army as being 'the bravest, the best, the finest disciplined and well-seasoned army in the world' or that a French officer could admiringly rate the British soldier as having '... no superior in the world; fortunately there are only a few of him'.

On the marriage of his favourite sister Pauline in 1803, Napoleon had instructed her '... the only nation you must never receive are the English'. Throughout his remarkable career, whether fighting by land amid alpine snows, in the sands of Egypt or on the endless plains of eastern Europe, Napoleon had never been able to forget that it was England who was his principal, uncompromising adversary. It was England who had mounted, and financed, the successive coalitions against France; yet, weak though her army might be in relation to his own apparently irresistible land forces, she remained protected by the wide moat of the English Channel and that ubiquitous Royal Navy. Napoleon had tried to strike at the arch-enemy by disrupting her communications with India, but Nelson had thwarted this design at Aboukir Bay in 1799. He had tried to strangle her by barring her trade with the north European ports, but Nelson had brought the League of Armed Neutrality to ruin at Copenhagen in 1801. There remained only a direct invasion of the British Isles.

As far back as 1797 the possibilities for such an invasion had looked enticing when a French raiding party landed in Ireland, pinning down for nearly three weeks the entire British garrison. That same year Napoleon, in his brief command of 'The Army of England', had begun the building of a flotilla of flat-bottomed vessels, and from the collapse of the peace in 1803 onwards he concentrated his thoughts on invasion. 'They want us to jump the ditch,' he declared in a fury, 'and we *will* jump it!' With characteristic vigour and resourcefulness, he set thousands of navvies to work dredging out the invasion ports and digging new basins to accommodate his flotilla of 2,000 craft. Shipyards all along France's Channel coast and the Low Countries reverberated with hammering and sawing. Napoleon himself specified the prototype of: 'A flat-bottomed boat able to transport 100 men across the Channel. There would be a mortar in the bows and stern ...'; he busied himself with such details as the numbers of cooking pots and pioneer spades to be carried in each barge, and even drew up an elementary rowing drill for the unfortunate troops who were to propel their own *péniches*. On the command 'Row!'

... every man holding the butt of the oars stretches forward together; they lean on the butt so that the blade does not plunge into the water until they have fully extended their arms ...

As it evolved, the invasion fleet comprised three kinds of vessel: large sail-driven *prames* over a hundred feet long, and each carrying 150 men; well-armed *chaloupes cannonières*, transporting guns, ammunition and horses; and – the most numerous – sixty-foot *péniches*, each containing 55 infantrymen. Ingenious 'terror' propaganda rumours were also circulated suggesting that Napoleon might also be planning to land troops by balloon, or even by a Channel tunnel or a bridge. He himself planned to be able to disembark 120,000 picked troops, plus 6,000 horse and supporting artillery; he was prepared to accept 20,000 casualties drowned on the way. 'One loses that number in battle every day,' he reckoned; 'and what battle ever promised such results as a landing in England?' No doubt as a result of misreading the scurrility of the British cartoonists, he also expected to '... have found partisans enough in England to effect a disunion sufficient to paralyze the rest of the nation.' He planned to reach London within five days.

Invasion, 1805, by air, sea and tunnel.
A French fantasy of the period which might in part
explain Britain's continued resistance to the
notion of a Channel Tunnel, two centuries later.

Throughout the glorious Indian Summer, continuing through the October of 1803, the east wind blew in the invaders' favour, but still the fleet did not leave its harbours. Napoleon moved his headquarters to a château at Pont-de-Briques near Boulogne, and at the end of November he instructed Cambacérès to 'have a song written to the tune of the *Chant du Départ* for the descent on England....' But in fact things had fallen badly out of joint; there were hopeless delays in the shipyards and money was running short; harbours were still so inadequate that it could take several days to get all the barges out to sea; and meanwhile the English frigates prowled everywhere, arrogantly close in-shore, like hungry sharks lurking to snap up an unwary vessel. Worst of all, the flat-bottomed barges, built without keels so as to ease beaching and unloading on the Kentish coast, proved hopelessly unseaworthy in anything but mill-pond waters rarely encountered in the notoriously capricious Channel. Sly jokes began to make the rounds in Paris about 'Don Quixote of *La Manche*'; in December winter gales closed down the invasion season, and almost immediately Napoleon's thoughts were distracted by the Cadoudal conspiracy.

Having examined one of the invasion barges that had been picked up, drifting helplessly in the Channel, a British admiral dismissed the prospects of such 'contemptible and ridiculous craft' achieving anything. Nevertheless, totally ill-prepared as England was to meet any invasion on land, the threat was received in deadly earnest (not altogether unmixed with the farcical). English babes went to bed terrified by such cautionary lullabies as:

> *Baby, baby naughty baby,*
> *Hush you squalling thing, I say;*
> *Hush your squalling, or it may be*
> *Bonaparte may pass this way.*
>
> *Baby, baby, he's a giant,*
> *Tall and black as Rouen steeple;*
> *And he dines and sups, rely on 't,*
> *Every day on naughty people.*

Church doors had Henry v's stirring words from the Siege of Harfleur pinned to them; the caricaturists took on a new note of belittling savagery, while blood-curdling posters depicted the horrors of invasion – mass rape of women and slaughter of infants – not to be improved on even in 1914. Songsters so bad they might have been hard-pressed to find employment with the BBC in a later age, had a heyday:

> *The French are coming, so they declare,*
> *Of their floats and balloons all the papers advise us,*
> *They're to swim through the ocean and ride on the air,*
> *In some foggy evening to land and surprise us!* ...
>
> *We'll announce to the world his detestable Fame;*
> *How the traitor* RENOUNCED HIS REDEEMER *and then*
> *How he murdered his Prisoner and poison'd his Men!*

Spymania was rife, with innocent holidaymakers being arrested for raising a telescope to their eye as a ship passed by, and there were more ugly rumours about a rising in Dublin.

Jingoism was orchestrated by none less than Pitt, who cheerfully toasted 'a speedy meeting with our enemies on our *own* shores'. Then still out of power, he found himself so preoccupied in training his battalions of Kentish Volunteers that, even by December 1803 when the danger had (at least temporarily) passed, it was 'impossible for me to think of going to town until the week after'. To Winston Churchill, writing a century-and-a-half later and with a detectable note of envy:

Few things in England's history are more remarkable than this picture of an ex-Prime Minister, riding his horse at the head of a motley company of yokels, drilling on the fields of the South Coast, while a bare twenty miles away across the Channel the Grand Army of Napoleon waited only for a fair wind and a clear passage.[6]

Meanwhile, in London even the pacific Addington took to appearing in the House in uniform; further north, Dorothy Wordsworth watched the Grasmere Volunteers marching back and forth, while in Scotland Walter Scott polished up his swordsmanship by slashing at turnips stuck on poles, and at Selkirk a forebear of the Fourteenth Earl of Home amused his Volunteers by singing an old Border song: 'Up with the souters [shoemakers] of Selkirk and down with the Earl of Hume!' Lord Auckland was even convinced that, if the invasion came, '... you would see all the ladies letting their nails grow that they might scratch at the invader'[7] for 'You never saw so military a country,' he observed; 'nothing but fighting is talked of.'

In its spirit of defiant determination, the mood of England then seems to have resembled that of the summer of 1940. Martello towers were built at key points along the coast, and floating batteries anchored off the more vulnerable beaches. At first the Government talked seriously of countering the invaders with a desperate 'scorched earth' policy in southern England; but more sensible was the proposal by Major-General John Moore (later of Corunna fame) to harass them with guerrilla tactics.

In the event, winter passed, followed by an unusually calm and lovely spring and summer, and still no invasion came. The fervour abated in England. Neglected, Boulogne harbour began to silt up with sand again, and, because of the Royal Navy's successful blockade, the training of Napoleon's crews suffered, as did the equipment of their vessels. Yet still he persisted with the project, to the extent of striking a superbly over-confident victory medal, with the inscription: *Descente en Angleterre, frappé à Londres en 1804.*

On 20 July 1804, against the advice of his admirals, Napoleon insisted on holding a review of the invasion flotillas, in the teeth of an onshore gale. Over two thousand men were drowned as a result. On 16 August 1804, amid magnificent panoply with 1,300 drummers on parade, he revisited the Army of Boulogne to bestow on its leaders the coveted *Légion d'Honneur* created by him two years earlier. By the time of his coronation as Emperor that December, he had assembled 177,000 men and more than 2,000 invasion craft on the Channel. As a fighting force it was incomparable, and morale was still magnificent:

> *From England we'll bring back treasure*
> *That won't have cost us a sou....*

NAPOLÉON AU CAMP DE BOULOGNE.

Napoleon at the Camp of Boulogne, seated on the ancient throne of Charlemagne's successor Dagobert, and distributing the *Légion d'Honneur*; 'it is by such baubles that men are governed.' 100,000 troops attended the ceremony; 2,000 drummers announced the arrival of the Emperor. The axe-bearing veteran being decorated is probably a member of the Corps of Engineers. Idle ships lie impotently in the harbour.

they sang with lusty expectancy in the taverns of Boulogne. After repeated exercises, Napoleon had proved that 25,000 men could now be embarked in ten minutes, but he had also at last come to the realization that he could not invade by means of his flat-bottomed barges alone. Everything depended on his weaker navy being able to achieve local supremacy for a limited period, to cover the invasion force.

'Let us be master of the Channel for six hours and we are masters of the world,' he wrote to Admiral Latouche-Tréville in July 1804. That Admiral, France's best, died however of a sudden heart attack. He was replaced by the more timid Villeneuve, and – once again – the invasion was called off for 1804. But the intent remained, with Napoleon vowing to his new Empress: 'I will take you to London, madam. I intend the wife of the modern Caesar to be crowned in Westminster.' Meanwhile, British heavy-handedness had come to his aid that winter by bringing Spain into the war against her. This meant that the campaigning season of 1805 would open with France granted useful naval bases at Cadiz and Ferrol (on the north-west tip of Spain), and her naval strength reinforced by the addition of 32 Spanish ships-of-the-line.

Although war had reopened between France and England in May 1803, there had continued to be virtually no fighting through that year and 1804, while France threatened invasion and both camps armed and trained for the next round. However in the realm of diplomacy Pitt had not been idle. Despite the dislike and distrust most red-blooded Englishmen felt for Russia and the Russians – which was mutual, and which Nelson exemplified when, at Copenhagen in 1801, he had told the battered Danes he only wished they had been Russians – Pitt had skilfully been fanning Tsar Alexander's indignation at the murder of d'Enghien. Equally he had been exploiting the Austrians' still smarting sense of humiliation, compounded with their anger at Napoleon's fresh annexations in northern Italy. On 11 April 1805, a secret 'provisional' treaty signed in St Petersburg laid the foundation of the Third Coalition, consisting of England, Austria, Sweden and Naples, with a big question-mark hovering over hitherto neutral Prussia. Through the dangerous early summer months, however, all continued to hang on a thread. Russia had still to be persuaded of the altruism of England's continued occupation of Malta,[8] while at home Pitt was very much at bay. In the Commons he had sat helplessly with tears streaming down his face as MPs voted to impeach his friend, Melville, now Treasurer of the Navy, for speculative improprieties. There was bad news from the West Indies about raiding successes by the French Navy, while the shortage of British ships was giving rise to serious fears that the continental blockade could not long be sustained.

It was the British blockade, however, that drove Napoleon into the ultimate act of provocation. In June he annexed the Ligurian Republic, with the excuse that he had to have its ships and seamen to help defeat England. This was in flagrant violation of his treaty with Austria, and it threw Tsar Alexander into an implacable rage. Napoleon, he declared '. . . is a scourge of the world; he wants a war and he shall have it'. Russia now committed herself to a new war against France. Combined with Austria, and with contingents from a host of lesser German states as well as Sweden, this Third Coalition would – so Pitt hoped – be able to field more than half a million troops by Christmas. On top of this, there also seemed a fair hope that Prussia might finally make up its mind to join the Allies. Apart from the war at sea, England's role in all this was to finance her continental allies to the tune of £1,250,000 per 100,000 soldiers per year, an astronomic sum in those days. Altogether, at least on paper, France would now be confronted by the most powerful land force yet mounted against her.

The war aims of the Third Coalition were to 'return peace to Europe', forcing France to withdraw from her conquests and accept, in essence, the territorial *status quo ante* of 1791. To achieve these aims, the basic Allied strategy for 1805 was as follows: in the south, the Austrian Archduke Charles (who had proved himself the most competent Austrian leader during the 1797 campaign) would attack in Northern Italy with the intention of pinning down a substantial portion of Napoleon's forces on the wrong side of the Alps; to the north, an imposing body of some two hundred thousand Russian troops, under Kutuzov and Buxhöwden, would join up with the main strength of the Austrian Army, led by Archdukes Ferdinand and John, to thrust through the territory of Napoleon's Bavarian ally. The Russo-Austrian force would then strike across the Upper Rhine, into France's vulnerable eastern flank. At the same time expeditionary forces comprised of 50,000 English, Swedes and Neapolitans would open other diversionary fronts along the European periphery. On paper, at least, it looked like a perfectly sound strategy. Secret as the Allied designs were, however, they were not to escape Napoleon for long as the summer of 1805 wore on.

Notes to chapter 4

1 'L'Oracle, 1803–1804'.
2 Nearly half the total death-roll during the twenty-two years of war (about 100,000 for Britain) was suffered in Pitt's West Indies' campaign.
3 *A History of the English-Speaking Peoples*, pp. 239–40.
4 An archaic honour later also bestowed on that other custodian of an embattled Britain, Winston Churchill.
5 *English Social* History, p. 503.
6 Op. cit., Vol. III, p. 241. There is a Churchillian inaccuracy here, the 'Grand Army' had not yet come into being.
7 *Journal and Correspondence of William Lord Auckland*, 1862.
8 In her traditional quest for warm-water ports, Russia herself cast covetous eyes on the Island of Malta.

5

'Rely on my Activity'

Rely on my activity; I will surprise the world by the grandeur and rapidity of my strokes!

Napoleon to Cambacérès, August 1805

O N 3 AUGUST 1805, Napoleon had arrived at Boulogne. Three days later he summoned his élite shock formation, the Imperial Guard. Day by day his stocky, impatient figure paced the coastal heights gazing in frustration at those famous white cliffs just visible in the distant haze, waiting impatiently for Admiral Villeneuve and the Combined Fleet to appear in the Channel. Today, as that narrow strip of water presents a rather less imposing obstacle, those white cliffs an altogether less alluring goal, it is hard to avoid the parallel between Napoleon and that other warlord of 135 summers later. Both had risen from lowly station to command, in a short space of time, the world's most invincible land force; both were restlessly daemonic men of small stature and both were at the zenith of their power as a commander; it was almost the same time of year; the grand design was approximately similar; and each would end, in frustration, by turning his great war machine eastwards instead. For Hitler too, the omens for the grand project (which had occupied Napoleon's fantasies intermittently over the previous seven years) had never seemed more propitious.

Experience had taught Napoleon that, even with the added strength of the Spaniards, there was still no prospect of his matching the Royal Navy, ship for ship. Therefore he would aim, as he had intended the previous year, to obtain local superiority in the Channel, just long enough for him to load and discharge onto British soil his overwhelming land force. To achieve this, in his third and final Grand Design issued on 22 March 1805, Napoleon ordered his scattered fleet to take to sea and make for the West Indies. By threatening British possessions there, and recalling how mistakenly Pitt had reacted to the threat in the previous decade, Napoleon reckoned he would draw Nelson and the main weight of the British battle fleets after him. Villeneuve and Ganteaume would then elude the British in the Caribbean, and double back with all speed and force, to appear in the Channel in July with the Combined Fleet of nearly 60 battleships.

It was with considerable misgiving that Villeneuve, driven on the one hand by fear of his master, on the other hand of interception by Nelson's blockaders, left Toulon for the Straits of Gibraltar. Already that January his fleet, with its inexperienced sailors and unbattleworthy tackle, had nearly met disaster when making a sortie in a storm. Nelson and the Mediterranean Fleet narrowly missed Villeneuve off Majorca; and then the French had disappeared, according to plan, into the Atlantic. Napoleon's expectations also appeared to be fulfilled by Nelson following his quarry, westwards. Although he made the trip from Gibraltar to Barbados in the record

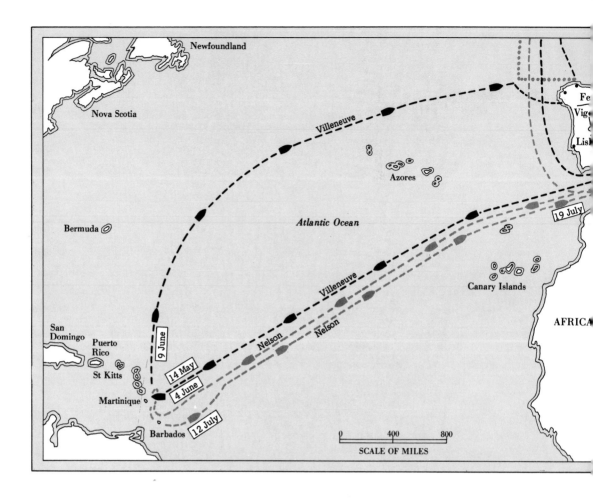

Newfoundland

Nova Scotia

Villeneuve

Azores

Atlantic Ocean

Bermuda

Canary Islands

San Domingo

Puerto Rico

St Kitts

Martinique

Barbados

Villeneuve

Nelson

Nelson

9 June

14 May

4 June

12 July

19 July

AFRICA

Fe
Vig
Lis

0   400   800

SCALE OF MILES

time of little over three weeks, misled by faulty intelligence, Nelson proved equally unable to overhaul the French in the West Indies. Obeying his orders, Villeneuve headed back eastwards for the Channel, but, pursuing him, Nelson was still able to make the return Atlantic crossing in a fortnight less than Villeneuve. What was even more crucial for Napoleon's Grand Design, however, was that Barham and his admirals had not been taken in by the French fleet's 'deception play'. The Duc de Decrès, Napoleon's able Minister of the Marine, had warned him that – whatever the crisis – the Royal Navy would *never* be enticed to disperse its effectives so as to leave the Western Approaches unguarded. It was a tradition that was to run through to the 1940s, and Decrès was to be proved right, Napoleon wrong. As if by radio communication, in an era when the fastest and farthest-reaching signal was the flag and the swift sloop, but in fact as a consequence of years of superlative training the British admirals seemed to know instinctively what to do without waiting for orders from above. When Nelson left for the West Indies, reinforcements were mustered in readiness to bolster the Channel Fleet – just in case.

The danger, for Britain, remained extreme. The enemy had all but succeeded in concentrating a superior force at the decisive point. Nelson, still off Cadiz, beating northwards on the day that Napoleon had arrived at Boulogne (3 August), wrote gloomily in his diary: 'I feel every moment of this foul wind ... I am dreadfully uneasy.' In England the invasion alarms were

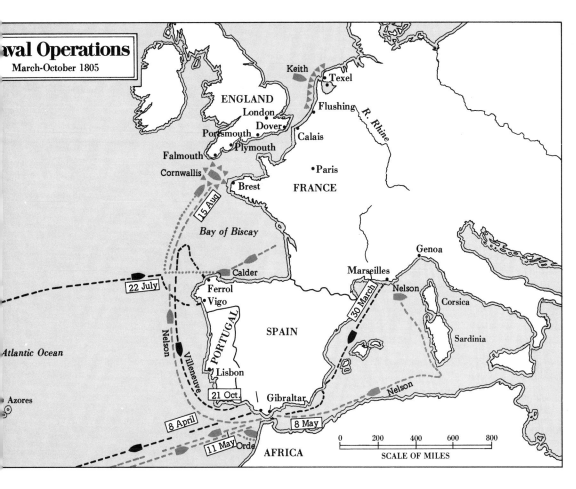

aval Operations
March-October 1805

Keith
Texel
ENGLAND
Flushing
London
R. Rhine
Dover
Portsmouth
Calais
Plymouth
Falmouth
Paris
Cornwallis
FRANCE
Brest
15 Aug
Bay of Biscay
Genoa
Marseilles
Calder
Nelson
22 July
Ferrol
Corsica
Vigo
30 March
Nelson
PORTUGAL
SPAIN
Atlantic Ocean
Sardinia
Nelson
Lisbon
Azores
21 Oct
Villeneuve
Gibraltar
Nelson
8 April
8 May
11 May Orde
AFRICA
0   200   400   600   800
SCALE OF MILES

RIGHT Admiral Villeneuve, by
Quenedey. Nelson's unhappy
adversary, insulted by Napoleon
as a '*Jean-Foûtre*' for his
excessive prudence, Villeneuve
eventually committed suicide
after Trafalgar.

sounding again; the Volunteers were on alert; Walter Scott galloped a hundred miles in a day to attend the muster of Dalkeith, while Sir John Moore's men practised combating invaders breast-high in the sea. On 18 August, the *Victory* brought Nelson back to England on his final homecoming. After hunting Villeneuve for 14,000 miles with total lack of success, he had hardly expected a friendly reception; as it was, he was quite overcome by the affection and admiration he encountered everywhere. When he re-embarked less than a month later many were in tears, recorded Southey, and 'knelt down before him and blessed him as he passed'. Returning to his weary ships, *en route* for Trafalgar, Nelson remarked simply to Hardy: 'I had their huzzas before. I have their hearts now.'

By this time, however, the immediate threat to England had passed, though it was by no means apparent at the time. A brig carrying Nelson's dispatches, the *Curieux*, had sighted Villeneuve heading for the Bay of Biscay and reached London with this vital information on 9 July. Naval reinforcements were rushed to bottle up the Channel off Cape Finisterre. On 22 July Rear-Admiral Sir Robert Calder with fifteen battleships joined battle there with Villeneuve's twenty. An elderly officer apparently concerned at his inferiority in numbers, Calder did not press the attack and – after an inconclusive action – Villeneuve was allowed to escape. Although Calder had only acted with a circumspection which would not have shamed Admiral Jellicoe at Jutland a century later, all England cried out for his blood and he returned to a court-martial and disgrace. Nevertheless, the Battle of Finisterre was enough to have a decisive influence upon Villeneuve's subsequent moves. In sharp contrast to Nelson's forces, after the summer's arduous sailing Villeneuve's ships were in poor shape, his crews reduced by scurvy and dysentery and those of his Spanish allies verging on mutiny: 'Our condition,' he reported to Decrès, 'is frightful.' He personally had also never held much faith in Napoleon's invasion scheme. Thus, after the brush with Calder, instead of continuing northwards, Villeneuve retired nervously into Ferrol. On 13 August he sailed southwards again, for the greater safety of Cadiz, where he was promptly sealed in again by Nelson's returning fleet, ultimately to be driven out to his doom off Trafalgar two months later.

Meanwhile, unaware of what had happened to Villeneuve, Napoleon was pursuing his plans to their climax at Boulogne. One hundred thousand men were drawn up on parade in a single line along the shore, an awe-inspiring spectacle. But time was not standing still. Napoleon – well-informed by spies – was well aware of the ponderously mounting threat of the land forces of Austria and Russia, combined under Pitt's Third Coalition. Yet he still considered that he had time to invade England, then return to deal Austria a crippling blow. Back and forth across the cliffs he strode, waiting impotently for the change of wind (which would never, in any event, bring Villeneuve). Reproachfully he wrote, on 13 August, to his Empress, absent at a spa:

It is not often one hears from you. You forget your friends, which is wrong. I did not know that the waters of Plombières had the same effect as those of Lethe. It seems to me that it was drinking these same Plombières waters that once made you say, 'Ah, Bonaparte, if ever I die, who will there be to love you?' That was a very long time ago, wasn't it? Everything passes, beauty, wit, sentiment, even the sun, all but one thing that is endless; the good I wish you, your happiness. I cannot be more loving even if you laugh at me for my pains. Goodbye, dear friend. I had the English cruisers attacked yesterday; everything passed off well....

Summer would not last forever. The letter to Josephine coincided with fresh orders to Villeneuve to hasten with all forces to the Channel, Napoleon being unaware that it was also the same day that Villeneuve was setting his sails in the opposite direction, for Cadiz. Uncertainty about Villeneuve's movements threw Napoleon into a terrible rage. Grossly calling the unhappy admiral a *'Jean-Foûtre'*, he accused him of little short of cowardice and treason, charges which drove Villeneuve to despair and, later, to suicide. The three days, 18–20 August, marked the period of Napoleon's highest expectations for the Channel crossing, although he was constantly receiving fresh warnings from Foreign Minister Talleyrand of Austria's warlike preparations to his rear. On 22 August, still ignorant of Villeneuve's true movements (of which the latter had not dared inform him), Napoleon wrote again to him at Brest, commanding:

Sail, do not lose a moment, and with my squadrons reunited enter the Channel. England is ours. We are ready and embarked. Appear for twenty-four hours, and all will be ended....

It was perhaps significant of Napoleon's own waning confidence that the six hours' mastery of the Channel he had required of Admiral Latouche-Tréville the previous year had now grown to twenty-four by August 1805. On 23 August a letter to Talleyrand reveals his restless thoughts already beginning to move elsewhere. If Villeneuve were suddenly (and magically) to appear, then there would still be time to launch the invasion; otherwise 'I shall raise my camp and march on Vienna.' An abject letter from Decrès assured him that Villeneuve had sailed to Cadiz, and urged him to regard this as a decree of Fate and cut his losses. 'It is a misery for me,' he lamented, 'to know the trade of the sea, for this knowledge wins no confidence nor produces any effect on Your Majesty's plans.' For several days longer, Napoleon remained in a state of indecision, intolerable to his nature. Then, abruptly, he set to preparing orders for the new operations. On 26 August he instructed his chief staff officer, Marshal Berthier, to move the Army of Boulogne against Austria. On 5 September, amid early autumn sunshine after a long, cold summer a captured schooner revealed to England the joyous news that the enemy had marched out of Boulogne, 'because of a new war with Russia'. England was saved!

Napoleon's decision to march east in 1805, and abandon (forever, as it was to turn out) his dream of leading a victorious army through the streets of London, looks to have been extraordinarily precipitate. But historians continue to argue as to whether he did *seriously* intend to invade England in 1805. Among other indications, however, the arrival of both the Imperial Guard and the cavalry suggest that it was more than a bluff. Equally, shortage of horses, and the far-from-complete marching array of the Grand Army when ordered to about-turn, indicate that there was little premeditation about his change of plan. Could an invasion have succeeded? Given the overall superiority of the Royal Navy in seamanship, if not in ships, it would have been a highly risky operation. But *if* Villeneuve had arrived in the Channel according to the Grand Design, and *if* the Third Coalition had not begun to menace France's back door, the risk might have seemed an acceptable one to the arch-gambler that Napoleon was. On the other hand, Arthur Bryant may not have been wrong in his estimation that 'Only the prudence or timidity of his admiral had saved his fleet from a fate as awful as that of the Spanish Armada.' As it was, his abandonment of the much-vaunted invasion project constituted perhaps the most serious strategic reverse in Napoleon's career up to that time; therefore, all the more did he

OVERLEAF *Napoleon at the Camp of Boulogne* by Bagetti. Napoleon inspecting his invasion fleet of *péniches, chaloupes, cannonières* and *prames*, uselessly harbour-bound in Boulogne. The ships standing out to sea are presumably the blockading Royal Navy squadrons, while the curious figure holding a large timber on the right perhaps represents Napoleon's fruitless ship-building programme.

who lived on success need a stunning victory elsewhere. Had the invasion aborted, however, as Thiers remarks,[1] it would

... at least have exposed him to a sort of ridicule, and would have exhibited him to the eyes of Europe as in a real state of impotence in opposition to England. The continental coalition, furnishing him with a field of battle which he needed ... drew him most seasonably from an indecisive and unpleasant situation.

Thus there was little doubt that, to some extent, Napoleon was himself relieved by what his despondent Minister of the Marine termed a 'decree of Fate'; certainly the new course of action imposed on him came as the most welcome kind of relief after all the months of frustrated inactivity facing out across the Channel. A brave new world of military possibilities in his own element (which, indubitably, the sea was not) opened itself to Napoleon – now, at last, the supreme war-lord of France. 'For the first time,' says Thiers, '... he was free, free as Caesar and Alexander had been. ... All Europe was open to his combinations.'

As it was to evolve, Napoleon's new plan of operations indeed seemed hardly less audacious than the one he had just abandoned. For six unbroken hours he dictated it to Daru, Lieutenant-General of the Army. The fact that he should have utilized so eminent a dignitary as a mere scribe denoted the extreme secrecy with which Napoleon prepared this campaign; for secrecy was absolutely essential to its success. Thus only Daru and Berthier – Napoleon's Minister of War, Master of Hounds, and chief staff officer, whom the *grognards* nicknamed 'the Emperor's wife' – were kept privy to the master-plan.

On the other hand, the total lack of secrecy of the Allies presented Napoleon's excellent intelligence service with as clear a picture of their intentions as if Napoleon himself 'had been present at the military conferences of M. de Winzingerode, the Austrian Chief-of-Staff, at Vienna'.[2] A great mass of 300,000 men (with more to follow) was mobilizing against him. Heading from south to north there was first of all Archduke Charles facing across the River Adige in northern Italy with some 100,000 troops. Next was Archduke Ferdinand, with roughly another hundred thousand, heading westward for Bavaria and already on the River Inn. Dividing the two archdukes, however, was the great mountain massif of the Tyrol, with its few viable and easily blocked passes, held by a small linking force under Archduke John. Then, far away to the east, were three ponderously moving Russian armies totalling another hundred thousand. Under Kutuzov and Buxhöwden, two were already on the borders of Austrian Galicia and clearly intending to join up with Archduke Ferdinand. Finally, further north, there was Bennigsen's army sitting on the eastern frontier of Prussia so as to exert pressure on its wavering king, Frederick William III, and with the (rather distant) ambition of awaiting Swedish and English reinforcements to move through Pomerania on Hanover and Holland.

Thus there would be three main Allied efforts developing across the continent of Europe: south, centre and north. All this was evident to Napoleon. It was equally evident that the gravest threat to France would come in the centre, once Ferdinand was joined by the Russians. His extraordinary intuition, aided by a comprehension of the rigid traditionalism of the Austrian military mind and its passion for fortresses, led Napoleon to calculate that Ferdinand would aim to establish himself in the Bavarian stronghold of Ulm on the Upper Danube Valley (a favourite

Marshal Berthier, later Prince of Neuchâtel. A somewhat romanticized portrayal of Napoleon's devoted chief of staff, nicknamed 'the Emperor's wife'.

standby of past Austrian tacticians). There he would wait for the Russians, then thrust into the French flank at Strasbourg with crushingly superior forces. With what was to prove uncanny accuracy, Napoleon predicted the positions the Austrians and Russians would reach several weeks ahead, and the routes they would take.

Above all, however, his genius for the *coup d'œil* immediately revealed to him the essential flaw in the Allied strategy. The enemy forces were widely dispersed over Europe. Because of the obstacle of the Tyrolean Alps, the Austrian Archdukes would have extreme difficulty in supporting each other. But what most attracted his gaze was the immense distance that separated Ferdinand, pressing on aggressively westwards towards Ulm, and the slow-moving Russians coming up behind him. They must inevitably be several weeks' march apart. (Kutuzov had in fact already started ten days later than reckoned; it appears, unbelievably, that one of the problems of the Allied timetable was the unallowed-for fact that the Russians were still using the Julian Calendar, which was twelve days behind that of their western confederates!)

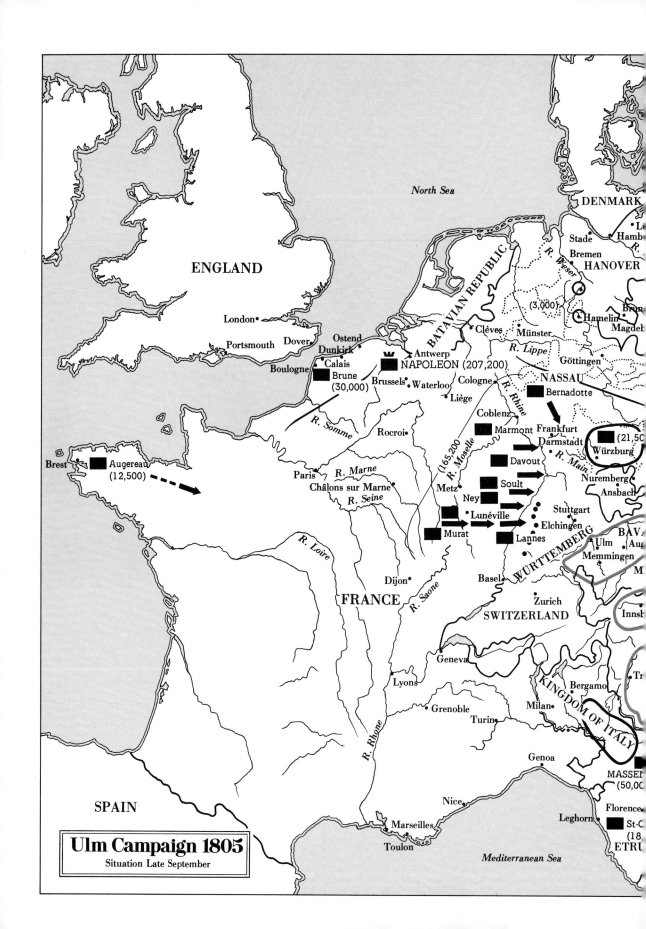

North Sea

DENMARK

ENGLAND

London•

Portsmouth•   Dover•

Boulogne•   Calais

Dunkirk
Ostend

Antwerp

NAPOLEON (207,200)

Brune
(30,000)

Brussels•   •Waterloo

Liège

Cologne•

NASSAU

Bernadotte

R. Somme

Rocroi•

Coblenz•

Frankfurt

Darmstadt

Würzburg

(21,5

Marmont

Paris•   R. Marne

Châlons sur Marne•

R. Seine

Metz•

Davout

R. Main

Soult

Nuremberg•

Ansbach•

Brest•

Augereau
(12,500)

R. Loire

Ney

Stuttgart•

R. Moselle

Lunéville•

Elchingen

BAV

Murat

Lannes

Ulm   Aug

Memmingen•

M

Dijon•

FRANCE

R. Saone

Basel•

Zurich•

SWITZERLAND

Innsb

Geneva•

Lyons•

Grenoble•

Milan•

Bergamo•

Turin•

KINGDOM OF ITALY

Tr

R. Rhone

Genoa•

MASSE
(50,0

Nice•

SPAIN

Marseilles•

Toulon•

Mediterranean Sea

Florence•

Leghorn•   St-C
(18

ETRU

Ulm Campaign 1805

Situation Late September

Cleves•   Münster•

R. Lippe

Göttingen•

Stade•   Hamb

Bremen•   HANOVER

(3,000)

Hamelin•

Magdeb

Brun

L

R. Rhine

R. Weser

SWEDEN

Copenhagen

sund

Lauenbourg

Königsberg

Tilsit

R. Niemen

Eylau

Friedland

Allenstein

Grodno

BENNIGSEN
(20,000)

PRUSSIA

Stettin

R. Narew

Bialystok

R. Oder

Thorn

Berlin R. Spree

Posen

Pultusk

R. Vistula

Warsaw

Brest-Litovsk

BUXHÖWDEN
(40,000)

RUSSIA

Potsdam

Leipzig Dresden

Breslau

Liegnitz

SILESIA

R. Vistula

SAXONY

Krakow

R. Bug

(2,500)

BOHEMIA

Olmütz

KUTUZOV (38,000)

Lemberg

R. Moldau

MORAVIA

GALICIA

Austerlitz

AUSTRIA

ARCHDUKE
FERDINAND (72,000)

Wagram

Linz

Vienna

Pressburg

Aspern

Essling

Salzburg

Buda

Pest

Leoben

HUNGARY

ARCHDUKE
JOHN (22,000)

TRANSYLVANIA

ARCHDUKE
CHARLES (94,000)

Trieste

R. Drave

nice

R. Danube

Adriatic Sea

DALMATIA

OTTOMAN EMPIRE

PAPAL
STATES

0   20 40 60 80 100 120 140

SCALE OF MILES

Here lay the key to Napoleon's hopes. He could reckon that at Boulogne he was closer to Ulm than was Kutuzov. If he could but move quickly enough he could isolate Ferdinand from his allies, and smash him before the Russians arrived, then hasten eastwards toward Vienna, to deal with Kutuzov. The campaign would be decided by two battles of annihilation in the Danube Valley. Everything would depend on speed – and this was a predominantly Napoleonic quality.

In a series of staccato orders, letters and decrees, the Emperor poured forth his campaign plan to the overworked Daru. Napoleon once claimed 'I never had a plan of operations.' It was quite untrue. He was, recalls Baron Jomini (the Liddell Hart of the era)

... in reality his own Chief of the Staff; holding in his hand a pair of compasses ... bent, nay, often lying over his map, on which the positions of his army corps and the supposed positions of the enemy were marked by pins of different colours, he arranged his own movements with a certainty of which we can scarcely form a just idea ...

Aided by an elaborate card index system, every detail, down to regimental level, came out of this one voluminous mind. Once when Napoleon came across a unit that had got lost during the approach march to the Rhine, he was able to inform its astonished officer, without consulting any orders, of the whereabouts of its division, and where it would be on the next three nights; throwing in for good measure a resumé of its commander's military record.

The essential component of Napoleon's strategy was that the Austrians at Ulm must not be attacked frontally; otherwise they might simply fall back on their Russian allies advancing from the east. 'My only fear,' he confided later to Talleyrand, 'is that we shall scare them too much. . . .' The Austrians would expect him to approach, conventionally, from the west via the Black Forest; so, instead, he would swing his armies southwards through Germany to throw an unbreakable barrier across the Danube downstream from Ulm, then roll up the enemy from the rear. Marlborough had followed roughly the same route, to Blenheim, a century earlier with 40,000 men; but to transport an army five times as big with all their cannon and impedimenta from Boulogne (500 miles as the crow flies) in an epoch when the fastest speed was that of his slowest grenadier's feet, and still take the enemy by surprise, presupposed no mean feat.

Thus, for speed and secrecy (and in conformity with his axiom of 'separate to live, gather to fight'), Napoleon split his forces into seven 'streams'. From the north Bernadotte, already stationed in Hanover, would push almost due south, through Würzburg. Next to him, Marmont's corps from Holland was to cross the Rhine by Mainz, and then wheel south; on his right came Davout, then Soult, rated as 'the most skilful at moving large masses of troops' of any European commander, and with the largest force (41,000), Ney and Lannes, later famous names of the Empire – all performing a similar manœuvre at intervals lower down the Rhine. Finally, Augereau, hurrying all the way from Brittany, would constitute the army reserve. Ahead of them all was to hasten the world's most formidable cavalry force, 22,000 strong, under the impetuous and dashing Murat, with the task of providing a screen to hide Napoleon's true design. Once across the Rhine, Murat would move ostentatiously through the Black Forest. He departed immediately to reconnoitre the way himself, under the *nom de guerre* of 'Colonel Beaumont'. On 25 August, General Bertrand was despatched to Bavaria to make notes of all

Mort de Monseigneur le Duc D'ENGHIEN.

The execution of the Duc d'Enghien, which Talleyrand
described as being 'worse than a crime, it was a blunder'.
A contemporary woodcut by an unknown Frenchman.

rejected the British terms. It was the first big mistake of his career. Instead of the years of
peace he had hoped for, in which he could have made his power virtually unassailable, on 18
May 1803 France found herself again at war with England. The following day the blockading
ships of Admiral Cornwallis were once more in position outside Brest.

Then, nearly a year later, Napoleon followed up this error with an even greater one. Shaken
by the Cadoudal conspiracy against him, he decided upon an act of sheer terror that would
deter his royalist foes once and for all. The thirty-two-year-old Duc d'Enghien was (says Duff
Cooper[14]):

... not only the least blameworthy but the most admirable of the Bourbon princes. ... Young, handsome
and chivalrous he resembled more a hero of romance than a prince of the nineteenth century.

While prepared to fight for his family rights with the *Armée des Emigrés*, he alone had steadfastly
refused to have any dealings with the conspirators against Napoleon, and lived quietly – following the pursuit of love – in the independent German state of Baden. On the night of 14 March
1804, he was kidnapped by a French cavalry detachment sent by Napoleon, and spirited off
to the sinister Château de Vincennes. A week later, after a perfunctory court martial which
produced no evidence against him, he was executed by firing squad, with his inseparable

area as the whole of the existing United States. Three weeks later the Louisiana Purchase was signed, at a price of $12 million – or only $4·5 million more than Monroe had been briefed to offer for New Orleans alone – and this regardless of Napoleon's promise to Spain never to sell to a third power.

'You will fight England again,' Napoleon remarked hopefully as he shook hands on the deal with the Americans. But at least the US would remain strictly neutral in the now imminent War of the Third Coalition; and on 7 November, as Napoleon was closing in on Vienna, Jefferson's army explorers, Lewis and Clark, were to reach the Pacific, thereby blazing the trail for America's 'Manifest Destiny' from burning sea to burning sea while the rest of the world, distracted, grappled in the heart of Europe. "*from sea to shining sea.*"

Thus to Napoleon all the omens could not help but look favourable to getting what he wanted – hegemony over Europe – and preferably by peaceful means. The United States had opted for neutrality, and his former enemies in Europe seemed reluctant to face war again. With twenty-seven million[12] to England's fifteen, Prussia's six, and Austria's twenty million, France had the largest population from which to draw fresh soldiers – except for Mother Russia's thirty-nine million – and the efficiency of her existing forces showed that she could beat any combination that might attack her. The potential coalition powers had, as previously noted, no common interest to bind them together, except opposition to France, and England and Russia looked as if they might easily come to blows over conflicting interests in the Near East and the island of Malta; while, internally, England herself seemed anarchic, led by a weak and aimless government under 'Doctor' Addington, and with no land forces worth mentioning.[13] The only four remaining factors of menace were the Royal Navy, the manpower resources of the Russian Army, the plottings of the Bourbons and 'Pitt's gold', the British funds capable of mounting a fresh coalition. However – especially with Pitt ailing and safely out of power – these factors showed no serious sign of combining against him, and by the beginning of 1803, Napoleon's voice had taken on a more strident note. He annexed Piedmont (although his guarantee of the integrity of the Italian states had been a *quid pro quo* for England's surrender of Malta), and sent Marshal Ney to invade Switzerland, which enraged even 'Doctor' Addington.

On her side, England by 1803 was becoming increasingly alarmed at France's naval activity, which included large numbers of flat-bottomed invasion barges. Her fears were not without reason; Napoleon intended to use the years of peace to construct twenty-five ships-of-the-line annually which, within six or seven years, would make him (at least theoretically) unbeatable at sea. Addington infuriated Napoleon by refusing to withdraw from the key naval bastion of Malta. What Fox called 'reciprocal Billingsgate' mounted in the press of both countries, and with it national feeling. In March, Napoleon had lost his temper at a public *levée*, shaking his cane at the English ambassador, Lord Whitworth, to the point where Whitworth expected to be struck, and exclaiming: 'Now you mean to force me to fight for fifteen more years!'

After another month of terse negotiations, Whitworth received what amounted to a final ultimatum to pass on to Napoleon; England would recognize the Italian annexations, in exchange for Napoleon's evacuating Holland and Switzerland and accepting a ten-year English tenure of Malta. Enraged that anybody should present *him* with an ultimatum, at the same time taking it no more seriously than Hitler was to take Chamberlain's 1939 guarantee to the Poles, Napoleon

LEFT Talleyrand, former Bishop of Autun, Prince of Benevento, wit and libertine, and Napoleon's Foreign Secretary. He later defected to Tsar Alexander and served under the Restoration as France's adroit representative at the Congress of Vienna (1814–15), ending his career as King Louis-Philippe's ambassador to England. The painter, Pierre Paul Prud'hon, had tactfully concealed his deformed foot.

Charles-Jean Bernadotte (1763–1844), later Charles XIV, King of
Sweden and Norway, was first general, then marshal under
Napoleon. Bernadotte was given command of the I Corps in 1805.

he saw, particularly the Danube crossings in the area around Donauwörth; and then to study
the terrain all the way to Vienna. 'Everywhere his language is to be pacific,' ordered Napoleon;
'he will speak of the invasion of England as imminent....'[3]

In fact, only a minimal covering force consisting of the third battalions of a few regiments
was to be left on the Channel in the role of guard against any English diversionary raids. As
part of the grand deception plan, Napoleon himself would remain at Boulogne to the very last;
rigorous censorship was applied, with post-offices occupied and newspapers muzzled. To all
but the handful conversant with the plan, Napoleon declared that he was sending only a defensive contingent of 30,000 men to the Rhine: and Talleyrand was instructed to spin out negotiations with the Russians and Austrians as long as possible.

Finally, down in Italy with only 50,000 men, Napoleon's most reliable tactician, Masséna, was instructed to pin down Archduke Charles' vastly superior army by adopting a defensively aggressive stance.

Already on 27 August the great machine, nearly two hundred thousand men strong – or roughly half of all the effectives of the Empire – began its immense march. By any standard the plan was one of the most brilliantly conceived, and speedily executed, of all time. However, of the many risks it entailed there hovered one above all others: Prussia. As with the two great encirclement strategies by which Germany nearly defeated France in 1914, and did succeed in 1940, Napoleon's plan depended on an infringement of neutrality. The *Blitzkrieg*-speed marches of Bernadotte and Marmont could not be made without traversing the Prussian state of Ansbach. Napoleon told Talleyrand to soften Prussia's indignation by offering her Hanover as a sop. Talleyrand was thrown into despair; as he once sighed, 'the most difficult person with whom Napoleon's Foreign Minister had to negotiate was Napoleon himself'. Opposed to the new war in the first place, he had admitted to the Prussian Minister in Paris that if he were able to prevent it 'he would consider such an action the most glorious event in his tenure of office'; now, by marching through Ansbach, it seemed inevitable that the nation of Frederick the Great must sooner or later range itself with the rest of Napoleon's enemies.

To Napoleon it was a calculated risk; if he violated Prussian territory to inflict a terrible blow upon the Allies it would probably serve to frighten the hesitant Prussians onto his side. In fact Prussia was outraged; the following year she would declare war on Napoleon, but too late; and it would only lead her to defeat at Jena. Had Prussia fought at once, Napoleon might have been defeated in 1805; as it was, though only Hardy's 'Spirit of the Years' could then have seen the prospects of Blücher and Waterloo shimmering in the distance, Napoleon's act of arrogance was to contribute to his ultimate downfall.

The Army of England now became designated the *Grande Armée*, heading for eastern Europe and the unknown instead of Kent and London. After all the months of intensive training put in while waiting at Boulogne, it was, in the Emperor's own view, 'the finest army that has ever existed'. Indeed, his confidence that it could execute so phenomenally a taxing manoeuvre seemed indicative of its quality.

Notes to chapter 5
1 Thiers, *Consulate and Empire*, Vol. VI, p. 5.
2 Op. cit.
3 Letter 9133.

6

'La Grande Armée'

... he (Napoleon) kept on winning his battles, not because he was a genius (I am convinced he was very far from that), but on the contrary because he was more stupid than his enemies, could not be carried away by logical deductions and only bothered about seeing that his soldiers were well-fed, embittered and as numerous as possible.

Tolstoy

IF ONE WERE TO CONSIDER the immense advances in military technique witnessed in the twentieth century, the purely technical aspects of warfare in Napoleon's day seem not to have progressed dramatically when compared with the previous century. In all armies, the basic infantry weapon was still the flintlock, smooth-bored musket with its detachable socket bayonet; the latter used more to frighten than to kill.[1] Capable of an accurate range of little more than 170 yards (although in the heat of battle, the average infantry man often missed at 50 yards) and a maximum rate of fire of two rounds per minute, rapidly fouled and unserviceabe in wet weather, the infantry musket was virtually the same as in the day of Marlborough or Frederick the Great. The cannon, too, showed an evolution that was largely relative. A 12-pounder, the standard 'heavy' field-piece, had a maximum range of a little over 1000 yards, or only 700 with canister;[2] muzzle-loading, a good gun crew could get off no more than one round a minute, and had to relay after each shot because of the lack of any recoil mechanism. The cavalry still charged with *arme blanche* (literally 'cold steel') – swords or sabres according to whether they were heavy or light cavalry, both weapons which had developed perhaps least of all over many centuries. It was only well after Waterloo that, with the flowering of the industrial revolution, warfare was to be truly revolutionized by such delights as the rapid-firing rifle, followed by the machine-gun and steel breech-loading artillery capable of hurling a high-explosive shell five, ten or fifteen miles.

As a result, by 1805 anyway, the battlefield had changed but little in terms of geographical scale and character. Although the clouds of smoke obscured most of it from the average participant (one thinks of the British commander ordered to advance at Waterloo who asked Wellington 'In which direction, my Lord?'), the short range of weapons compressed it into an area where one individual could usually exercise effective overall control. (At Austerlitz, during much of the battle, Napoleon would actually have most of his units in sight.) Because of problems of supply and logistics, battles – even Waterloo – were largely one day affairs, unlike the protracted slogging matches of the First World War or even the American Civil War. It is also to be noted that the successes of the Revolutionary and Napoleonic Armies were due in part at least to innovations brought in, or at least proposed, during the *ancien régime*. Therefore it is elsewhere that one needs to look for what distinguished the Napoleonic battle.

To begin with, the coming of the French Revolution had completely modified the style and objectives of warfare; the same was to happen in the twentieth century, in the aftermath of the Soviet Revolution of 1917. Before 1792, a battle had been a passionless, elegant and gentlemanly affair (*Messieurs les gardes françaises, tirez!*), fought between professionals for a limited advantage, usually dynastic rather than ideological or even territorial. In the eighteenth century, it was considered proper to declare war, and plunder was restrained so that even Adam Smith, who deplored its wastefulness, could reckon that it '. . . is so far from being a disadvantage in a well-cultivated country that many get rich by it . . .'

Commanders took along with them their hairdressers, and sometimes even their wives; weighed down by their vast administrative tails, armies moved slowly and deliberately, and at the onset of mud and frost they disappeared, like squirrels, to re-emerge in the spring. The height of strategy, suggested Major-General Henry Lloyd in his *History of the Late War in Germany* (published in 1781) about Frederick the Great's campaigns, was to: 'Initiate military operations with mathematical precision and to keep on waging war without ever being under the necessity to strike a blow.' Such Barry Lyndon kind of battles were rarely fought 'to the last man'. It was a world that began to vanish with the cannonade of Valmy on 20 September 1792 (shots that were, indeed, 'heard around the world'), when a French 'people's army' defeated the Duke of Brunswick's regulars. Goethe, accompanying the Prussians, declared prophetically: 'From this place and day commenced a new epoch in the world's history.'

After Valmy came the revolutionary *levée en masse*, which – almost overnight – was to furnish 450,000 men for the French armies; conscripts who, in the words of a French historian, Louis Madelin: '. . . driven in their thousands to the frontiers, trembled as they reached them, and then made all of Europe tremble.' The day had arrived of the mass, and ever-expanding, conscript army, which, imbued with fanaticism, would turn the battlefield into a place of mounting carnage and horror. Whereas in the Augustan eighteenth century, Saxe and Turenne had never maintained an army of more than 50,000, and the highest number even Frederick the Great had mustered at any one battle had been 77,000 (at Hohenfriedberg), at *seven* of his battles Napoleon would command over 100,000 men) reaching 175,000 on the bloody field of Leigpzig (1813), in which was also suffered the previously unheard-of total casualties to both sides of 120,000. Finally, it was left to Napoleon to introduce, or re-introduce, the 'total war' that toppled dynasties and shattered existing balances-of-power.

Under the old European purchase system, an officer could well reach the rank of colonel at the age of twenty, having spent more time at court than with his regiment. But in France, with the Revolution, birth ceased to be a prerogative for advancement; many of the old, aristocratic officers were purged and commissions were made open to all. At first the purges seriously impaired the effectiveness of the army (the navy, as has already been noted, possibly never recovered), but later this democratization provided Napoleon with an immense advantage. By 1802, when he created the *École Spéciale Militaire*, the new French officer corps was already becoming an imposingly élite body. In 1804 he reinstituted the title of Marshal, abolished by the Revolution, and it could be said with truth that every French soldier carried a marshal's baton in his knapsack. A ranker and lawyer's son called Bernadotte would become King of Sweden, while Masséna, one of Napoleon's finest Marshals, was the orphaned son of a grocer,

RIGHT A French infantryman of the line, by
Marinet, *circa* 1807, with notes added subsequently
describing his uniform in detail.

Troupes Françaises

Inf. de ligne. Chasseur (1807)

2e reg.t

probabl.t en 1810

habit, gilet, culotte guêtres blanches.

buffle.t en croix

pompon

Cordon du Sch. } vert foncé
épaulettes }

torsade d'épaulette rouge

plaque & boutons j.

Cocarde comme ici

Collet
revers
retroussis
douf... de bas
parlemens } Rouge
& pattes de parem.

d'après les notes à la main
l'unif. serait ainsi modifié
pompon rouge, cordon
de Schako blanc
épaulettes blanches,
p. poil rouge.

ailleurs:
le pompon rouge & blanc
pattes de parem. blanches
guêtres noires

A Paris chez Martinet Libraire, rue du Coq N.º 13.

Dep. à la Bib.que

INFANTERIE DE LIGNE
1.er Regiment
Garde de Paris

and went to sea as a cabin-boy at the age of thirteen. Only two out of the twenty-six marshals had noble antecedents, and, by 1805, half of the whole officer corps had risen from the ranks. They were also young, because the Emperor reckoned no commander had any enterprise left in him after his forty-fifth year; of the corps commanders at Austerlitz, Bernadotte at forty-two was the oldest, Davout was only thirty-five. He was exacting in what he demanded of his senior officers, who were expected to share the privations of the simple soldier, sleep in the open, and lead from the front (later, as the victorious generals and marshals grew grander this keenness for the rough life tended to wain). If Napoleon's generals had a fault it was that they lacked initiative on the wider tactical level; for – such was his ascendancy – they always looked to him for guidance on every issue. It was a shortcoming that was to lead to serious problems in the 1805 campaign.

Organizationally, the French Army had been totally transformed since 1792. First, Napoleon had institutionalized the compact division,[3] composed of 6,000 to 9,000 men and never more than five or six infantry regiments strong, which, with its rapid mobility, had proved the key to his early victories. Next, in the Camp of Boulogne, he had the Army Corps, self-contained, fast-moving and hard-hitting formations, each consisting of two or three divisions, with its own artillery and cavalry, and commanded by one of the stars in the imperial firmament. In order to confuse enemy intelligence Napoleon would frequently vary their battle strengths. Each corps was, in effect, a miniature army capable of engaging or pinning down a vastly superior force for several hours, until its neighbouring corps could hasten up in support or prise the enemy apart from a flank. The corps would advance to battle behind a reconnaissance screen of light cavalry, their infantry columns preceded by a dense swarm of 'skirmishers' ('. . . as sharp-sighted as ferrets and as active as squirrels'). These light infantry sharp-shooters picked holes in the enemy lines, while the main punch formed up behind them. During the months at Boulogne, infantry, cavalry and artillery arms within each corps had trained more closely together than ever before, with the result that the First *Grande Armée* of 1805 was probably the best trained force Napoleon ever commanded.

To a large extent, the striking power of Napoleon's new army corps was provided by their self-sufficiency, and therefore speed, on the approach march, as will be seen shortly. It was a cardinal principle that baggage had to be reduced to the barest minimum. This, in effect, meant living off the land, or in Napoleon's own parlance 'making war support war'. Already, twenty years before the Revolution, the French military philosopher, the Comte de Guibert, had urged this procedure and the revolutionary armies had taken to it with gusto. By breaking away from the depot system of supply of the eighteenth century, they had profited immensely from mobility; but, if carried too far, the policy of 'living-off-the-land' could eventually prove to be a wasting asset, in more than just the literal sense. Of General Jourdan's revolutionary army invading Germany in 1796, Marshal Soult said it '. . . could exist only by plunder, and this both raised the country against us and destroyed the discipline of the troops'.

Here was a predicament that would plague Napoleon in the course of time. The supply trains bringing up ammunition and stores were still, strangely enough, in the hands of civilian contractors; in 1805 they would *just* prove adequate, but two years later the system was to break down seriously in the Polish campaign. Always verging on the ramshackle, always within an inch or two of collapse, Napoleon's logistics system was both a strength and a grave weakness. At Austerlitz, Davout's corps would save the day by covering 100 miles in 48 hours, and arrive fit to fight. But it was also these demands on the local populace that would, eventually, prove a factor in unleashing the 'war of peoples'.

Under Napoleon (but more especially under the dashing Murat) the French cavalry was transformed from a laughing stock into a very potent instrument. It fell into two main types, light and heavy, each with clearly differentiated functions. The light squadrons belonged to the divisional and army corps cavalry, and were employed for deep reconnaissance and protective screening in front of an advance, a role that was to assume particular importance in the advance to Ulm during the first part of the 1805 campaign. They were also used for pursuit following a victorious engagement – notably at Jena in 1806. Unlike the daring generals of the American Civil War, however, Napoleon never used these cavalry squadrons for large scale raids any distance away from the main body of the army. They were comprised, in 1805, of twenty-four regiments of *chasseurs à cheval* and ten of Hussars; in later years, having noted painfully the expertise of the Russian Cossacks with their 16-foot-long lances, Napoleon was to introduce new Units of Lancers, originally Polish levies. The Hussars, a reckless and hard-swearing lot clad in heavily-braided dolmans (tight-fitting jackets of Hungarian origin and the showiest uniforms in the army) and wearing long pigtails, seemed particularly to embody much of the panache associated with the French cavalry as a whole, which had changed but little from pre-revolutionary times. General Marbot describes a typical *maréchal de logis* (sergeant-major) who had trained him:

Shako over the ear, sabre trailing, face disfigured and divided into two by an immense scar; upturned moustaches half-a-foot long, stiffened with wax ... two great plaited tresses of hair hanging from the temples ... and with this what an air! – the air of a swaggering ruffian ...

Another cavalry general, Lasalle, allegedly claimed that any Hussar 'not dead at thirty' must have been a malingerer.

The heavy cavalry consisted of two regiments of Carabiniers, twelve of Cuirassiers heavily armoured with bullet-proof breast- and back-plates and thirty of Dragoons.[4] It was held in massed formations ready to launch powerful charges against weak points in the enemy line at the critical moment – a fundamental feature of the Napoleonic battle. In contrast to the curved, slashing sabre of the light cavalry, the principal weapon of the heavy regiments was a straight thrusting sword; at varying times both categories also carried short muskets or carbines, and pistols. Until they were able, after 1806, to remount their regiments with captured steeds, the French heavy cavalry was notably less well mounted than its continental enemies; particularly the Russians, who had perhaps the best horses of any army. The French rode lumbering Norman and Flemish animals, probably not unlike a percheron, that were great weight carriers but very slow; far removed from the traditional image of the charge at the full gallop, they would sometimes be unable to break out of trot. But this deficiency was, in Wellington's view, more than made up for by the fact that the French heavy cavalry '... excelled in battle drill and tactical handling, and the larger the formation the more this superiority told.'

Napoleon's philosophy of boldness was not unlike Guderian's handling of his tanks in 1940,

LEFT A French Dragoon. The standard cavalry of the line, and the 'maids of all work', the Dragoons were less heavily armoured than the Cuirassiers, and would sometimes charge with the heavy cavalry, or bolster up the screening operations of the light cavalry.

RIGHT A selection of Tsar Alexander's 'irregular cavalry' – Siberian Cossacks, Kalmucks, Bashkir and Don Cossacks – often of doubtful reliability, and equally happy plundering an ally as a foe. Note the 14-foot lances of the Cossacks, later adopted by Napoleon.

Cavalier Kalmouk. — *Cosaque de la Siberie.* — *Chef de Baskirs.* — *Cavalier Kalmouk.* — *Officiers des Cosaques du Don.* — *Cosaque de la Mer Noire.* — *Cosaque d'Irkoutsk.* — *Chef des Tartares d'Oczakow.*

the cavalry was never to be used '... with any miserly desire to keep it intact ... I do not wish the horses to be spared if they can catch men ...' For the opposing infantry, a charge by the French Cuirassiers was always a terrifying experience.

Although its basic weapons and their capabilities remained much the same, the artillery arm – which was, after all, Napoleon's own speciality – was constantly being expanded and stream-lined. 'Today the artillery indeed decrees the destiny of armies and of people,' he once declared. In numbers, however, his artillery was relatively small, hardly larger than that mustered by Frederick the Great. Among his earliest triumphs he had won the battle at Rivoli in 1796 with less than 20 cannon; but they had been well-placed. These numbers were to rise to a maximum of 700 guns at Leipzig, but here – as on several other occasions – he was to be considerably outnumbered by the Allied artillery. (At Eylau in 1807, for instance, the Russians – historically renowned for their mass use of cannon – actually had a superiority of more than two-to-one, while of Soult's 48 guns, all but 6 were Austrian booty.) In 1805, the First *Grande Armée* counted a ratio of roughly 2 pieces to every 1,000 men, arriving at Austerlitz with 139 cannon to the 278 of the Allies.

However it was how Napoleon deployed his guns that was decisive. As in many other things,

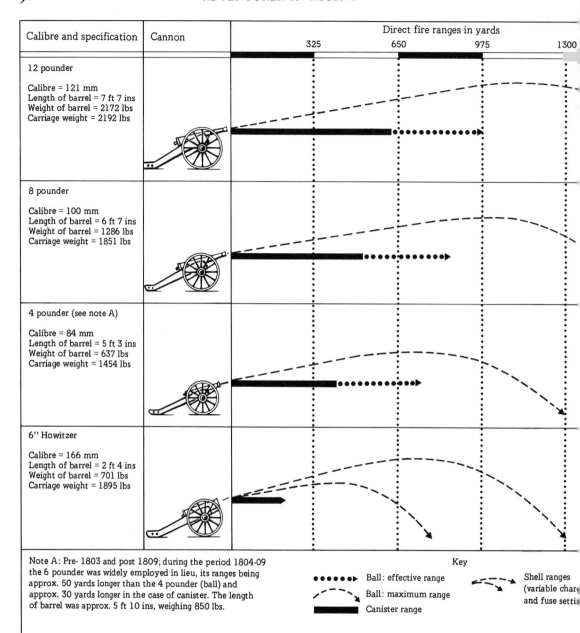

Calibre and specification	Cannon	Direct fire ranges in yards

Direct fire ranges in yards: 325 | 650 | 975 | 1300

12 pounder

Calibre = 121 mm
Length of barrel = 7 ft 7 ins
Weight of barrel = 2172 lbs
Carriage weight = 2192 lbs

8 pounder

Calibre = 100 mm
Length of barrel = 6 ft 7 ins
Weight of barrel = 1286 lbs
Carriage weight = 1851 lbs

4 pounder (see note A)

Calibre = 84 mm
Length of barrel = 5 ft 3 ins
Weight of barrel = 637 lbs
Carriage weight = 1454 lbs

6" Howitzer

Calibre = 166 mm
Length of barrel = 2 ft 4 ins
Weight of barrel = 701 lbs
Carriage weight = 1895 lbs

Note A: Pre- 1803 and post 1809; during the period 1804-09
the 6 pounder was widely employed in lieu, its ranges being
approx. 50 yards longer than the 4 pounder (ball) and
approx. 30 yards longer in the case of canister. The length
of barrel was approx. 5 ft 10 ins, weighing 850 lbs.

Key

●●●●●● Ball: effective range

– – – Ball: maximum range

▬▬▬ Canister range

Shell ranges
(variable char[ge]
and fuse setti[ng])

1625 1950	Gun crews ■ Specialist ⊠ Non-specialist	Ammunition Trail chest Caisson			Average rate of fire	Location (see note B)
	8 7/15	Ball 9	Ball 48	Canister 20	One round per minute	Artillery reserve and corps reserves (one battery of eight guns per corps)
	8 5/13	Ball 15	Ball 62	Canister 20	Two rounds per minute	Divisional reserves
	5 3/8	Ball 18	Ball 100	Canister 50	Two to three rounds per minute	Advance guards and divisional reserves and artillery reserve (horse batteries)
Shell burst danger zone 45 yards diameter	8 5/13	Shell 4	Shell 49	Canister 11	One shell per minute	Divisional reserves and artillery reserve

In the case of the 12, 8 and 4 pounders, the employment of riccochet fire could increase the maximum range by between 50% and 75%; each 'bound' of the cannon-ball theoretically decreased in distance by 50% each time it hit the ground; i.e 600/300/150/75/37 yards.

Note B: Most guns were organized into 'companies' of eight cannon; in the case of many divisional and artillery reserve formations (and some corps reserves) a proportion of six cannon to two howitzers was observed.

Artillery of the Grande Armée

he had benefited from innovations that had preceded him. Already before the Revolution, a Frenchman, Comte Jean de Gribeauval, had greatly enhanced the mobility of cannons by substantially reducing their weight. This had been achieved by casting barrels thinner and shorter, and making the carriage lighter; with the result that, for instance, a Gribeauval 8-pounder weighed just half as much as its predecessor. This meant, in effect, that the guns could now keep pace with the infantry on an approach march, and, drawn by horses instead of oxen, would not even lag too far behind the cavalry. Tested with success during the American War of Independence, the Gribeauval guns also attained a remarkable degree of standardization. Napoleon further reduced his standard pieces to four: the 6-pounder, the 8-pounder, the 12-pounder (he affectionately called them his *belles filles*) which still weighed two tons and required twelve horses to move it, and a $5\frac{1}{2}$-inch howitzer, designed for indirect fire over crests, with explosive shell. Typical of Napoleon's rationalization, this last weapon – replacing a 6-inch one – meant that each ammunition waggon could carry 75 rounds instead of the 50 previously. The standardization of calibres resulted, initially, in Napoleon having fewer guns to draw upon; on the other hand their reduced weight enabled him to gallop his pieces from one end of the battlefield to the other, thereby diminishing the drawback of their short range and affording himself a rapid concentration of firepower to batter the enemy to shreds at the critical point. 'It is the artillery of my Guard,' declared Napoleon, 'which generally decides my battles, for, as I have it always at hand, I can bring it to bear wherever it becomes necessary.' Here, in its tactical handling, lay the true superiority of Napoleon's artillery.

Eye-witnesses at Napoleonic battlefields speak of the constant, sinister and mysterious humming noise of the cannon-balls flying overhead. While, in their support the artillery played an immense part in sustaining the morale of the French infantry, to advance towards enemy guns firing directly at you at short range was perhaps the worst of all battle experiences; a hit from one round shot could disembowel or smash to a pulp three men at a time. At Waterloo, one British company square suffered 25 killed and wounded from the same shot. The effects of exploding shell, such as mortally wounded Tolstoy's Prince Andrei at Borodino, were immeasurably less lethal than those of a century later; on the other hand, the impact of cannon firing grape-shot at point-blank range into charging cavalry was appalling. In return, the gunners were often overrun and sabred by the cavalry; but, as the latter seldom had time to stop and spike the pieces, they would often be brought back into action again by courageous and resourceful gunners.

Napoleon's infantrymen looked more like an army in rout after a long march, straggling, dishevelled and apparently indisciplined; perhaps not unlike the Israeli soldier of today, and appearances were equally deceptive. Carrying no baggage trains, they were often dangerously short of ammunition, ill-paid, ill-shod and ill-fed; and yet they constituted the finest fighting force in Europe. 'The first quality of a soldier,' declared Napoleon, 'is fortitude in enduring fatigue and hardship.' He also considered that 'tents are not healthy, it is better for the soldier to sleep out'. The French infantryman marched weighed down by a 58-pound pack (the Guard, burdened with its extra 'ceremonials' was privileged to carry 65 pounds),[5] which contained 60 rounds of musket ammunition, rations for a week, a spare pair of pants, two shirts, and two extra pairs of boots; but, mass-produced and glued rather than sewn together, the boots often

A *vivandière* in an army camp. A doubtless glamourized view of a tough
profession, one of the hazards of which is suggested by the lady's
somewhat extended apron. An engraving by J. B. Seele.

fell apart on the march and so the infantrymen were happiest when they could relieve their
better-equipped enemy (or sometimes, allies!) of their footwear. Also with Napoleon's troops,
courageous and robust *vivandières* sometimes travelled. They, in addition to other services
rendered, did their best to repair tattered uniforms.

On paper the basic ration of one pound of 'munition' bread, four ounces of meat, two ounces
of dried vegetables and one ounce of brandy meant that the infantryman was better fed than
many a French civilian, but because of the afore-noted vagaries of the supply system theory
quite often did not become practice; the bread ration more frequently took the form of a hard
biscuit, tied by string around the soldier's neck. To compensate for all these hardships there
was no corporal punishment, as in the British Army; instead men were goaded on by a coveted
system of awards and decorations. Nevertheless, like the fighting men of the other nations, they
would inevitably arrive on the battlefield wet and cold, hungry and fatigued.

The standard infantry weapon was still, with small improvements, the Model 1777 musket,
with all its limitations and unreliability. (According to one expert, at reasonable ranges hits
were seldom registered at a better rate than one in every 3,000 to 4,000 shots fired.) Yet, John
Keegan[6] suggests that, because of its greater concentration and control, an infantry regiment
of the Napoleonic era was 'arguably more dangerous to approach than a late nineteenth-century
– Boer War – one'. To obtain this maximum advantage of fire-power, all depended on formations

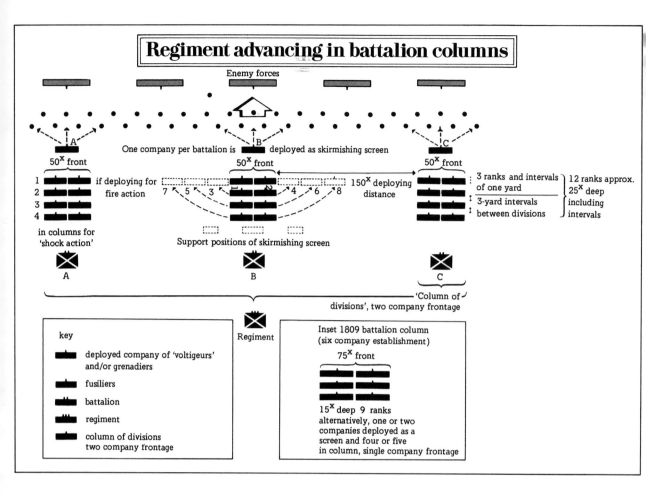

and their tactical deployment. At this, of course, Napoleon was unbeatable. Breaking away from the eighteenth-century tradition of advancing to the attack in a beautifully 'dressed' line, Napoleon had come to prefer the principle of the 'battalion column'. This was much more adaptable to an approach through broken country (such as Napoleon was to encounter at Austerlitz); with an exposed front of perhaps no more than fifty yards, it presented the minimum target to the enemy, and, with skilful control, could very swiftly be spread out into line order for 'fire action'. Later Napoleon experimented successfully with various forms of *ordre mixte* in which battalions would advance part in column, part in line, according to the circumstances, preceded by those clouds of infuriating and damaging 'skirmishers', a role greatly suited to the born individualism of the French soldier.

To his confidant on St Helena, General Gourgaud, Napoleon expounded that, as far as his strategy was concerned, the whole art of war was 'just like all beautiful things, simple; the simplest manoeuvres are the best'. (This simplicity inevitably brought with it a degree of predictability, so that after 1807, Napoleon's opponents became less liable to being taken by surprise.) That great American naval historian, Admiral Mahan once observed that: '... not by rambling operations ... are wars decided, but by force massed and handled in skilful combinations.' Combined with his superb – indeed unique – comprehension of the interactions of time and space,

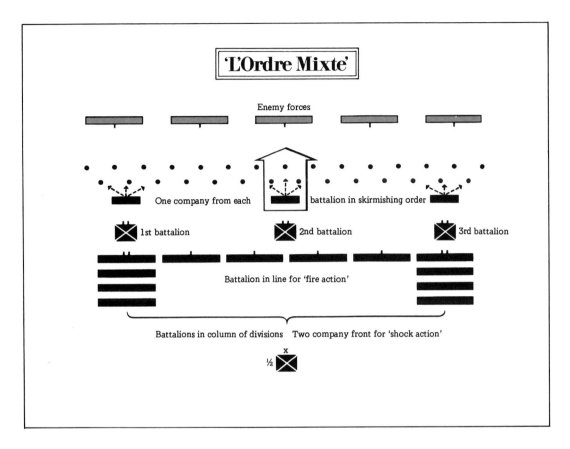

this very much conformed with Napoleon's basic philosophy. As a key to his strategy, he had declared in 1797:

There are in Europe many good generals, but they see too many things at once; as for me I see only one thing, namely the enemy's main body. And I try to crush it, confident that secondary matters will then settle themselves....

Again, two years later (to General Moreau), he had stressed the imperativeness of moving so as always to achieve local superiority, even against a force that was in total superior to his own, then 'beat it (the broken remnants) in detail'. In consequence '... the victory which was the result was always, as you see, the triumph of the larger numbers over the lesser.' At no battle would this policy work to better effect than at Austerlitz, and it was cardinal among his five principles for conducting a campaign. Others included moving his main force so that it was always placed on the enemy's flank or rear,[7] and enabling it to act against enemy lines of communication, while guaranteeing its own. Between 1796 and 1815, Napoleon would employ his famous *manœuvre sur les derrières* (or what Liddell Hart called the 'indirect approach') no less than thirty times; again, never with greater effect than at Austerlitz. Once on the battlefield, the image of Napoleon as the daring gambler without limits has also been over-stressed; in various respects he would show extreme prudence, especially when it came to keeping in hand powerful tactical reserves for an opportunity, or against the contingency, of a reverse.

Although there was no aspect of staff planning over which Napoleon would not exert a personal influence, behind him he had a far more impressive and weighty back-up machinery than is often assumed. Already by 1805 Imperial *Grand-Quartier-Général* numbered more than 400 officers and 5,000 men; by 1812 the officer complement had escalated to 3,500. Headquarters was divided between two separate organizations: Napoleon's *Maison*, or Military Household – which David Chandler[8] rightly describes as 'the true nerve centre of the French war effort' – and the General Staff proper. The most important personage in the staff bureaucracy was Louis-Alexandre Berthier, 'small, stout, ever laughing, very full of business' and known to the soldiers as 'the Emperor's wife'. Although rated (by David Chandler) as having 'rarely served as more than a glorified chief clerk', because of the way Napoleon took so much on his own shoulders, Berthier was rather more important than this by reason of the nexus and the factor of continuity which he represented. Already aged fifty-two in 1805, as the son of a high-ranking officer and a pre-Revolutionary officer himself he was one of the few to provide a continuum with the Staff Corps of the *ancien régime*; promoted general in the Revolutionary armies in 1795, he became Napoleon's Chief-of-Staff the following year and was to hold the post until he switched to the monarchy at the end of the 1814 campaign. (He died falling out of a window in 1815, and is strongly suspected of suicide.) At the same time, by being Vice-Constable, Minister of War and Master of Hounds, he also held a key position in the *Maison*. Although Napoleon's proclivity for secrecy was such that he would occasionally keep even Berthier in the dark, he regarded him as quite indispensable.

Important figures later in the *Maison* were Duroc, the Grand Marshal, and Caulaincourt, Master of the Horse, as well as a cluster of lesser generals entrusted with the most vital missions as aides-de-camp. At the heart of the *Maison* was the Imperial Cabinet, from which emanated in genesis all Napoleon's plans. It consisted of only a handful of personnel, among whom the geographer, Bacler d'Albe, was the most essential cog. A 'little dark man, handsome, pleasant, well-educated, talented and a good draughtsman', the poor fellow would be summoned by Napoleon at any hour of day or night. As soon as the site for Imperial Headquarters in the field had been decided, d'Albe would set up Napoleon's 'operations room', the centre-piece of which would be a vast map table of the theatre of war, so large that the Emperor and his topographer would often be forced to lie on it full length together. 'I have seen them more than once,' wrote Baron de Fain, the Cabinet archivist[9] '... interrupting each other by a sudden exclamation, right in the midst of their work, when their heads had come into collision.' It was symptomatic of the immense importance which Napoleon always attached to topography, which was to pay dividends particularly at Austerlitz.

After such a session on the map table, Napoleon would then begin dictating orders like a machine-gun, walking slowly about the room. 'As inspiration came to him,' says his private secretary, Baron de Méneval;

... his voice assumed a more animated tone, and was accompanied by a sort of habit, which consisted in a movement of the right arm, which he twisted, at the same time pulling the cuff of the sleeve of his coat with his hand ... expressions came without effort. ...

Because of the speed of his dictation, this would be scribbled down by the secretaries in rough draft and finally worked up on large sheets of 'elephant paper', sometimes a metre in length.

On the march, Napoleon's entourage would be further compressed to a 'Little Headquarters', or tactical headquarters, which might move several days ahead of the main body. Napoleon himself normally travelled in a light *calèche* when distances were small, but more often in a heavy *barouche*, drawn by six powerful horses. On the box would be Roustam, Napoleon's Mameluke *valet de chambre* (acquired during the Egyptian campaign); inside, Berthier, sitting up attentively while

... with his head covered by a checkered handkerchief, the Emperor could sleep in his carriage as though in his bed. In the interior of the carriage were a number of drawers with locks and keys containing news from Paris, reports, and books. ... A large lantern hung at the back of the carriage and lit up the interior, whilst four other lanterns illuminated the road. ...

Though he was an indifferent horseman (Odeleben[10] says scathingly: 'Napoleon rode like a butcher. ... Whilst galloping, his body rolled backwards and forwards and sideways') and was thrown more than once, when roads were poor he would take to horseback, once covering 86 miles in five-and-a-half hours.

At the hub of the whole Napoleonic war machine stood – and would continue to stand, right up to the last dreadful minutes at Waterloo – the Imperial Guard. Consisting of all arms, it was about 7,000 strong in 1805, but by 1814 it would escalate to 100,000, virtually an army in its own right. Élite of the élite, and envy of other nations, the Guardsman had to be over 1.78 metres tall (5ft. 6ins.) – a fair height in those days of undernourishment – must have fought in three campaigns or have been wounded twice, and must read and write. He was not allowed to frequent places of ill repute, and if he should escort a proper lady under no circumstances was she to be seen on his arm. To the Horse Grenadiers (sometimes nicknamed 'big heels', because of their vast boots, or simply 'gods' because of their haughtiness) it was forbidden that 'any woman under forty come in to make soup for them'. Old in experience rather than age, they averaged between twenty-five and thirty. Respectfully addressed as 'Monsieur' by their officers (the ordinary soldier of the line even used to joke that donkeys used by the Guard were promoted to 'mules'), the Guard enjoyed many special privileges such as higher pay and better rations and quarters. (Before Eylau, for instance, after the Russians had pillaged everything, only the Guard had its own ration waggons; the rest of the army came close to starving). Above all, theirs was the privilege of guarding the Emperor; and, in turn, of being thrown into battle at the decisive moment as a constantly dependable reserve. The *grognards* – as Napoleon himself had nicknamed the 'Old Guard' – grumbled and groused, but always went on, and on. As was to be said of it, immortally, at Waterloo, the Guard 'died, but never surrendered'. On the other side of the coin, some military historians hold the Imperial Guard to have played an injurious role, to the extent that its élitism drained the rest of the line. Nevertheless, its morale was unbeatable, and set the tone for the whole army.

Certainly, if there was one quality the *Grande Armée* of 1805 had to excess, it was morale, or sheer fighting spirit. 'If you discover how,' wrote one of Britain's most revered commanders, Field-Marshal Wavell, many years later '... he inspired a ragged, mutinous, half-starved army

and made it fight as it did ... then you will have learned something.' Like so much else, the explanation had its roots in Revolutionary times. After the initial setbacks against the First Coalition, special 'political commissars' (not unlike those introduced by the Soviet Army), called 'Deputies-on-Mission' were despatched to the armies to instil a new spirit. Although the purges and punishments they carried out were – as might have been expected – often bloody and unjust, they did succeed in their mission. The early urgency that the Republic was fighting for its life, on its own territory; the new egalitarianism, as far as advancement was concerned; the awareness that, unlike the impressed serfs of the other continental nations, the French soldier alone felt he had a personal cause worth fighting for, plus that extra indefinable something to be found in almost all 'revolutionary armies' of the twentieth century, provided the rest of the mix. Napoleon simply carried on all that was best of the revolutionary zeal; 'We suffered, but were proud of our sufferings,' wrote a Grenadier, 'Because our officers, with their packs on their backs, shared our meagre rations.' But Napoleon, of course, grafted his own special – indeed unique – morale-boosting magic onto the Revolutionary stock.

First of all, even though he was a Corsican, he understood the mentality of the French soldier quite uncannily well. The soldier, said Napoleon: '... is not a machine to be put into motion, but a reasonable being that must be directed ... [he] loves to argue, because he is intelligent....' Like Montgomery with his Eighth Army, he believed in making the simplest soldier party to his plan, and understand what was to be demanded of him. As has already been noted the degradation of corporal punishment had been abolished and replaced by a system of glory, awards and riches. On the other hand, no flogging-through-the-ranks could be more searing than a flaying from the Emperor's tongue when in one of his terrifying rages. Describing his outburst against a regiment that had lost an 'Eagle' at Austerlitz, the Comte de Saint-Chamans[11] was to admit:

... my flesh crawled. I broke into a cold sweat, and at times my eyes were coursing with tears. I do not doubt that the regiment would have performed miracles if it had been led into action at the very next instant.

Equally no one was more aware of the positive force of his personality than Napoleon himself. 'The 32nd Brigade would have died for me,' he once observed; 'Because after Lonato, I wrote: "The 32nd was there, I was calm." The power of words on men is astonishing.' Napoleon also used this 'power of words' often quite unscrupulously when framing his famous Bulletins in the aftermath of a battle. Mediocre victories would be transformed into epic triumphs; while, particularly after assuming the Imperial Crown, Napoleon himself did his best to foster super-human legends, *inter alia* in popular engravings, all designed to suggest he was endowed with powers beyond the natural. This mixture of half-truths and downright lies employed in his Bulletins was probably designed as much to exhilarate his own forces as to demoralize the enemy. Throughout his career Napoleon was conscious of having constantly to keep up a certain moral momentum to hold the enthusiasm of the French army: 'I had to act with *éclat*,' he said after his first triumph in the 1796 Italian Campaign; 'to win the trust and affection of the common soldier.' 'A man does not have himself killed for a few halfpence a day, or for a petty distinction,' Napoleon recognized; 'you must speak to the soul in order to electrify the man ...' and this was

LEFT A Grenadier of the Old Guard or '*grognard*'.
The soldier's height is characteristic of the Guard,
as is the favoured clay-pipe.

a skill at which he was unrivalled. As Marshal Marmont wrote a long time later: 'We marched surrounded by a kind of radiance whose warmth I can still feel as I did fifty years ago.'

The troops of the *Grande Armée* with habitual cheeriness spoke of 'setting off for the marriage feast' as a campaign approached, and as the Emperor personally took leave of his departing cohorts at Boulogne, their display of ardour after the long months of boredom and frustration waiting on the Channel was quite overwhelming. It was only rivalled by the glumness of those left behind to protect the coast (to whom Berthier promised an invasion next spring, once the Emperor had 'punished the continent for its aggression'). Those Frenchmen of 1805 had already defeated most of the soldiers of Europe, and consequently despised them. The long, perilous march into the heart of the continent held little horror or fear for them. Says Thiers:

> They set off singing and shouting '*Vive l'Empereur!*', begging for as speedy a meeting as possible with the enemy. It is true, that, in those hearts, boiling over with courage, there was less pure patriotism than in the soldiers of '92; there was more ambition, but a noble ambition, that of glory. . . . The volunteers of '92 were eager to defend their country against an unjust invasion; the veteran soldiers of 1805, to render it the first power in the world.[12]

It was a valid distinction. And, though that mesmeric spell of Napoleon, under which his *grognards* would march to Hell and back for him, would endure through 1812 and beyond, now it was at its all-time peak of potency. These soldiers of 1805 would never be surpassed.

Notes to chapter 6

1 Studying wounds suffered in a number of hand-to-hand combats, Napoleon's Surgeon-General, Larrey, could count only five actually caused by bayonets compared with 119 bullet wounds; a conclusion that could be paralleled with remarkable accuracy in two World Wars, where the majority of bayoneted men were generally on the point of surrender anyway!
2 Charged with small balls, this was principally used against massed infantry at short range. In 1784, the British had invented the shrapnel (named after its inventor), a shell that exploded above the heads of the infantry, but it was still not widely in use.
3 The compact division was in fact introduced by the French Revolutionary armies.
4 The Dragoons were the standard cavalry of the line, less heavily armoured than the Cuirassiers they would sometimes charge with heavy cavalry, or support the light cavalry.
5 In the Peninsular War, British riflemen staggered under 80 lbs of equipment which sometimes led led to needless deaths from exhaustion on the march.
6 *The Face of Battle* (1976).
7 'They sent a young madman,' an Austrian officer complained characteristically during the Italian campaign, 'who attacks right, left and from the rear. It's an intolerable way of making war.'
8 In *The Campaigns of Napoleon* (see bibliography).
9 '*Mémoires*' from *Napoleon at Work* by Vachée (translated 1914).
10 Baron von Odeleben, *A Circumstantial Narrative of the Campaign in Saxony* (1820).
11 *Mémoires du Général Comte de Saint-Chamans* (Paris 1896).
12 Thiers, *Consulate and Empire*, Vol. VI, p. 13.

PART TWO

Austerlitz

Napoleon's triumphal entry into Vienna, 14 November 1805.

L'ARMÉE FRANÇAISE
PASSE LE RHIN A STRASBOURG
25 Septembre 1805.

Napoleon points out the way, crossing
the Rhine at Strasbourg. A decorative
panel from Versailles by E. May.

7

Ulm

2 September – 21 October

The Emperor has discovered a new way of waging war; he makes use of our legs instead of our bayonets...

Anonymous French soldier, 1805

HAVING DISPATCHED his troops, Napoleon set out for Malmaison on 2 September 1805. In Paris there were some distractingly aggravating domestic problems to be dealt with; a disappointing harvest had made bread prices soar and finances were in a mess. The budget showed an immense deficit, and as it was against all Napoleon's principles either to borrow or to print paper money, a heavy increase in taxation was his only recourse. Rumours that he was reaching down into the bottom of the national coffers in order to pay for the new war were spreading financial panic. This, plus a call-up of 80,000 to provide him with a contingency reserve, did not enhance his popularity in the capital. On 23 September when he explained to the Senate the causes of the new war, laying the blame squarely on the Allies, the Senators evinced little more than token enthusiasm. During his return to the Tuileries, he was vexed by the unwonted lack of warmth shown by the populace. Disagreeably aware that civilian morale was not of the same high order as that of the *Grande Armée*, Napoleon left Paris for Strasbourg knowing how imperative it was for him to win a swift and decisive victory; if for no other reason than that the country might otherwise face bankruptcy.

At Strasbourg, the gloom was intensified by Talleyrand, the venal ex-Bishop of Autun, turned Minister of Foreign Affairs. There are no shortage of *bons mots* describing Talleyrand; most of them unflattering. To one Scottish duke, he was '... the most disgusting individual I ever saw. His complexion is that of a corpse considerably advanced in corruption.' There was Chateaubriand's immortal description of his re-appearance after the final defeat of his master, declaring loyalty for the restored monarch: '... there came in silently Vice leaning on the arm of Crime; M. de Talleyrand supported by M. Fouché'; and there was, finally the King's own epitaph on hearing of his death: '... but there is no judging from appearances with Talleyrand!' Nevertheless, there was equally no gainsaying that he was one of the most brilliant diplomatists of all time, with considerably longer vision than Napoleon himself.

For both national and personal reasons, Talleyrand disapproved of the new war. With his club-foot and love of comfort, he dreaded the pain that resulted from the long marches trailing behind his master. The rest of his entourage was also suffering from presentiments that, like Turenne or Charles XII, the irreplaceable leader might possibly be struck down by a stray ball.

The Empress herself, so Thiers alleged with just a touch of cynicism, 'was the more strongly attached to him the more fear she felt about the duration of her union with him'. Having got over his latest transient infatuation with twenty-year-old, musical Mme Duchatel that spring, Napoleon displayed a renewal of his passion for Josephine and there was an emotional (and public) farewell scene. Napoleon wept and vomited, and according to Talleyrand suffered something like a convulsion – news which was warmly received in London as signifying that the arch-enemy had been laid low with an epileptic fit. 'It really is painful to leave two people one most loves,' grieved the Emperor, embracing them both and then setting forth, on 1 October, on one of his rare campaigns without a woman.

Once the other side of the Rhine, things immediately looked brighter. Only a short time behind the schedule laid down by Napoleon, on 26 August the *Grande Armée* was concentrated perfectly in conformity with Napoleon's plans and was marching superbly. It was probably one of the first times in warfare that roads were to be used so extensively for transportation of an army on a large scale. The infantry strode forth in two parallel files at the side of the dusty roads, leaving the centre free for the cavalry and heavy waggons, each division spread out over three miles in precise march discipline. With straws between their teeth so as to keep their mouths closed, the troops would begin their march at between 4 a.m. and 6 a.m. and bivouac before midday. Every hour there was a five-minute halt when the music – clarinets, flute and horn – played, and when the men showed signs of sleepiness on the march the drums began to beat. Anything to keep them on the move.

Among the Guard, even though they carried heavier packs than the Line, discipline was of course superb; at Ettlingen they rendered honours in immaculate full dress when the Emperor was received by the Grand Duke of Baden. Desertions were minimal; out of Marmont's 20,000-strong 2nd Corps, only 9 men were missing when it reached Würzburg. 'The Emperor has discovered a new way of waging war,' grumbled the infantry, 'he uses our legs instead of our bayonets.' As previously noted, the speed of Napoleon's forces on the march was legendary. Advancing into the German states, the *Grande Armée*, travelling light, was preceded by the quartermasters who arranged billeting and requisitioning. Fortunately, at any rate in the early stages, food was readily available in rich Württemberg and Bavaria. 'It was the height of the potato season,' Corporal Jean-Pierre Blaise wrote to his parents from Germany; 'How many times did we blight the hopes of a villager! We plundered him of the fruits of a whole year's work. However we were, as you might say, forced to do so ...' The unhappy German peasants tried to bury their food supplies, but the French foragers soon ferreted them out.

Then bad weather struck and in the sodden bivouacs morale slumped. François-Joseph Joskin wrote: 'Oh, mother, what a great misfortune has befallen me to become a conscript! What an unhappy life it is to be a soldier!' Food supplies were uncertain; boots were holed and the horses were beginning to break down. Davout was asking permission to shoot hungry marauders. Something of that Boulogne euphoria began to dissolve under the icy rain. But Napoleon was in no way dejected; to Josephine he wrote exuberantly on 2 October: 'Our grand manoeuvres are in full swing. The armies of Württemberg and Baden are joining mine. I am in good health, and I love you....' Then, on 7 October, Murat's cavalry had already crossed the Danube downstream from Ulm. The *Grande Armée*'s front concentrated from 125 down to 50 miles.

In contrast to his own performance, Napoleon noted (on 2 October) how 'the enemy is marching and countermarching and appears to be embarrassed'. Though nominally under Archduke Ferdinand, the Austrian expeditionary force on the Danube was in effect commanded by his quartermaster-general, General Karl Mack. Aged forty-three at this time, Mack had been born in Bavaria of a lower-middle-class Protestant family and had worked his way up through the ranks. In 1799 he had been defeated by Napoleon in Italy and captured, escaping the following year. He had not handled that campaign with particular distinction, and Nelson – with whom he had collaborated in Naples – went so far as to declare him 'a rascal, a scoundrel and a coward!' This was unduly harsh, and Mack seems to have been a courageous soldier at least as competent as most of the leaders thrown up either previously or subsequently by a nation whose greatest talent never lay in the art of warfare. As *Generalquartiermeister*, Mack had done his best to modernize the Austrian Army, but his efforts had been resisted as too 'revolutionary' by Vienna's hidebound military establishment.

Basically, the Austrian Army of 1805 remained that of Maria Theresa and Joseph II. Its bible was still the *Generals-Reglement* of 1769, which stressed drill and rigidly linear tactics and a cautious strategy based on secure communications, coupled with a traditional Austrian proclivity for fortified bases. The Commissariat was regarded as too socially inferior to be administered by officers-and-gentlemen; hence it was rotten with corruption, and barely functioned. Between 1801 and 1804 the national military budget had been cut by more than half. Most of the Austrian infantry still carried the 1754 musket, and had very little practice with it. Artillery was sprinkled about in penny-packets among the infantry, much as the French were to use their tanks in 1940. Baggage trains were huge, partly due to the requirements of officers' personal kit.

Greatly impressed by the mobility of Napoleon's army, Mack had undertaken a series of fairly far-reaching reforms in the spring of 1805; but it had been too late, and Mack himself seems to have been somewhat carried away by optimism at what he had already achieved. More realistically, the best Austrian commander, Archduke Charles, had unsuccessfully resisted involvement in a new war on the grounds that the army was simply not ready for it. He was overruled by the 'hawks'; thus, when war came, the Austrian Army was caught in the middle of change and reform, its organization still antiquated and its movements ponderous. The High Command was in the hands of the slow-witted and argumentative Aulic Council. Its deliberations with the Russian leaders were sadly shown up by Napoleon's axiom that

... nothing is so important in war as an undivided command. For this reason, when war is carried on against a single power, there should be only one army, acting upon one base, and conducted by one chief.

Moreover, within the Ulm camp, there was already a fundamental clash of personalities between the aristocratic, overbearing Catholic Archduke (given titular command not least to keep it out of the hands of the mistrusted Russian ally) and the despised Lutheran ex-ranker, Mack, who was to bear the shame and responsibility of the coming disaster.

Under the impulse of Ferdinand and the Aulic Council, Mack had committed the fatal error of crossing the River Inn into Bavaria on 8 September, without waiting for the Russians who were still east of Vienna. This was exactly what Napoleon had foreseen (he also seems to have

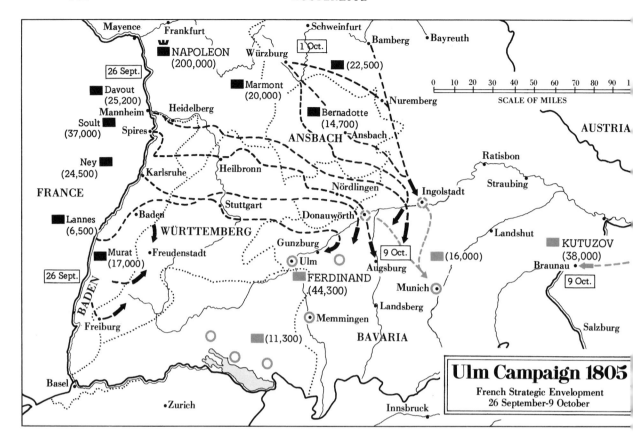

Ulm Campaign 1805
French Strategic Envelopment
26 September-9 October

been aided by having a skilful double-agent, Charles Schulmeister, insinuated into Mack's own headquarters, who kept Napoleon informed of just how far the Russians were from joining up with Mack at Ulm). Equally Mack and Ferdinand had perfectly swallowed Napoleon's deception plan, expecting the main French offensive to be delivered in Northern Italy, as in 1796 and again in 1800; they were also distracted by such carefully-planted rumours as that the British had landed in Boulogne and that a *coup* had been launched in France against Napoleon. Refusing to believe that he would risk breaching Prussian neutrality by marching through Ansbach, they had their eyes riveted to their west, on the Black Forest where Murat's cavalry had been ostentatiously swarming about. A series of contradictory intelligence reports were reaching Mack. As a result he continued to sit paralysed at Ulm, ordering up reinforcements from the Tyrol – only to increase Napoleon's eventual bag of prisoners. When Marshal Soult's corps crossed the Danube at Donauwörth on 8 October, the officers of a reconnaissance force dispatched by Mack were taken by surprise in the middle of their dinner. The surprise was universal. As Thiers remarks:

Never was astonishment equal to that which filled all Europe on the unexpected arrival of this army. It was supposed to be on the shores of the ocean, and, in twenty days, that is to say the time required for the report of its march to begin to spread, it appeared on the Rhine, and inundated South Germany.

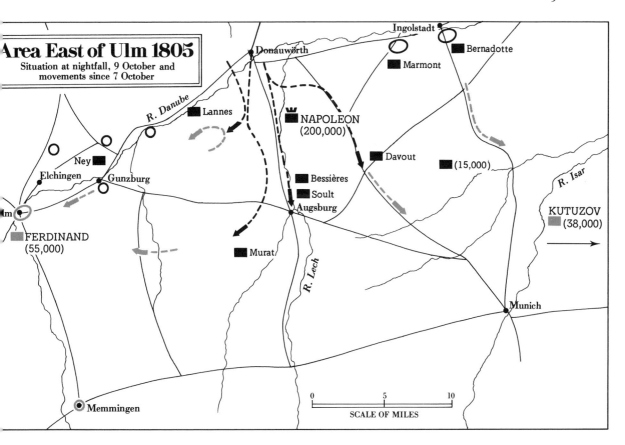

Although, with the arrival of the *Grande Armée* on the Danube, the curtain was now rent asunder, Mack could still not be sure of precisely what Napoleon was planning to do. He seems to have nursed a wishful belief that, since Napoleon had crossed the Danube and then swung westward again, he might be heading back to Paris to cope with the domestic crises that Mack too had heard about. Consequently he went on wavering, adopting scheme after scheme and then abandoning them. In turn Mack's irresolution made it the more difficult for Napoleon to form an appreciation of how his enemy would react once the jaws of the trap closed behind Ulm. There were basically three options open to Mack. He could stay in Ulm and sit it out until the Russians arrived; a contingency for which he had neither the strength nor the provisions. He could try to break out of the trap and retreat on Vienna along the north bank of the Danube; but this route lay across the main line of march of Napoleon's forces and he would be sacrificing his own communications with the Tyrol. Or he could withdraw southwards up the River Iller, to withdraw on Vienna through the Tyrol, linking up on the way with Archdukes John and Charles.

This last seemed to Napoleon the most logical contingency, and upon this judgement he went on to commit his first major error of the campaign, which, had the Austrians been less ineffectual, might easily have led to catastrophe. To prevent Mack breaking out southwards,

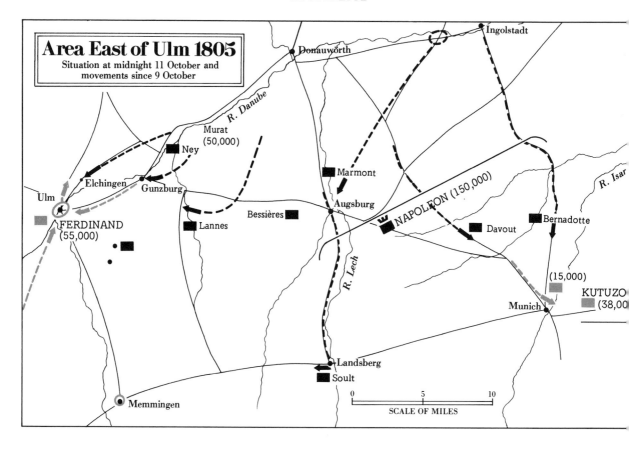

Area East of Ulm 1805
Situation at midnight 11 October and
movements since 9 October

Ingolstadt

Donauwörth

R. Danube

Murat
(50,000)

Ney

Marmont

Elchingen

Gunzburg

Ulm

Augsburg

NAPOLEON (150,000)

R. Isar

Davout

Bernadotte

FERDINAND
(55,000)

Lannes

Bessières

R. Lech

(15,000)

KUTUZO

Munich

(38,00

Landsberg

Soult

Memmingen

0   5   10

SCALE OF MILES

LEFT Marshal Michel Ney (1769–1819),
Duke of Elchingen and later Prince of
Moscow. 'The bravest of the brave', and a
true front-line leader, he was shot after
Waterloo by the Restoration.

Napoleon dispatched the main weight of his army – Lannes, Soult, Davout, Marmont and the Guard – across the Danube, concentrating on Augsburg. Bernadotte was sent eastwards, as a covering force against the Russians; leaving only Murat, with Ney under his command, to control the Danube River itself on both sides.

With their vaunting pride, rivalry and ambition, one of the chief faults of Napoleon's marshals was that they seldom took well to being subordinated to one another. Murat, the thirty-eight-year-old innkeeper's son, created commander-in-chief of the newly formed Guard in 1799 and Napoleon's brother-in-law the following year, was the most over-weaningly ambitious of them all. Tall, vain, handsome and a brilliant horseman with a passion for fine horses and extravagant uniforms, Murat was renowned in the army for his rash courage (even though he was bullied by his wife, Caroline). General Savary remarked acidly that 'it would be better if he was endowed with rather less courage and rather more common sense', and his mixture of impetuousness and self-interest was to lead Napoleon to the brink of disaster on more than one occasion during the Austerlitz campaign. He was the most resented of Napoleon's marshals, and Ney, the thirty-six-year-old cooper's son, immediately chafed at being placed under his command. Red-headed Ney was also courageous to a fault; of only moderate intelligence he could show initiative, but often at the wrong time, and his front-line style of leadership tended to lead him to ignore units not immediately within his sight.

Relations between the two marshals were thus immediately strained. On 11 October, when (in interpretation of Napoleon's instructions) Murat ordered Ney to move his whole corps across to the south bank of the Danube, there was a violent row in front of many witnesses which nearly ended in a duel between the two commanders. Finally only General Dupont's division of 6,000 men was left on the north bank of the Danube, muddled by conflicting orders that resulted from the marshals' altercation. Murat – and certainly Napoleon – was unaware of just how weak the French forces now were that side of the river.

Meanwhile, Mack had captured orders revealing Ney's dispositions and realized that an escape route north was open. Suddenly the unfortunate General Dupont found himself confronted by 60,000 Austrians 'in an imposing attitude', some twenty miles north-east of Ulm. Typically of the spirit of the *Grande Armée*, however, Dupont hurled forward two regiments in a savage bayonet attack. The Austrian front line recoiled, leaving behind 1,500 prisoners. For the next five hours there was violent fighting in and around the village of Haslach, between Dupont and 25,000 Austrians. Dupont's division was cut to pieces, and possibly only saved from being overrun by the fact that Mack himself had been wounded in the battle. But Dupont held; if he had not, the Austrians – says Thiers – 'would have fled into Bohemia, and one of Napoleon's most splendid combinations would have been completely frustrated....' Certainly there would have been no Austerlitz.

Opinions differ as to who was to blame for this near-disaster; Thiers says it was Murat, Ségur blames Napoleon. Wherever the fault lay, Napoleon on hearing of Dupont's plight immediately took over the reins himself, ordering Ney to push vigorously across the Danube upstream from Dupont. On 14 October, Ney, enraged by this decimation of one of his divisions and Murat's overbearing manner, seized Murat's arm and shook him violently in front of the Emperor, exclaiming angrily: 'Come, prince, come along with me and make your plans in face of the enemy.' He then galloped off, in full uniform and decorations, to supervise the relief operation 'amidst a shower of balls and grape, having the water up to his horse's belly'.

Dupont's valour, however, had provoked fatal dissension in the Austrian camp. On 12 October, Archduke Ferdinand wrote bitterly to his kinsman, the Emperor: 'General Mack has already projected and put into execution today three absolutely different plans.' Although the French error had opened an escape route out of the Ulm trap, Ferdinand had thrown it away by pressing the attack on Dupont so half-heartedly; yet he now urged Mack to agree to his escaping from Ulm in that same direction with at least a part of the army. Mack protested that, left with only 30,000 men until the Russians should arrive, this would abandon him completely to the mercy of Bonaparte, while Ferdinand's force would just be chopped up piecemeal by the French cavalry. But, with true Habsburg arrogance, the Archduke challenged him: 'Confine me in the fortress if you wish to prevent me. Does your power extend to that!'

Ulm, and the Austrian army there, was doomed. On 12 October Napoleon wrote triumphantly to Josephine: 'The enemy are beaten and don't know what they are about. It all looks like the most successful, the shortest and the most brilliant campaign ever fought. . . .' The following day he issued a proclamation to the army, declaring: 'Soldiers! It is only one month since we were encamped on the Ocean, facing England. . . . Soldiers! Tomorrow will be a hundred times more famous than the day of Marengo; I have placed the enemy in the same position.'

By the night of 15 October, Ney had retrieved the situation on the left bank of the Danube by winning a brilliant victory at Elchingen (which was later to earn him the title of Duke of Elchingen), and had established himself on the Michaelsberg heights overlooking the city from the north-west. That day the Emperor, while gazing down on Ulm, came under heavy fire himself when a concealed Austrian battery poured grape-shot into the Imperial group, and Lannes had to seize the reins of his horse to lead him hastily out of danger. (At another time, on the River Lech, the Emperor had also narrowly escaped death or serious injury when his horse, stumbling, had fallen on top of him. The episode had been kept a strict secret from the rest of the army.)

The citadel of Ulm was now held in a vice on three sides, with Soult moving up on the fourth from the south-west. Napoleon called on Mack to surrender; Mack refused. On 16 October, Napoleon ordered Ulm to be bombarded with a few warning shells. Conditions in the city, largely as a result of the Austrians' chaotic Commissariat, were already appalling: '. . . Many thousands of men made their quarters on the open streets, where they cooked and slept. . . . The whole city was a latrine, permeated with a pestilential stench. . . .' Meanwhile, as threatened, Ferdinand had pulled out with 20,000 men, abandoning Mack altogether. Equally, just as Mack had predicted, the Horse Guards pursued them, putting the unhappy fugitives to the sword at every turn; the Bavarian peasants plundered them as well, cutting the traces of the artillery to steal the horses. Finally, only 2,000 men struggled into Prague.

Blindfolded, Napoleon's aide, the Comte de Ségur, was led into Mack's citadel to renew cease-fire negotiations. Until that moment the unfortunate Mack had still no idea that he was encircled by 100,000 enemy troops, plus another 60,000 between him and the Russians. With his own army now divided in half, his position was clearly hopeless but still he refused to surrender. Finally, on 19 October he gave in and on the following day Napoleon, mounted on a white horse, watched as the army that was to have taken Strasbourg and Paris passed into captivity.

RIGHT *The Battle of Elchingen*, 14 October 1805,
by Rugendas. A key victory won by Ney and Lannes,
this battle sealed the fate of Mack at Ulm.

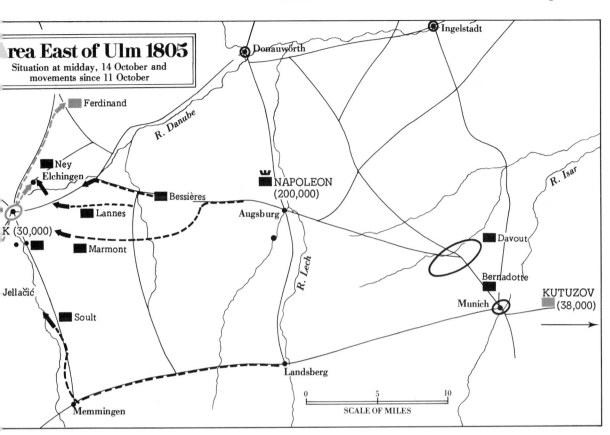

rea East of Ulm 1805
Situation at midday, 14 October and
movements since 11 October

ABOVE Napoleon receiving the sword of the surrendering Austrian commander at Ulm. A sketch by Antoine Jean Gros done on the field.
RIGHT *Trafalgar* by J.M.W.Turner. A distant reverse that, at the time, seemed to do little to diminish Napoleon's triumph at Ulm.

The incessant rain of the previous weeks had suddenly turned to glorious sunshine. A conversation took place between Mack and Napoleon, whom a captured Austrian officer described in his moment of glory as dressed 'in the uniform of a common soldier, with a grey coat singed[1] on the elbows and tails, a slouch hat without any badge of distinction on his head, his arms crossed behind his back, and warming himself at a camp-fire'. To Mack, a 'powdered old man in a splendid uniform of blue and white', Napoleon remarked, 'I don't know why we are fighting each other. ... I did not wish it; I did not intend to fight any but the English, when your master came along and provoked me,' adding (prophetically, as far as his own was concerned), 'All empires come to an end.'

Mack disappeared into ignominy. While Archduke Ferdinand was to become the darling of Vienna for his flight from Ulm, the plebeian Mack was made scapegoat for the defeat; he was court-martialled, broken from service, and thrown into a dungeon for several years.

On the 21 October, Napoleon issued his victorious proclamation:

Soldiers of the *Grande Armée*:

In a fortnight we have made a campaign; we have accomplished what we intended. We have driven the troops of the house of Austria out of Bavaria. ... The army, which, with equal ostentation and imprudence, came and placed itself on our frontiers, is annihilated....

Of the hundred thousand men who composed that army, sixty thousand are prisoners; they shall go and replace our conscripts in the labours of our fields. ... Soldiers, this success is owing to your unbounded confidence in your Emperor, to your patience in enduring fatigues and privations of every kind....But we shall not stop there; you are impatient to commence a second campaign. That Russian army, which the gold of England has brought from the extremities of the earth, shall share the same fate...

It was a classic victory, and won with an extraordinary economy in casualties on the French side; however Austrian losses (including those inflicted in the ensuing sweeping-up operations) are reckoned to have totalled almost 60,000 men. Including those lamed by the long march, Napoleon lost no more than 2,000 men *hors de combat*, most of them from the single, battered division of General Dupont.

News of Ulm, when it reached England, was greeted with a mixture of shock and outrage. Lord Auckland declared that a Captain of the London Volunteers would have done better than Mack. Lady Bessborough wrote: 'I am so terrified, so shocked with the news I scarcely know what to wish. This man moves like a torrent ...' while Lord Grenville was incredulous: '... An army of 100,000 men, reckoned the best troops in Europe, totally destroyed in three weeks ... Yet even this, I am afraid, is only the beginning of our misfortunes....'[2]

Events would prove this to be no exaggeration. Yet there was one shadow in Napoleon's triumph; the shadow that would always haunt him. That same glorious day of 21 October was also the day that Admiral Villeneuve, driven out of Cadiz by his Emperor's repeated taunts of cowardice, had been smashed by Nelson's fleet at Trafalgar. In the oft-repeated words of Admiral Mahan: 'Those distant, storm-beaten ships, upon which the Grand Army never looked, stood between it and the dominion of the world.'[3] Though British glory at Trafalgar was hardly of any immediate consolation to the humiliated Austrians, whatever successes might now fall to Napoleon on land, ultimate victory would henceforth always elude him.

It was not until some time later that Napoleon learned of the disaster at Trafalgar; he expressed himself 'mortified', ordered the minimum to be made of it in the French press, otherwise showed only moderate distress, and refused to be distracted from the pursuit of the decisive contest ahead. After Ulm he wrote to his Empress:

I have been rather overdone, my good Josephine. Eight days spent in the soaking rain and with cold feet have told on me a little; but ... I have accomplished my object; I have destroyed the Austrian army by simple marching ... I am on the point of marching against the Russians; they are ruined....

Notes to chapter 7
1 A hole had apparently been burned in it by a spark from a bonfire.
2 As quoted by Arthur Bryant in *Years of Victory*, pp. 179–80.
3 In one sense this was an obvious, if not faintly absurd, remark; how *could* the *Grande Armée* have set eyes on the Royal Navy's ships, any more than the Kaiser's or Hitler's land-locked armies were to do a century later?

8

On to Vienna and Austerlitz

21 October – 28 November

A consecutive series of great actions never is the result of chance and luck; it is always
the product of planning and genius … What is luck? The ability to exploit accidents.

Napoleon

NAPOLEON RESTED four or five days longer at Ulm before moving on eastwards down
the Danube Valley – first stop Munich. Accorded a warm welcome there by his
'liberated' Bavarian allies, Napoleon was in an ebullient and generous mood, presenting his Guard with one thousand pairs of new boots. At Munich, however, he was
caught up by his hobbling and fatigued Foreign Minister, bringing with him a variety of head-
aches. In France, the financial crisis was worsening; several bankers had been declared bankrupt,
including M. Recamier, husband of the famous Empire beauty. An outraged Prussia was taking
the French violation of Ansbach's neutrality worse than anticipated. In revenge, Russian troops
were being allowed passage through Silesia, and on his way to Vienna young Tsar Alexander
had paused in Berlin to captivate the Queen and cajole her vacillating husband into signing
the Potsdam Treaty, whereby Prussia would intervene on the Allied side as soon as her mobilization could be completed, early in December. Thus, as Napoleon advanced further 'into the
very entrails of Europe', there was the ever-increasing danger that the jaws of a gigantic trap
– sprung by Prussia in the north and Archduke Charles moving up from Italy in the south
– would close on his rear.

Seeing all this, Talleyrand beseeched Napoleon to try now to seduce the battered Austrians
out of the coalition by means of 'soft' peace terms. Austria – urged Talleyrand, as always, taking
the longer view – must be transmuted into the ally of France, as an eastern bulwark against
Russia. With the scent of military victory in his nostrils, however, Napoleon was little inclined
to heed Talleyrand. On 28 October he left Munich to begin the march to Vienna, 250 miles
distant. Either way the risks were the greatest he had ever taken. If, instead of advancing, he
adopted a defensive posture, within little more than a month he would have to face the combined
weight of 120,000 Austrians, 100,000 Russians and 150,000 Prussians. On balance, comments
Thiers, his decision to press on 'was the wisest, though apparently the rashest'. Napoleon's
strategy now was, on the one hand, to continue to keep the Austrian Armies of Archdukes John
and Charles (in the Tyrol and Northern Italy respectively) out of the Danubian theatre of war;
on the other, to catch and destroy Kutuzov somewhere *south* of the Danube, before Russian
reinforcements could reach him. The one fear that dominated all Napoleon's thinking from

this time onwards was that the Russians might escape northwards, back across the great river barrier.

On the day of his departure from Munich, the southern jaw of the potential Allied trap was in fact badly bruised when the dependable Masséna, with his 50,000 men, forcefully attacked Archduke Charles's 80,000 troops outside Verona. The Second Battle of Caldiero (as it came to be known) was a model of aggressive defence. It inflicted 11,000 casualties on the Austrians, and pinned them down so that they would be unable to join in developments north of the Tyrol. Napoleon could now march eastwards along the narrow, vulnerable route between the Alps and the Danube, fairly confident that his southern flank would be safe. However, he did take the precaution of establishing supply dumps at various intervals which could serve either for the advance, or a withdrawal if it were to be forced upon him. He also organized a flotilla of mobile pontoon barges to link the forces moving along both sides of the Danube.

Conditions on the new march were far from excellent. On All Saints' Day, a foot of snow covered the ground; at times the revictualling broke down, and the army was scourged with hunger. Corporal Jean-Pierre Blaise wrote: 'It was again one of the most wretched nights that we had spent; we could hardly remain lying down, such was the steepness of the slope....' The Corps Commanders were constantly receiving such bossy reminders from Berthier as:

... I repeat that in a war of invasion and of rapid movements which the Emperor is waging there can be no depots, and the generals in command have themselves to see to it that they procure the necessary supplies from the countries which they traverse.

Then, on 5 November, Murat and Lannes caught up with the Russians at Amstetten, just south of the Danube and 100 miles west of Vienna. It was the *Grande Armée*'s first encounter with this new, redoubtable enemy. Kutuzov – who had only recently heard of the disaster at Ulm, since Archduke Ferdinand had persisted in sending him nothing but optimistic news – fought a brief battle to save his baggage train, then disengaged.

Since 25 August, when, under the Allied grand strategy, the one-eyed old Russian veteran had set off westwards from Galicia, Kutuzov's columns had had a wearisome time. Under orders from the Tsar, a sixth column had been sent back to watch the frontier with Turkey; then the order had been countermanded, the column wearily trying to catch up with the main body. Pressed by Emperor Francis, Kutuzov had been urged, in September, to speed his march so as to join up with Mack, though grumbling to Czartoryski, Alexander's Foreign Minister: '...our soldiers have already endured much fatigue, and they are suffering badly'[1] and again, on 1 October: '... They have had to march barefoot, and their feet have suffered so badly on the sharp stones of the highways that the men are incapable of service ...'

By 26 October he had been reinforced by some 27,000 fatigued Russians and 18,000 Austrian survivors from Ulm and elsewhere. Relations between the two Allies were already strained, with the Austrian commander, Lieutenant-General Max Merveldt, complaining to Vienna that Kutuzov '... seems unacquainted with the art of war ... He leaves time and distance completely out of account, and is most unwilling to risk his troops.' In fact, Kutuzov had already made up his own, highly independent mind to conduct one of those long, stubborn retreats for which he was to earn his place in history.

RIGHT The dashing cavalryman, in characteristic pose, and suitably adorned. Marshal Murat (1767–1815), later King of Naples, turned on his brother-in-law in 1814, but was executed in a hare-brained attempt to recapture Naples in 1815. Portrait by Gros.

Whereas the Austrians' obvious priority was now the defence of their capital, Vienna, Kutuzov's was the preservation of his unbattleworthy army. In the event, a compromise was forced on him. He was to concentrate on holding the permanent bridge over the Danube at Krems, some forty miles upstream from Vienna. This would enable him both to cover the approaches to Vienna, and also keep open an escape route northwards. Then, as a result of conflicting orders received from the Aulic Council (but what at the time looked remarkably like cowardice), on 1 November Merveldt had withdrawn his main force south-eastwards, leaving Kutuzov unsupported at Amstetten to fend off Murat's cavalry. Three days later Merveldt was fallen upon by the combined forces of Davout and Marmont and destroyed on the snow-covered field of Mariazell. It was a further episode hardly calculated to improve Austro-Russian relations. Kutuzov proceeded with a savage 'scorched earth' withdrawal, burning everything behind him – something the French had never yet encountered, but would learn more about in 1812. Arriving at Krems, Kutuzov discovered that the Austrians had not fortified the bridgehead. He now took the major strategic decision to pull his army out, northwards across the Danube.

Misjudging his new adversary, Napoleon calculated (and hoped) that Kutuzov might stand and fight a decisive battle at St Pölten, some thirty miles further east from Amstetten. At this moment the Emperor and his staff were still at Linz, further behind the vanguard and more out of touch with developments than was his wont, which was perhaps a contributory factor in the second[2] major error of the campaign that the French were about to commit. On 7 November Murat intercepted messages revealing Kutuzov's intention to retreat across the Danube at Krems. From this it seemed clear that the Russians were planning to abandon the capital of their allies, and fall back northeastwards into Moravia whence they had only recently arrived. If they succeeded it meant that they would escape Napoleon's trap, and his grand strategy of a swift battle of annihilation would collapse. However, the dazzling prospect of the open, defenceless city of Vienna lying just ahead was too much for the vainglorious Murat to resist. After Marengo, the victorious French had come close to Vienna in 1800, but otherwise no western army had ever occupied it. Here indeed was a prize worthy of Murat's boundless ambition; perhaps he already thought of himself as Duke, or even King, of Vienna? Momentarily he was like a head-strong stallion that had ripped the bridle out of the grasp of its handler and bolted.

Kutuzov, his forces increased to 40,000 by the arrival of the jaded sixth column, soon perceived that – with Murat and Lannes galloping for Vienna – the French had only one *ad hoc* army corps, Mortier's, advancing in extended order along the north bank of the Danube. The supporting troops were well behind him, as was the Danube flotilla which provided the only means of transferring troops from one side to the other of the now wide and largely bridgeless river. Kutuzov swiftly turned about and, on 11 November, despatched nearly 15,000 men to strike Mortier's 6,000 from the front, flank, and rear in a narrow defile at Dürrenstein. The situation was almost a repeat of Dupont's reverse before Ulm, except that, this time, the odds were not so great. The Russians, however, pressed their attack with much more vigour; although allegedly impeded by the weight of their heavy overcoats. The rugged but rather slow-witted General Mortier,[3] fighting sword in hand at the head of his Grenadiers, was nearly captured. It was Dupont, again, who came to the rescue and the Russians were driven back; but with heavy French losses – 4,000 on each side.

Subsequent Russian historians claim that, at Dürrenstein, Napoleon had been dealt 'a serious blow in the eyes of all Europe' for the first time in his military career. Indeed, it was a close-run thing, and if Mortier's corps had been wiped out it would have gone far to dilute the results of Napoleon's triumph at Ulm. In all probability the set-back would not have happened had Napoleon been more closely in touch with the advance troops.[4] As it was, with his usual alacrity he restored the imbalance, taking it out on his brother-in-law Murat, with one of his most searing reprimands:

I cannot approve your method of advance; you proceed like a scatterbrain (*étourdi*), and you pay no heed to the orders I send you. Instead of covering Vienna, the Russians have recrossed the Danube at Krems. This extraordinary circumstance should have made you realize that you ought not to move without fresh instructions. . . . Without knowing what plans the enemy might have had, or being aware what my intentions were in this new state of affairs, you go and set my army at Vienna. . . . You have made me lose two days, and have considered nothing but the petty triumph of entering Vienna. There is no glory except where there is danger. There is none in entering a defenceless capital.

Napoleon should perhaps have remembered this in 1812.

Kutuzov had escaped Napoleon's first trap, and a chastened Murat now redeemed himself by a Machiavellian ruse the following day. Arriving at the great bridge leading over the Danube to Vienna, he realized at once that the bridge was mined; in fact, an Austrian gunner was standing by with a lighted fuse as the French approached. But the Austrian troops guarding it were commanded by a general brought out of cold storage after a dozen years' retirement – Prince Auersperg. Disingenuously shouting 'Armistice, Armistice!', Murat and Lannes talked their way across the vital bridge, and at the other end they managed persuasively to assure the defenders that an armistice had been signed: 'How is it that you have heard nothing about it? Peace is being negotiated! Lead us to your general.'

While the bemused Auersperg was pondering what to do, a detachment of French Grenadiers doubled across the bridge, and the key to the Austrian capital was in Napoleon's hands. Emperor Francis declared himself '. . . all the more hurt since this stupid and unpardonable blunder has destroyed the whole trust of my allies at a single stroke.' In fact, by uncovering the flank of the retreating Kutuzov, considerably more than just trust was now at risk. Among the francophone Russian officers, a bitter jest (according to Tolstoy in *War and Peace*) went the rounds: '. . . *c'est comme à Ulm . . . c'est du Mack. Nous sommes Mackés!*'

Napoleon was delighted by this rather underhand *coup*, and promptly forgave Murat his earlier transgression. On 14 November, seventy-three days after leaving the English Channel, the Emperor rode with calm dignity and a much beplumed train into the Austrian capital. Hating the savage Russians whom they reckoned to have left them in the lurch, those Viennese who had not abandoned the city greeted him more like some conquering Austrian general (though they could hardly have seen many).

Mozart's *The Magic Flute* was currently being performed at the Opera; a week later, the first night of Beethoven's just-completed *Fidelio* would flop in front of an audience full of French uniforms (Beethoven himself, disillusioned with Napoleon whom he had once venerated, refused to watch his procession through Vienna). In the Vienna arsenals Napoleon discovered 2,000 cannon, 100,000 muskets and a vast store of ammunition negligently left behind by the

ABOVE Marshal Jean Lannes (1769–1809) by Gérard. Lannes was an aggressive Gascon who, among other things, found it hard to take orders from Murat. Later he was mortally wounded at Essling. Napoleon said of him: 'He was a swordsman when I found him, and a paladin when I lost him.'

RIGHT Murat deceiving the Austrian defenders before crossing the Vienna bridge, by Lethière.

Austrians. They would prove useful against the Austrians and their allies at Austerlitz, and the city itself provided the French with an invaluable supply and hospital base.

Meanwhile, in the south, Archduke Charles had withdrawn from Italy. With Masséna close on his tail,[5] he was obliged to keep up a running fight while trying to come to the aid of Vienna. Napoleon now sent Marmont southwards to Leoben in Styria to block him off. As a result, Archduke Charles's army and Archduke John's force from the Tyrol were harried eastwards across what is now Yugoslav Slovenia and into Hungary. Neither would be able to play any role in the coming operations. Here Napoleon's original strategy had been perfectly executed.

Kutuzov now hastened his pace north-eastwards. Behind him came the *Grande Armée* in pursuit, looting as it went. An old Austrian cavalry officer described one French unit as clad

... in sheepskin or the fur of some wild animal; others are rigged out in the most strange manner and carry long sides of bacon, ham, pieces of meat hanging from their belts. They are veritable walking larders. Others march with their bodies hung all over with loaves of bread and bottles of wine ...

The Austrians, however, suffered even more from their own allies – in the best tradition of Russian armies down through the ages – acting as if they were in enemy territory. On the withdrawal from Krems, they 'plundered, ravaged, even murdered, behaving like downright barbarians, so that the French were almost regarded as deliverers ...' They so stripped the surrounding area of both food and horses as to make a prolonged stand there improbable, and disease began to run through the cold, hungry army. They treated the Austrian troops with arrogance and contempt, sneering at them and blaming them (not without reason) for the disasters of the campaign to date. Relations between the two armies were noticeably deteriorating.

Commanding the advance guard, which he had spurred on at a killing pace, on 15 November a red-eyed Murat beat the Russians to Hollabrünn, a small centre where he was able to revictual his forces. However, remembering the disaster that had nearly overtaken Mortier, and conscious of the presence of the bulk of Kutuzov's army somewhere close by, he felt distinctly nervous. So it was with ill-disguised relief that he was suddenly informed of the arrival, under a flag of truce, of Russian emissaries, asking for a temporary armistice in advance of peace negotiations. Lannes was suspicious, but Murat acceded, falling into a trap which suitably paid him out for his own deceit on the Vienna bridge. According to Weyrother, the Austrian Chief-of-Staff, '... if the Russians, with their peculiarly Byzantine cunning, had not contrived to repay the deceitful French in their own coin, ...' it seemed as if Kutuzov must have been destroyed. As it was, the twenty-four hours during which Murat stood still were sufficient for him to extricate his tired forces, and put a healthy distance between them and Murat. When (simultaneously with the arrival of fresh details about the disaster at Trafalgar) Napoleon heard of Murat's latest error of judgement, he flew into a terrible rage and unleashed yet another venomous shaft against his headstrong brother-in-law:

It is impossible for me to find words with which to express my displeasure to you.... You are causing me to lose the fruits of a campaign. Break the armistice at once and march on the enemy.... The Austrians let themselves be taken in over the passage of the Vienna bridges; you have let yourself be taken in by an aide-de-camp of the Tsar!

Kutuzov had escaped a second trap, causing Napoleon to lose more time that he could ill afford. As he wrote to his brother Joseph on 15 November: 'The fate of the world may depend on a day.'

Stung by this latest rebuke, Murat thrust ahead once again, fighting a brisk engagement at Schöngrabern – immortalized in *War and Peace* – against Prince Bagration's rearguard; which cost it 3,000 men. The following night was passed by one French colonel in a grisly enough bivouac prepared by his Carabiniers: '... they dragged together a number of Russian corpses, face to the ground, and spread a layer of hay on top.' Kutuzov, nevertheless, congratulated the Georgian prince: 'I shall not ask after your losses. You are alive, and that is enough for me.'

On 19 November Murat occupied the Moravian capital of Brünn (Brno), happy to find it full of badly needed provisions. Some of the French officers were also happy to discover in the city 'extremely pretty women, got up in the most tasteful and tempting way'. Less fortunate troops, frozen with the damp cold, dismantled entire houses and their furnishings to fuel camp fires, to the dismay of the wretched peasants who had greeted them as liberators from the Russians. On that same day, Kutuzov came to rest in Olmütz, some forty miles away to the north-east. Here he linked up with the second Russian army under Buxhöwden, at last arrived from Galicia, 'completely fresh and in splendid order', in contrast to Kutuzov's force which (as described by one of its officers)

... had been ruined by perpetual hardship, and broken down by the lack of supplies and the foul weather of late autumn ... their footwear had almost ceased to exist. Even our commanders were arrayed in ill-assorted, almost comic attire.

Five days later the splendid Russian Imperial Guard, 10,000 strong, arrived all the way from St Petersburg: '... a magnificent force, composed of enormous men, who appeared by no means exhausted by such a long march.'

The two great opposing forces now stood and contemplated each other, for the first time in the campaign; equally for the first time it seemed as if the strategic advantage might lie with the Allies. It was also plain that a full-scale confrontation on the battlefield could not now be long postponed. For Napoleon, irrevocably committed in the very heart of Europe, the critical moment had arrived. The alternatives open to him were either to win a decisive victory, and quickly; or to face annihilation. With Prussia's entry into the war seeming to come closer every day, the whole of Europe had become, potentially, a deadly trap for the *Grande Armée*. Certainly, this is how it must have looked, unmistakably, to any neutral observer. The future held four daunting prospects for Napoleon. If Kutuzov withdrew out of reach again, denying him the decisive battle he sought, Napoleon would be lost. He would be equally lost if he were to fight a drawn game, leaving the enemy forces undestroyed. Thirdly, if he were forced to attack a superior enemy force on ground of its own choosing, Napoleon would be at a grave tactical disadvantage. He was thus left with a fourth, and risky option: to entice the Allies to attack him where and when he wanted. And this is what he intended to do.

Everything depended on the Russians taking Napoleon's bait. He would have to persuade them that they now outnumbered him by two to one, and that – become suddenly aware of

BATAVIAN
REPUBLIC

OLDENBURG

MECKLENBURG

R. Elbe

• Hamburg

• Bremen

HANOVER

R. Weser

• Hanover

• Magdeburg

Berlin

• Potsdam

• Münster

• Wittenberg

Wesel •

R. Lippe

R. Saale

• Halle

• Leipzig

SAXONY

Kassel •

Naumburg •

Dresden

Cologne •

• Erfurt

• Jena

• Chemnitz

R. Rhine

Weimar •

Ilm

• Saalfeld

• Meiningen

Karlsbad

Koblenz •

Coburg •

Hof •

R. Moselle

Frankfurt •

• Bamberg

Bayreuth •

Mayence •

Pilsen •

Aschaffenburg •

• Würzburg

FRANCE

Mannheim •

ANSBACH

• Nuremberg

BAVARIA

Spires •

Heidelberg •

• Ansbach

Ratisbon •

Karlsruhe •

Heilbronn •

Straubing •

Aalen •

Nordlingen •

Baden •

Stuttgart •

Donauwörth •

Ingolstadt •

Landshut •

Strasbourg

Freudenstadt •

WÜRTTEMBERG

Ulm

Günzburg •

Pas

Braunau

Augsburg •

Munich •

BADEN

Augereau
(12,000)

Freiburg •

Memmingen •

Landsberg •

Salzburg •

Ney
(7,500)

Zurich •

Innsbruck •

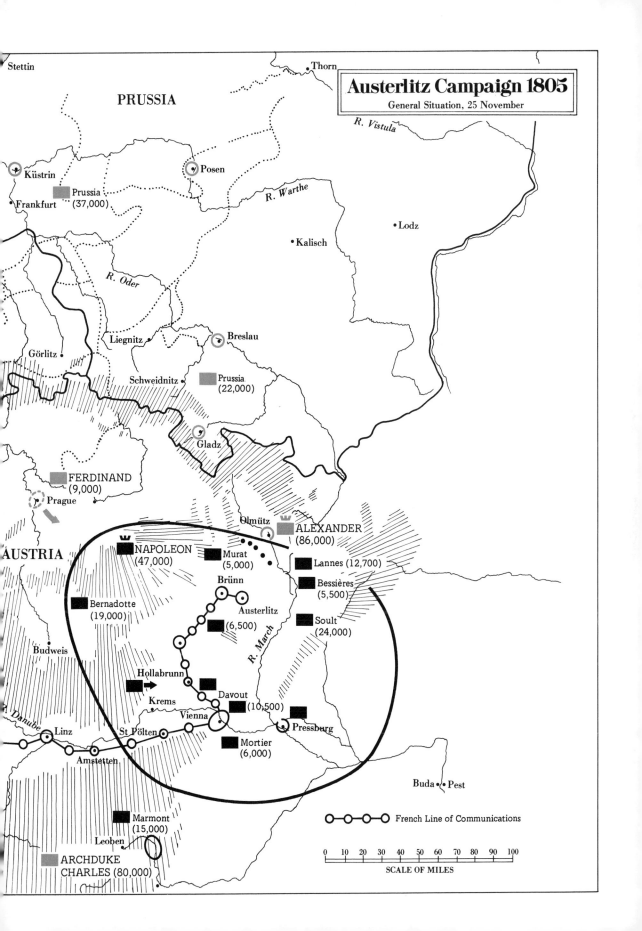

Stettin

Thorn

PRUSSIA

Austerlitz Campaign 1805
General Situation, 25 November

R. Vistula

Küstrin

Posen

Frankfurt

Prussia
(37,000)

R. Warthe

Lodz

Kalisch

R. Oder

Liegnitz

Breslau

Görlitz

Schweidnitz

Prussia
(22,000)

Gladz

FERDINAND
(9,000)

Prague

Olmütz

ALEXANDER
(86,000)

AUSTRIA

NAPOLEON
(47,000)

Murat
(5,000)

Lannes (12,700)

Brünn

Bessières
(5,500)

Bernadotte
(19,000)

Austerlitz
(6,500)

Soult
(24,000)

Budweis

R. March

Hollabrunn

Krems

Davout
(10,500)

Danube

Linz

St Pölten

Vienna

Pressburg

Amstetten

Mortier
(6,000)

Buda • Pest

Marmont
(15,000)

French Line of Communications

Leoben

ARCHDUKE
CHARLES (80,000)

0   10   20   30   40   50   60   70   80   90   100

SCALE OF MILES

his extended position – he was frightened. For the next ten days he busied himself with reconnaissance and espionage, bluff and counter-bluff, and – a skill in which he had few rivals – play-acting. Thirty-one-year-old General Savary, an adept at intelligence work, was despatched to the Tsar's camp at Olmütz; to spy out the land and gauge the Russian mood, but also to drop meaningful hints that a worried Napoleon would now be quite grateful for a negotiated peace. While the army sat unprovocatively motionless, liaison officers sped out to summon up the corps of Davout and Bernadotte and all other available forces for the coming confrontation. Ceaselessly Napoleon himself roamed over the countryside between Brünn and Olmütz, poring over maps with Bacler d'Albe, and consulting accounts of battles that had been fought in the Moravian hills by Frederick the Great. He also had with him some useful notes which that twenty-six-year-old Swiss military genius, Colonel Jomini, currently accompanying Ney on the campaign, had written only the previous year in his *Traité des Grandes Opérations Militaires*:

... Between Olmütz and Brünn there are several little rivers tucked away among the mountains which provide very favourable camps. On the whole, Moravia can be defended against a superior army ...

According to one of Napoleon's officers, Brigadier Thiébault, however, the name Moravia had sinister connotations for the French. It

... signified for them *mort à vie*.... In ten years of campaigning many of our officers had risked their lives in one battle after another, without ever thinking that they ought to draw up their wills. But they made them now ...

Suddenly Napoleon stuck his pin in the map midway between Brünn and the small village of Austerlitz, some thirteen miles to the east. Notwithstanding all his minute study and deep reflection of the past days, it seemed almost as if a divine intuition was guiding his hand at this moment.

Notes to Chapter 8

1 Letter to Czartoryski, 23 September.
2 His first had been to leave the north bank of the Danube so weakly held by Dupont's division on 11 October.
3 A contemporary pun about him was 'the big mortar (*mortier*) has a short range'.
4 Thiers goes so far as to criticize it as a 'negligence scarcely ever to be met with in operations directed by Napoleon', and largely exculpates Murat.
5 Napoleon's orders to Masséna (on 22 November) were: '... pursue the enemy with your sword in his ribs so that he may not be able to attack us, as we are now in the presence of the whole Russian army.'

9

Austerlitz: the Eve of Battle

28 November – 1 December

Gentlemen, examine this ground carefully; it is going to be a battlefield; you will
have a part to play upon it.

Napoleon: 21 November 1805

AS NOVEMBER drew to its end, inside Olmütz Castle the highest councils on the Allied
side found themselves, once again, in a state of discord, as they had been during
the critical moments before Ulm. There were the 'hawks' convinced that now, at
last, they had the archfiend, Bonaparte, beautifully cornered – and the 'doves' who
were urging caution. Chief among the 'hawks' was Count Dolgorukov, aide-de-camp to the Tsar
and exerting a potent influence on the twenty-eight-year-old autocrat; arrogant in the extreme
he was a kind of Russian counterpart to the headstrong Murat. On 28 November Napoleon,
hinting at negotiations, had requested a personal interview with the Tsar, and Dolgorukov had
been sent to the French camp as spokesman. Haughtily he offered the enemy emperor 'peace
at once if you give up all Italy immediately. ... But if France goes on with the war, it will
be Belgium, Savoy, Piedmont ...' With difficulty Napoleon had controlled his temper, keeping
up the role that his strategy dictated, but afterwards he had exploded, slashing at the ground
with his riding crop and slating Dolgorukov as 'a youthful trumpeter of England': 'These people
must be mad to expect me to evacuate Italy when they find it impossible to get me out of Vienna!'

Dolgorukov, however, had conveyed exactly the desired impression back to his master; Napoleon he described as 'a little figure, extremely dirty and ill-dressed' and his army on the brink
of doom. In particular, he delivered one nugget of intelligence. The previous day Soult, on
Napoleon's orders, had abandoned both Austerlitz and the dominant Pratzen Heights behind
it. This, declared Dolgorukov triumphantly, must provide evidence of Napoleon wanting to
avoid battle. The young Tsar, who (according to the émigré general, Langeron) above all 'wished
to experience and win a battle', and the firebrands of his entourage had been persuaded.

Among the 'doves' stood the 'honest and grave' Prince Adam Czartoryski, Alexander's Polish
Minister of Foreign Affairs. He felt strongly that the Tsar, sickly and subject to occasional
fits bordering on epilepsy, should not have been with the army in the first place. 'He had never
served; he could not know how to command ... surrounded by young, giddy, ignorant, pre-
sumptuous men ...' Czartoryski recommended that the Allies should withdraw further north-
eastwards into Silesia until Prussia entered the game. Equally cautious was Emperor Francis
of Austria, at thirty-seven years old already prematurely old, with a complexion blotchy from

Tsar Alexander I of Russia (1777–1825), by
George Dawe, looking rather more self-assured than
he did during most of the Battle of Austerlitz.

Emperor Francis I of Austria (1768–1835) in
later life, by Anton Einsle; he was prematurely
aged even by the time of Austerlitz.

good living and in his Habsburg eyes 'the look of the crowned conserver of the existing order'. Still shaken by Mack's downfall at Ulm, he also knew (many times over) what it was like to be mangled by Napoleon. Another 'dove' was the sardonic emigré Frenchman, the Comte de Langeron, probably one of the smartest intellects in the Allied camp.

Most noteworthy of the 'doves', however, was Tolstoy's hero of *War and Peace*, General Mikhail Golenishchev Kutuzov. Already sixty, but with his greatest fame still seven years ahead of him, Kutuzov had fought in Poland and under the great Suvorov during the Turkish Wars. His character revealed a mass of typically Slav contradictions: he was in turn lazy and ambitious, ill-read and obtuse, but he had an earthy shrewdness, and combined extremes of refinement and coarse grossness. A tremendous drinker, he habitually travelled with three wenches in his baggage train, and on the eve of an important battle he would often summon all three. In his various defensive actions along the Danube, he had deserved far more credit than historians have given him. But, as a result of these earlier experiences, he had also derived the poorest opinion of Austrian generalship, which at Olmütz he made little attempt to hide. (The Russian dislike of their Austrian allies, lumped together with other Teutons as 'Germans',[1] comes through in every line of *War and Peace*, often seeming to eclipse their hatred of the French. Typical of the Russian view is Prince Bolkonsky's contemptuous dismissal: 'Ever since the world began, everybody has beaten the Germans. But they never beat anybody. Only one another. He [Napoleon] made his reputation fighting them.')

In the Allied councils, Kutuzov urged a fighting withdrawal into the Carpathians; '... for the further we entice Napoleon, the weaker he will become.' It was very much the strategy he would adopt in 1812. In 1805, however, it was clear from the start that he did not enjoy the hawkish Tsar's confidence, who on one occasion told him curtly 'that is none of your business' when the Commander-in-Chief had enquired about his operational intentions.

In their turn, the Austrians were full of mistrust for their blustering, semi-barbarian Russian ally who constantly reminded them that they had come to save the poor incompetent Austrian army. By 1 December – or 19 November in the Julian calendar of the Russians – relations were more strained than ever. Over the previous ten days twice that number of plans had been put forward: '... everybody had an opinion ... and everybody expressed it.' But eventually the 'hawk' party had triumphed, headed by the Tsar whose lust for glory had been further seasoned by the arrival of a courier from St Petersburg who declared: 'All Russia is quivering with joy, Sire, at the thought of their beloved leader taking into his own hands the fate of the army ...'

So an offensive battle was decided upon for the following day; but not till after midnight (because of the still-raging arguments and counter-arguments) did the joint Allied staffs meet to receive their orders. Kutuzov, in disgust, had by now more or less washed his hands of the coming battle; as the baggage train with his ladies had got bogged down somewhere, he comforted himself by getting drunk instead ('hardly a good beginning to a battle' writes that renowned puritan, Field-Marshal Montgomery of Alamein!). During much of this crucial meeting he was half-, or completely, asleep – and many of the other participants were semi-comatose. Of all the generals present, says Langeron, only little Dokhturov even bothered to study the map.

The briefing was conducted by General Weyrother, the Austrian Chief-of-Staff, described as 'a veteran of the Viennese offices', who had become a 'hawk' in opposition to his own Emperor. He was (or should have been) intimately acquainted with the terrain, as he had recently conducted manoeuvres over it, and it was his battle plan that had finally been accepted for the next day. In a boringly pedantic, Teutonic fashion Weyrother droned on, unfolding on the table (wrote Langeron):

'... an immense and most accurate map of the environs of Brünn and Austerlitz, and read the dispositions to us in a loud tone and with a self-satisfied air which indicated a thorough persuasion of his own merit and of our incapacity. He was really like a college teacher reading a lesson to young students.

Weyrother's strategy was to fix Napoleon opposite the commanding Pratzen Heights (which Soult had abandoned with such apparent folly), and give the impression that he faced the main threat of a frontal attack there, by superior Allied weight of men. In fact, however, 55,000 men out of the total force of approximately 89,000 (under command of Buxhöwden) would be slipping southwards to smash into the French right flank between Telnitz and Sokolnitz. Once across the Goldbach brook and through the French defence, Buxhöwden's powerful spearhead would fan out to sever French lines of communication with Vienna, roll up the *Grande Armée* from the rear, and encircle it. This grandiose flanking manoeuvre was indeed a leaf borrowed from Napoleon's own book. While it was under way, the rest of the Russian line would be held defensively on the right by Bagration (13,700 men), and the Pratzen Heights in the centre by little more than the 10,000 élite troops of the Russian Imperial Guard, the sole reserve, under command of Grand Duke Constantine.

At this point only Langeron[2] asked the key question: 'If the enemy forestalls us, and attacks us near Pratzen, what would we do?' Weyrother parried this by stressing Napoleon's weakness ('If he has 40,000 men, that's putting it too high'), and therefore his inability to launch a dangerous attack himself. In addition to this crucial flaw in his *Disposition*, Weyrother also erred in presuming that the Allied army could act in conformity and with speed, and – indeed – that the Russian commanders would be able to understand the orders given them. Apart from this, says a modern Sandhurst historian, Christopher Duffy,[3] Weyrother's *Dispositions* '... would gain high marks as an operational order in a military academy today...'

Finally, after three hours' silence, Kutuzov emerged from his coma to break up the meeting with: 'There is nothing more important than to sleep well. Gentlemen, let us take some rest.' The die was cast.

From the vast Allied camp, six miles long, rose a mounting hum of activity. One Russian major expressed admiration for the apparent precision with which the Austrian staff moved such masses of troops – but it was not a view that would outlast the battle. The preparations, says Tolstoy in *War and Peace*, were like:

... the first movement of the centre wheel of a great tower-clock. One wheel moved slowly, another set in motion, then a third, and wheels began to revolve faster and faster, levers and dogwheels to work, chimes to play, figures to pop out and the hands to advance in measured time, as a result of that activity.

How may one evaluate this new enemy Napoleon now faced? Under 'mad' Paul I, and his

Prince Mikhail Golenishchev Kutuzov (1745–1813), the Russian
commander-in-chief. A not very flattering English portrait, but
then he was in no way a particularly handsome figure.

brutal favourite, Alexei Arakcheev, the Russian Army was reckoned to have been 'set back by half a century'. Alexander had attempted reforms from his accession in 1801 onwards, but Arakcheev remained on for many a year; now Inspector General of the Artillery, he had been known to scalp his men by wrenching out their hair, and – on the long march from Russia – had personally sliced off several heads for 'insolence'. In sharp contrast to the French, the Russian soldiery was still driven on by fear and the lash of the knout; army service had been reduced from life to twenty-five years but during this time the soldier-serf hardly ever had leave,[4] so that a common social phenomenon in Russia was the 'soldier's wife' who became a part-time whore, raising children her husband knew nothing of. About the only way the soldier could escape was by such self-inflicted injuries as knocking out his front teeth, which were essential to tearing open the nineteenth-century musket cartridge.

The standard of the senior officers was perhaps typified, if not by Kutuzov, certainly more by his fellow army commander, Buxhöwden, an Estonian German with the good sense to have married Catherine's illegitimate daughter, but described (by the Moravian parish priest on whom he was quartered) as being 'of very little education', and who

... carried about with him a train of hunting dogs, as well as other creatures which I shall not specify out of fear of offending the ears of decent people. The whole took up eleven coaches and as many carts ...

Probably the best of the Russian leaders was forty-year-old Prince Peter Bagration, normally taciturn and rather shy, but whose Georgian blood sometimes led to violent eruptions; he was fiery, utterly fearless, but also totally reliable, and an inspiring leader of men. Better than the average, too, were such column commanders as Lieutenant-Generals Dokhturov, Miloradovich, and the French emigré, Langeron. But, lower down, according to that critical British observer, Major-General Wilson,[5] the inadequacies '... of regimental officers is more felt in this army than in any other in Europe,' and, in the eyes of another British officer they '... spent their time drinking, gambling or sleeping.'

As already noted, the Russian heavy cavalry were the best-mounted of any army and supported by swarms of irregular Cossacks; incredibly dexterous with their 14- to 18-foot lances, they were also highly indisciplined, equally happy when raping and plundering friendly peasants as when attacking the enemy. The artillery was numerically imposing: 'No other army moves with so many guns and with no other army is there a better state of equipment, or more gallantly served,' Wilson was to write of the Russians in the 1806–7 campaigns,[5] but in 1805 the standard Russian 'unicorn' was badly out-ranged by the French field-pieces, and the Commissariat so hopeless that batteries were constantly running out of ammunition; to wit Tolstoy's superb account of the plight of the courageous little Captain Tushin. Clad in grey-green, the Russian infantryman was better camouflaged than others, but he was miserably fed and equipped, with inferior muskets and a passion for bayonet-work; though as an Austrian ally uncharitably remarked:[6] '... they are so clumsy that they never manage to catch anyone!'

The single greatest redeeming feature of Tsar Alexander's army, however, was the unquenchable courage and endurance – under every adversity – of the simple soldier, of all arms. As a French officer (Marbot) was to record of an episode in the 1807 campaign: '... our soldiers

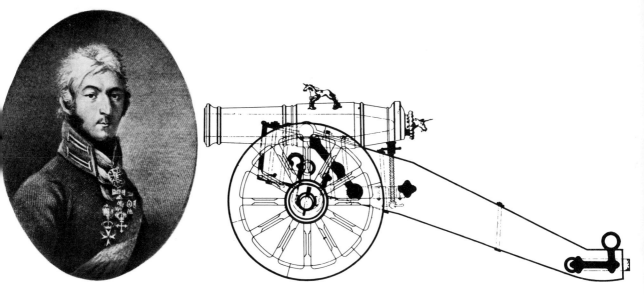

ABOVE LEFT Prince Peter Bagration (1765–1812), the fiery Georgian who was probably Russia's ablest commander, especially on the defensive. Mortally wounded at Borodino in 1812, he was immortalized by Tolstoy in *War and Peace*.

ABOVE RIGHT The Russian 'unicorn' field-piece, out-classed and out-ranged by French artillery.

BELOW 'The arrival of the Russians to the aid of the Austrians', a cruel but not totally inaccurate French cartoonist's view of the breech-less Russian Muzhiks meeting the battered, effete Austrians.

Arrivée-des Russes au secours des Autrichiens

a ah! Mon Général il y a de l'Oignon ;   et bien Mes Amis qui a til de Nouveau

A Paris chez Bosset M.d d'Estampes et Fabricant de Papiers peints Rue S.t Jacques au coin de celle des Mathurins N.° 670.

fired at the enemy at 25 paces but he continued to march without a sound.' On the eve of Austerlitz, the Russian forces were still exhausted and undernourished from their gruelling three
months' march. Through the unwieldiness of their columns (each infantry regiment requiring
some 50 waggons and 300 horses) much of their battle supplies had not yet arrived; which
was one good reason why Kutuzov had wanted to avoid a major battle. Nevertheless, in their
stolid way, morale was excellent. Says Tolstoy: '... nine-tenths of the men in the Russian army
were at that moment in love ... with their Tsar and the glory of Russian arms.'

The terrain over which the gigantic clash was to take place was compressed into so small
an area that the whole of it could have been seen by a high-flying eagle. From Brünn to Austerlitz
was sixteen miles and the length of the front from north to south less than ten. There were
no outstandingly striking features in the landscape. The Goldbach Brook and its tributary
the Bosenitz, which divided the field, were marshy streams meandering roughly from north
to south, hard to find on any map. Nothing overlooking the Goldbach could be termed more
than a hillock, with the dominant Pratzen Heights standing at only 320 yards above sea level
and rising less than 100 yards in a gentle slope out of the Goldbach valley. The north of the
battlefield was bounded by the wooded hills of the so-called 'Moravian Mountains' in which
it would be impossible to fight a battle of manoeuvre, thus providing an anchor to the line
on both sides. Between them and the east-west Brünn to Olmütz highway there rose on the
French side of the lines, a mound 220 yards high which the French nicknamed the *Santon*,
because its curious shape reminded them of the pyramids they had seen in Egypt. It was to
play a crucial part in Napoleon's plan of battle. South of the highway came the Pratzen Heights,
now in Russian hands and commanding the whole battlefield; opposite across the valley, and
less dominant, rose high ground between the hamlets of Bellowitz and Schlappanitz. Further
southwards the hills dwindled, with the Goldbach weaving indeterminately between the villages
of Kobelnitz, Sokolnitz – with its game park and pheasantry, enclosed in a low wall – and Telnitz;
then it wended its way through boggy water meadows containing a series of small shallow lakes
or ponds that have since disappeared. Though the weather was thawing, making the ground
muddy and slippery, the ponds were still frozen over.

These, in effect, were the essential features of the battlefield; Austerlitz itself being little
more than a cluster of houses surrounding the small Castle of the Counts of Kaunitz which
had once entertained Empress Maria-Theresa.

As early as 21 November, Napoleon (according to Ségur) had warned his officers: 'Gentlemen,
examine this ground carefully; it is going to be a battlefield; you will have a part to play upon
it.' With his uncanny genius for the *coup d'oeil*, he had taken in all the features of the terrain,
his gaze lingering particularly on the Pratzen Heights. As he explained two days before the
battle:

If I wanted to prevent the enemy from passing, it is there that I should post myself; but that would
lead only to an ordinary battle and I want decisive success. If, on the other hand, I draw back my
right towards Brünn and the Russians pass these heights, they are irretrievably ruined ...

Over the next ten days Napoleon's plan was to evolve and be modified to meet shifts in the
enemy dispositions, but its basic aim would be to invite the Allies to outflank him to the south.

This, in turn, would involve the Allies in taking the risk of exposing their own flank on the Pratzen Heights as they swung southwards; a risk that Napoleon had endeavoured to make acceptable to them by his show of nervousness and his abandonment of the Heights.

The key was the *Santon*, which he intended to employ as a corner-stone in the battle and which, therefore, on no account should fall into enemy hands. Accordingly Lannes had been vigorously engaged in fortifying it, this activity promptly being interpreted by Weyrother and the 'hawks' as proof that Napoleon was preparing to fight a defensive battle against a frontal attack at the north end of the line. Napoleon further aided them in the formulation of their battle plan by denuding his defences between Kobelnitz and Telnitz so as to leave an enticing hole there. Meanwhile, his main punch, a powerful concentration of 30,000 men consisting of Soult's Corps backed by Bernadotte and Bessières with the Guard, would be forming up behind the centre of the line – out of sight of enemy eyes and shielded by the familiar light cavalry screen posted across the Goldbach. Once the Allies had committed themselves to their flanking march, and had moved the bulk of their forces off the Pratzen Heights, Soult would smash through there, apparently the most unassailable point of the enemy line and hence where an attack would be least expected. If successful, he would then envelop from the rear the enemy columns, pressing them back against the Menitz and Satschan ponds. Having shattered this main body of the Allied army, Napoleon intended to swing northwards to trap Bagration's force which Murat and Lannes would have been pinning down on the left of the line.

Like all Napoleon's major stratagems, it was superbly simple, but even more full of risk than normal. During the last days of November he had difficulty disguising his anxiety, which was, evidently, contagious. On that one evening he found three of his key marshals – Murat, Soult and Lannes – nervous and quarrelsome. Everything depended, still, on the Allies' willingness to conform to the plan he was imposing on them. Had Kutuzov been allowed to refuse battle, Napoleon would have found himself placed in the almost impossible predicament of having to withdraw sooner or later. As previously noted, however, the 'hawks' had already done almost everything Napoleon required of them; admittedly, under the circumstances, it would have been difficult for them to reject the bait offered. Thus, while the Allies remained unaware of Napoleon's plan, Napoleon had the supreme advantage of knowing theirs and – remarks Field-Marshal Montgomery[7] – 'knowing that it was bad, because he had forced it on them'. Herein lay Napoleon's mastery as king among generals. Yet, even after Weyrother had taken Napoleon's bait, the French would still face the grave danger that their deliberately-weakened right wing might indeed be pierced, bestowing success on the enemy plan. Here all depended on the arrival in time of Davout, whom Napoleon had kept off the stage (so as to reinforce his appearance of numerical weakness), and who was now hastening up from Vienna by rapid forced marches.

On the morning of 1 December, the French watched anxiously as the massive Allied formations manoeuvred across their front. The Russians '... stood in the open, and every here and there the green line of their infantry was interrupted by groups of stationary cossacks and regiments of cavalry uniformed in white.' They were so close that one of Napoleon's own escort, a crack marksman, unsaddled with a single shot '... a Russian officer who had drawn our attention by the startling whiteness of his uniform.'

That afternoon, Napoleon carried out his final inspection of the *Grande Armée*. For the first time he was wearing, over the green, white and red uniform of a colonel of the Guard's *chasseurs à cheval*, the *redingote gris* which was to become a legend after Austerlitz. Ignoring the scruffy dress of his men, the piercing eye missed nothing when it came to inspecting weapons. He tasted and smelt the gunpowder with all the knowledgeability of the artillery expert, and nagged and rended defaulters:

The tips of your flints must be rounded and set as the colonel ordered ...

And you: what have you done with your scouring rod? ... You've lost it? Admit it then, you fucker!

Few generals have ever used grosser language to the troops than Napoleon: the *grognards* feared it and loved it. Here the Emperor would pause to swap a coarse soldier's jest with a veteran whose face he recognized: there, to pinch the ear affectionately of another. It was a moment when that inexplicably magic touch sent morale soaring to the skies, as could no other great commander. 'Look how happy he is!' exclaimed Sergeant Coignet of the Guard, as Napoleon passed by. He managed to impart to his men a miraculous sense of immortality, and

Even if one had to die, what did it matter? Death was beautiful in those days, so great, so splendid in its crimson cloak. It looked so much like hope ... the very stuff of youth.[8]

By nightfall on 1 December, Napoleon had made all his dispositions, placing most of the guns himself. The enemy continued to react as he wished, steadily shifting their forces southwards, and he revealed himself filled with confidence; perhaps too much. He had selected his battle headquarters up on the high ground near Bellowitz, where his sappers had constructed him a sort of woodman's hut, and dictated his final orders to Berthier. In a proclamation to the *Grande Armée* he announced:

Soldiers:

The Russian army is presenting itself before you in order to avenge the Austrian army of Ulm....

The positions we occupy are strong, and as they advance to turn my right, they will expose their flank to me.

Soldiers, I shall direct your battalions myself. I will hold myself far from the firing if, with your accustomed bravery, you carry disorder and confusion into the ranks of the enemy. But, if victory should for a moment be uncertain, you will see your Emperor expose himself to the first blows ...

As usual his speech ended with a reference to the distant arch-enemy:

... we must defeat these hirelings of England, who are animated by so great a hatred for our nation. This victory will end the campaign ...

NAPOLEON[9]

As Jomini commented: 'Never in the history of the world has a leader of an army revealed his plan in this way to the whole of his forces.' It was taking a grave chance with security. Fortunately, however, the revealing proclamation never fell into enemy hands – and if it had, such was Weyrother's obsession with his own ploys, it would probably have been ignored.

At dinner that night Napoleon was unusually relaxed and expansive. 'Entering the thatched cottage near by with us,' writes Ségur, 'he sat down gaily at table.' Silver candlesticks and goblets appeared from nowhere, and the fare was sumptuous, although the Emperor's favourite

A French military hospital tending wounded Russian prisoners, by Roehn.
A considerably idealized view of what such hospitals were really like.

Chambertin suffered from having been shaken up on the long marches. Jovially, Napoleon called on General Junot for the latest news from Paris. Junot reported that a porpoise had been seen in the Seine, but was promptly cut short: 'I expected you to tell me about the arts.' The conversation passed to the opera, where Mozart's *Don Giovanni* had registered a great success, and thence to the theatre. Having castigated contemporary dramatists, the Emperor declaimed: 'Look at Corneille! What a creative force! He could have been a statesman!' From there the talk drifted back to war, with some of the wilder-eyed members of the Imperial entourage suggesting that the army should drive on to Constantinople. At this point, however, Napoleon's much-wounded aide, General Mouton, interjected with a Cassandra-like note that broke up the party:

My conscience obliges me to tell you that the army can do no more. If it were led still further, it would obey, but against its will. It is showing such fervour on the eve of battle only because it reckons on finishing tomorrow and returning home.

This douche of cold water was not exactly what Napoleon wanted in such a moment of transitory euphoria. He broke off to visit the field hospital where, on the morrow, Surgeon-Major

Baron Larrey (who, in contemporary portraits, looks like a curly-headed boy) would be operating up to his elbows in blood. Clausewitz was to reckon that, along with the shortcomings of Napoleon's food and supply system, neglect of medical requirements was among the most important factors in the ultimate destruction of the *Grande Armée*. Larrey, who by the end of his career would have been present at sixty battles, had striven to improve the prospects of the wounded by speeding treatment with 'flying hospitals', and had himself invented a rudimentary prototype of an evacuation ambulance. Yet, between 1801 and 1804 the numbers of surgeons had actually been halved, and Napoleon was not exaggerating when he rashly declared: '. . . strictly speaking there is no medical corps.' Thus in 1805 the medical services, such as they were, were inadequate and demoralized, making Larrey's domain the least inspiring component of the *Grande Armée*.[10]

Although disease still carried off ten soldiers for every combat death, and the actual damage inflicted by the low velocity musket ball was far less atrocious than that caused by HE shells in the First World War, or the high velocity conical bullet of today, the fate of the wounded in a Napoleonic battle was still a terrible one. Standing orders dictated that they were not to be removed from the line during the battle; yet within two hours from the start of it, Larrey's field hospitals might already be full. Piled on their straw-covered ground, for the wounded amputation was the treatment most frequently administered by the ill-trained, brutal and sometimes drunken apothecaries. There was always a shortage of sedatives, so that most of the butchery would be performed with no more than a swig of brandy to deaden pain. Chances of recovery from surgery were roughly 50 : 50.

But if things were bad on the French side, they were infinitely worse across the lines; afraid of contagion, senior Austrian physicians would often avoid the field hospitals completely; and Russian standards were summed up by a remark made to the Tsar by the Cossack General-in-Chief, Platow: 'God and your Majesty forbid; the fire of the enemy is not half as fatal as a drug.' The British observer, Wilson, was deeply shocked to hear a senior Russian officer declare (during the carnage at Friedland) that 'a cannon ball was the best doctor for men without limbs.'

Shortly before midnight, an exhausted Davout rode up to Napoleon's headquarters. His men had covered 100 miles in two days. They were broken with fatigue, and still some distance away. Nevertheless Davout promised they would be in position by 8 a.m. the next morning; but only just. Napoleon was overjoyed, and went to his bivouac to sleep, contented that one of his major worries was overcome. It was after 11 p.m., and Napoleon's custom on the eve of battle was to bed down for a few hours, then rise before the dawn to issue final orders based on the latest possible information; but within an hour he was roused by an aide reporting heavy musketry fire in the direction of Telnitz. Napoleon set off promptly, and typically, on a personal reconnaissance. In the darkness, he narrowly escaped falling into the hands of a Cossack outpost (and then how the course of history would have been changed!), but what he saw persuaded him of two things. First, the main weight of the Allied army was being committed southwards, as he had hoped; secondly, it was moving a few miles further south than he had expected. The shift made the hole which Davout was to plug look that much more vulnerable. Swiftly Napoleon despatched fresh orders to Soult, slightly tilting the axis of his thrust towards the south, and detaching a force of 3,000 men to reinforce the defence of Telnitz, if necessary.

Meanwhile, on the Allied side an unhappy omen had taken place; during a last inspection

RIGHT *Napoleon visiting a bivouac on the eve of Austerlitz*, by Louis-François Lejeune. While Napoleon talks with local peasants, urgent fortification work is being completed in the background on the Santon knoll.
OVERLEAF *The Surrender of Ulm*, by Thevenin. The long serpents of defeated Austrian troops file out of the city, while on the far left Napoleon's white charger, Marengo, is held by Roustam, his Mameluke valet.

the Tsar's horse had stumbled on a tussock and thrown its rider. The staff were also making heavy work on translating Weyrother's ponderous instructions into Russian, not even starting until 3 a.m., so that the battle would have begun before some of the commanding generals even received their orders.

On Napoleon's return from his reconnaissance, an extraordinary spontaneous demonstration took place. Suddenly an unknown Frenchman recalled that 2 December was the first anniversary of the Coronation. Cries of '*Vive l'Empereur!*' burst out through the camp, and excited soldiers began waving torches. Fire caught a pile of straw, and all at once the whole French camp turned into a mass of flame and wild enthusiasm. On the other side of the Goldbach, Allied sentinels gave the warning that the French were launching a night attack, and there was a brief moment of alarm. Napoleon himself was temporarily enraged by this breach of discipline. Yet the demonstration had also touched him and assured him, once and for all, of the unsurpassable morale of the *Grande Armée* on the eve of Austerlitz. As he finally returned to his bivouac towards 4 a.m. for what was left of the night, he was heard to admit:

This is the finest evening of my life.

Notes to chapter 9

1 The Russian word for a German, *Nemyets*, originally signified any alien who spoke 'incomprehensibly and unclearly', the Germans being the first group of aliens to come to the Slav countries.
2 Admittedly, this is on his own evidence, which may have been wisdom after the event.
3 In *Austerlitz 1805*, see bibliography.
4 This harshness of service was not even totally modified under the Soviet system; in the Second World War, Red Army soldiers often fought until killed or disabled, without ever returning home.
5 *Brief Remarks on the Character and Composition of the Russian Army* (London 1810).
6 As quoted by the British Ambassador, Sir Arthur Paget, in his reports to the Foreign Office.
7 *A History of Warfare*, see bibliography.
8 Alfred de Musset, *Confessions d'un Enfant du Siècle*.
9 There is some doubt as to the total authenticity of this proclamation which might have been fabricated or subsequently tampered with.
10 But it would be quite wrong to deduce from the deficiencies of medical arrangements that they 'strongly suggest that Bonaparte was in fact taken by surprise by the enemy's advance', as Correlli Barnett claims in *Bonaparte*.

ABOVE LEFT *The Battle of Jena* by Horace Vernet. Exploiting a privilege of the Guard, a Grenadier has evidently shouted out something that has startled Napoleon and his aides. According to Coignet, then a corporal of the Grenadiers, the Guard had spent the previous night consuming vast quantities of looted wine. Because of the proximity of the Prussians in the thick fog, they had been adjured to keep total silence; so Napoleon's apparent ire may well have been provoked by a pot-valiant *grognard* breaking this silence.

ABOVE RIGHT *Napoleon at Eylau 1807*, by Mauzaine after Gros. This was his grimmest battle to date, and Napoleon registers shock at the carnage on the snow-covered battlefield.

10

'Le Beau Soleil d'Austerlitz'

2 December, dawn – 9 a.m.

> When I read the story of the Battle of Austerlitz I saw every incident. The roar of
> the cannon, the cries of the fighting men rang in my ears and made my inmost self
> quiver.
>
> Balzac, *Louis Lambert*

AS FIRST LIGHT filtered through a heavy ground mist, 73,000 Frenchmen with
139 cannon faced 89,000 Allied troops (of which all but 15,700 were Russian) with
278 guns.[1] It was one of the heaviest concentrations seen in any battle of modern
history to date. By 7 a.m. the higher hilltops were beginning to appear like islands
floating in mid-air, with the mists shrinking down into the valleys in a milk-white sea. Above,
there was a dark clear sky. Near Allied headquarters up at Krzenowitz, just west of Austerlitz
itself, the two emperors were suddenly revealed to their troops riding side by side, the Austrian
in a white uniform on a black charger, the Russian in a black uniform with white plumes in
his hat and mounted on a bob-tailed chestnut. Kutuzov was there, looking worn and irritable,
and affecting a show of disinterested obsequiousness which little pleased his Tsar.

Shaking off the exhaustion and hunger with which the nineteenth-century infantryman inevitably entered battle, thousands were on the move, formed up behind their different colours,
each 'with face newly washed and shaven and weapons clean and rubbed up to the final glitter'.
Behind them

... with measured hoof beats and the jingling of trappings, rode the cavalry, elegant in blue, red and
green laced uniforms, mounted on black, roan or grey horses, bandsmen in front, their jackets covered
with lace. Yonder, the artillery was crawling slowly into place between infantry and cavalry, the long
line of polished shining cannon quivering on the gun-carriages.[2]

Further behind still bustled the busy staff officers in their grey cloaks, between the generals,
their red necks squeezed into stiff collars, and the flamboyant pomaded officers of the Court
of St Petersburg. Everywhere there was the clatter of hooves and the rumble of gun-carriages,
with an occasional sparkle as a bayonet caught the feeble sun on the heights. A testy exchange
now took place between Kutuzov and Alexander, later immortalized by Tolstoy.[3] To Kutuzov's
explanation of why the advance was not already under way, the Tsar retorted impatiently:
'But we are not on the Empress's Meadow, where we do not begin a parade until all the regiments
are formed up!' to which came the crushing reply: 'Your Highness! If I have not begun, it

Detail of a painting by Horace Vernet showing Napoleon giving his last orders before the Battle of Austerlitz. The artist has evidently used licence in prematurely dissipating the fog.

is because we are not on parade, and not on the Empress's Meadow. However, if such be Your Highness's order . . .'

With no show of enthusiasm, Lutuzov then gave the order to advance, and the vast bodies of men disappeared into the fog as they descended from the Pratzen Heights, heading southwards.

In command of the three Russian columns that constituted the massive and unwieldly flanking force was the unimpressive General Buxhöwden. Leading the advance guard, opposite Telnitz, was Kienmayer, a survivor of the Ulm debacle, with 6,800 men – most of them Austrian. It was Kienmayer's premature fumblings, during the night, which had warned Napoleon that the enemy thrust was aiming further south than expected. Next came little General Dokhturov with 13,700 men and Langeron, full of scepticism for the Allied plan, with 11,700. Further north came the Pole, Prszebyszewski with 7,800, and finally – the last to move off the Pratzen Heights – 23,000 men under the Austrian General Kollowrath and the florid faced Russian, Miloradovich.

In the valleys through which they were moving the fog was so dense it was impossible to see more than ten paces ahead. Bushes loomed up like gigantic trees, and level ground seemed like cliffs and slopes. Marching without any advance guard or proper liaison between units, some regiments of Kollowrath's column became horribly tangled together, and confusion reigned. To make matters considerably worse, Austrian Prince John of Lichtenstein (in command of the Allied cavalry) committed an appalling map-reading error. Instead of deploying opposite Murat at the north end of the line, his horses suddenly appeared three miles further south, cutting across the line of march of the three cumbersome great infantry columns. Commanders were enraged and the confidence of the troops shaken. Bitter reproaches passed between Austrian and Russian. Finally the situation was saved by Langeron grabbing Lichtenstein's bridle, and turning him and his thousands of chafing cavalrymen sharply about! But, as it was, the disorder caused was to delay the unleashing of Buxhöwden's assault by one critical hour.

At about 7 a.m. the first blow in the battle was struck when Kienmayer's Austrians, eager to avenge Ulm and vindicate themselves in the eyes of their supercilious Allies, hit the end of the French line at Telnitz. With Davout's III Corps still not yet in position, the whole of the danger area from Telnitz to Kobelnitz was held by General Legrand's thinly-spread division of 6,000 men – upon which Buxhöwden's 55,000 troops were ponderously converging. Telnitz itself was covered by just the 3rd Regiment of the Line, plus a battalion of Corsicans who, most skilful marksmen, were cunningly concealed in broken ground and vineyards. As the mist cleared in patches, the Corsican *voltigeurs* picked off the Austrian Hussars with deadly accuracy.

What began with an attack by a few squadrons of cavalry now escalated rapidly, with Kienmayer throwing in the Szekler Infantry Regiment, followed by the remainder of his foot battalions. The skirmishing surged back and forth, and within the first hour the Szeklers had lost two-thirds of their effectives. Then, at 8 a.m., an hour later than intended as a result of the disorder in the fog, Dokhturov's column appeared on the scene. The Russians pushed the 3rd of the Line out of Telnitz, and back across the Goldbach brook. Into the hole, Kienmayer threw his 14 squadrons of cavalry. These were bravely resisted by small light cavalry units belonging to General Margaron, which Napoleon had detached from Soult's IV Corps in the

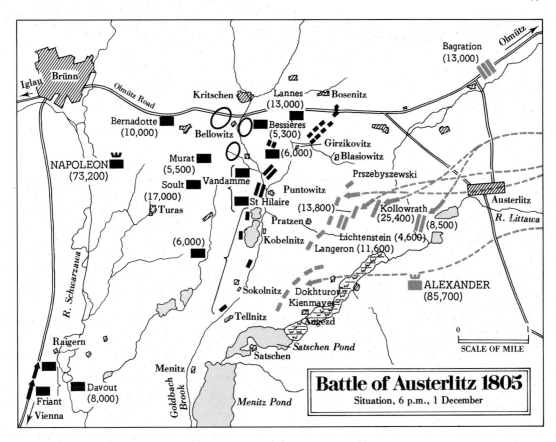

final amendment to his orders. But they could not hold against such odds for long, and the line behind Telnitz buckled.

Meanwhile, further north at Sokolnitz (which lies to the west of the Goldbach) the situation was even graver. Here both Langeron and Prszebyszewski (known to the Tsar as 'the Pole with the unpronounceable name') with nearly 20,000 men were attacking together in overwhelming force. But, once again, because of Lichtenstein's blunder they were an hour late, and a further delay was caused when the vast Russian columns jammed the crossings of the Goldbach. But for these delays, it seems probable that the bolt holding the whole of Napoleon's vulnerable right wing might have been prised open. Somehow his last-minute change of orders was late in getting to Davout at Reigern Abbey, so that III Corps' vanguard under General Friant was already heading northwards for Kobelnitz. A galloping liaison officer from Soult overtook Friant, however, and turned him at the double towards the endangered Telnitz-Sokolnitz sector. The Allied delays enabled the 1st Brigade, led by Friant himself, to reach it just in time.

In the fog and the excitement of the moment, one of those unnecessary tragedies of war now struck the French. The hard-pressed 26th Light of Legrand's division suddenly saw the 108th Regiment from Friant's vanguard loom up on the other side of the Goldbach and, thinking it was the enemy, fired into them. The 108th feared that their flank was being turned, and reeled backwards. The Allies were swift to profit from this disarray, and bit deeper into the French right wing. Fighting like a hero, General Friant himself rushed from one threatened battalion to another; but Langeron brought up 30 cannon and swept a hole through the thin French line. The odds were too great and thus, by 9 a.m., Dokhturov had taken Telnitz, Langeron was in Sokolnitz, and 'the unpronounceable Pole' in Sokolnitz Castle. From these bridge-heads across the Goldbach, the three powerful columns were preparing to debouch into the plain behind the French defences. At this end of the line, the day was beginning to look full of menace for Napoleon.

On the French side, various French commanders noted the uncanny hush with which the battle began. Shortly after dawn (according to Ségur), Napoleon said to his aides: 'And now, gentlemen, let's go and do great things!' Moving up to his battle command post on the high ground by Bellowitz, he had all his thoughts concentrated on the Pratzen Heights, wreathed in mist just three miles to the south-east. He had already ridden nervously about for two hours, seeking signs to confirm the movement of the Allied forces, and was now waiting impatiently, his eyes trying to pierce the pervading mist. The behaviour of that mist was a vital ingredient of the master plan; if it dissipated too soon, the great mass of Soult's assault force, marshalled down in the Bosenitz valley at his feet, would be exposed to the enemy's gaze; if it lingered too long, Napoleon would be unable to judge when Buxhöwden had moved off the Pratzen, and whether the *moment juste* for the attack had arrived. But, as with his other reckonings, the fog factor had not been left to chance; in his detailed reconnoitring of the field over the previous days, Napoleon had duly observed the regularity with which the nocturnal mists filled the low land and were then slowly burnt off by the watery winter sun in the early morning.

Suddenly, behind the enemy lines, there appeared the great, red orb of the sun. It was now about 8 a.m. A few minutes more, and through the last wisps of vapour rising off the Pratzen Heights, Napoleon and his entourage could clearly see the enemy forces pouring 'like a torrent', southwards off the Heights. *'Le beau soleil d'Austerlitz!'* Whoever made that exclamation has also been lost in mists of history, but it was to come to epitomize the Empire's summit of glory.

Short, bow-legged and supposedly with one foot slightly clubbed, thirty-six-year-old Nicolas Jean de Dieu Soult was the man of the moment. The son of a notary from the Midi, he had been captured with a broken leg by the Austrians in 1800, and received his *bâton* in 1804. Aptly nicknamed 'Iron Hand' by his troops and quite imperturbable, Soult was to gain at Austerlitz Napoleon's acclaim as 'Europe's first tactician'. 'How long will it take you to move your divisions to the top of the Pratzen Heights?' Napoleon now asked him. 'Less than twenty minutes, Sire,' Soult replied; 'for my troops are hidden at the foot of the valley, hidden by fog and campfire smoke.' 'In that case, we will wait a further quarter of an hour.'

Through his spyglass trained on the Pratzen, Napoleon watched attentively as Kollowrath and Miloradovich moved their columns off the vital plateau, leaving it almost empty. Then he gave the decisive order. 'One sharp blow and the war's over!' he declared in the hearing of Brigadier Thiébault. Hoarse voices shouted the command back and forth along the line, 200 drums beat the *pas de charge*. The 17,000 men of Soult's two divisions surged forward in the famous Napoleonic *ordre mixte*; skirmishers, then infantry battalions in both line and column, and the sombre blue batteries of gunners following up close behind.

Marshal Nicolas Jean de Dieu Soult
(1769–1851). Later Duke of Dalmatia,
he was the hero of the frontal attack on
the Pratzen Heights at Austerlitz,
and – with Marmont – the longest
surviving of Napoleon's marshals.
By an anonymous painter.

Up on top of the Pratzen, Tsar Alexander I had been watching the departure of Buxhöwden's imposing force, when the hand of his Foreign Minister, Czartoryski, touched him respectfully on the arm:

'Look, Sire, at the brisk and purposeful march of those Frenchmen scaling the plateau ...'

'I see nothing else, *mon cher*! ... What would you put their strength at? Two battalions? Three? Four?'

'Several regiments at least, Sire, if not several divisions. It's an attack by an army corps.'

'But they come out of a clear sky! How is it that we have had no warning?'

'Your Majesty should say rather that they come from hell. This cursed mist hid their troops from us.'

From that instant, says Thiers, the Tsar 'lost all the confidence which he had till then felt, and conceived a sinister presentiment which never left him during the engagement'.

After passing rapidly through a possibly dangerous Scylla-and-Charybdis bottleneck between Puntowitz and Girzikovitz, Soult's two divisions fanned out into two separate streams. On the right, St Hilaire (who had issued his troops a triple ration – almost half a pint – of the *Grande Armée*'s gut-rot brandy) swept like a tornado, on through the village of Pratzen (with explicit orders not to halt there) and up to the commanding knoll of Pratzeberg. Such was the total surprise of the attack that there was still little firing; most of the battle-noise being contributed by the drummers, the shouting of the company commanders and the untuneful bellowing of

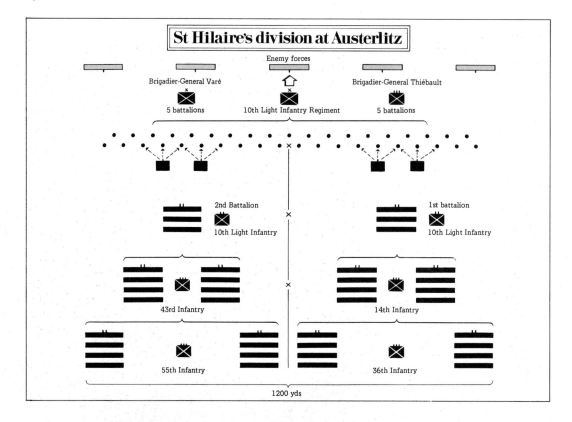

St Hilaire's division at Austerlitz

Enemy forces

Brigadier-General Varé   Brigadier-General Thiébault

5 battalions   10th Light Infantry Regiment   5 battalions

2nd Battalion   1st battalion

10th Light Infantry   10th Light Infantry

43rd Infantry   14th Infantry

55th Infantry   36th Infantry

1200 yds

ribald marching songs. On the left, Vandamme's division was held up briefly by determined enemy resistence in Girzikovitz. But Dominique José Vandamme – brutal, violent, high-handed and renowned for his insubordination and (later) his looting (Napoleon once remarked to him: 'If I had two of you, the only solution would be to have one hang the other') – was a fighting divisional commander, one of the *Grande Armée*'s best. Wounded already, he threw his men at the Russian infantry with the bayonet, routed them, then overran their supporting artillery. In his impetus he then actually rushed past his objective, the Stari Vinobrady knoll on the Pratzen, which was held by five Russian battalions and artillery. He swiftly wheeled round and, in the teeth of heavy plunging fire, swarmed up the knoll, dislodged the Russians and seized their guns.

Vandamme had marched for half-an-hour, and fought for half-an-hour; St Hilaire had been in action for little more than twenty minutes in all. Before 9.30 a.m., Soult was master of the Pratzen Heights, the routed Allies falling back hastily in the direction of Austerlitz.

All this was observed by Kutuzov, with a mixture of detached gloom and vindication. It was *his* soldiers that were being hammered, but it was not his plan that was causing the defeat, although he had lacked the strength of will to have it altered. As soon as he had seen Soult's infantry emerging out of the mist in front, the old veteran had realized what was going to happen; Soult, in order-of-battle, would smash into the unguarded Allied flank while it was in order-of-march. Nothing but total disaster could ensue. As he stood there in silence, an enemy musket

The carnage of the battlefield. A later Rowlandson cartoon of Napoleon in dialogue with Death – a theme frequently used by British cartoonists about both the Kaiser and Hitler in the First and Second World Wars.

ball creased his cheek. He dabbed at the blood with a silk scarf, waving away the personal physician sent him by the Tsar, with the words: 'Thank the Emperor and tell him that my wound is not serious, but that the fatal wound is here,' pointing to the advancing French.[4]

Notes to chapter 10

1 Accurate figures of the numbers involved at Austerlitz vary considerably from source to source. On both sides, a substantial number were infirm from the march, or *hors de combat* for one reason or another. One figure (Duffy) puts the actual French effectives at possibly no more than 60,000; while, according to the official French commentary after the battle less than 50,000 fired a shot. Thus the numerical disparity between the two forces may have been even greater than it seemed on paper.

2 Tolstoy, *War and Peace.*

3 ibid.

4 Tolstoy drew most of his historical material for Austerlitz from Mikhailovsky-Danilevsky's official account and generally with considerable fidelity, but here adds an interesting novelist's twist. In this memorable scene, in *War and Peace*, the physician is replaced by the fictional Prince Andrei, and it is to the fleeing *Russian* soldiers, not the French, that Kutuzov points.

11

'One Drop of Water'

2 December, 9 a.m. – 12 a.m.

There is a movement in engagements when the least manoeuvre is decisive and gives
a victory; it is the one drop of water which makes the vessel run over...

Napoleon

WITH THE SURPRISE and devastating impetus of Soult's attack, the scanty Allied
force left on the Pratzen had collapsed at once. Kutuzov bellowed to Miloradovich to form front with the rear of his column still in the area, but only a few
battalions could be turned about in time. He then called on Grand Duke Constantine to prepare to throw in the Imperial Guard, held in reserve back at Krzenowitz. These
were piece-meal remedies, and Kutuzov has been sharply criticized for his 'indolence' in not
pulling back the main weight of Buxhöwden's force, so as to retake the Pratzen and prevent
the Allied armies being cut in two. In this case, an orderly retreat could perhaps have been
made upon Austerlitz, and total catastrophe averted. Instead, however, Kutuzov was 'content
to parry the evil of which he was an eye-witness'. However, in Kutuzov's defence, although
Napoleon's nimble army corps might have been capable of so rapid a manoeuvre on such a
grand scale, this was simply not within the ponderous fighting style of the Russian army, and
would almost certainly have only led to a multiplication of the chaos of the early morning
approach marches. Meanwhile, the actual author of the disastrous Allied plan, Weyrother, seems
to have maintained a curiously low profile; later, at the height of the battle, he was to have
his horse shot from under him.

Napoleon was swift to exploit his initial success in the centre. He ordered Soult to consolidate
his gains on the Pratzen in anticipation of the inevitable counter-attack, while Bernadotte's
I Corps was pushed forward in support. At forty-two the oldest of the corps commanders at
Austerlitz, Bernadotte's height had earned him the nickname of *Sergeant 'Belle-Jambe'* in the
'Old Army'. With a Pyrenean's capacity for intrigue, he is generally reckoned to have been
better cast as a king of Sweden (1818–1844) than a general, and was one of Napoleon's least
aggressive commanders. By way of widening the breach, Bernadotte captured Blasowitz to the
left of Soult's breakthrough, but a determined attack by two battalions of the Russian Imperial
Guard promptly drove him out of it again.

Up to this point, the northern sector of the front had been relatively static but by about
10 a.m., while there was a brief respite in the centre, the whole of it erupted into violent combat.
Napoleon had designated it as the secondary battle area, ordering the two Gascons who loathed

A detail of *The Battle of Austerlitz* by Rugendas. Amid the chaos, a coolly pointing Napoleon is depicted surrounded by his Mameluke, Dragoon and Hussar aides-de-camp.

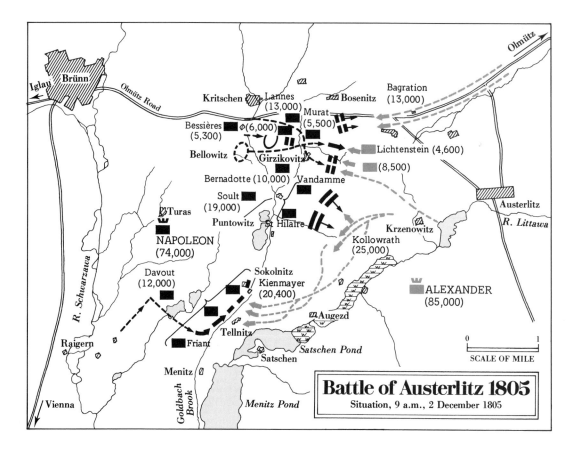

Iglau
Brünn
Olmütz Road
Kritschen
Lannes
(13,000)
Bosenitz
Bagration
(13,000)
Olmütz
Murat
(5,500)
Bessières
(6,000)
(5,300)
Lichtenstein (4,600)
Bellowitz
Girzikovitz
(8,500)
Bernadotte (10,000)
Vandamme
Soult
(19,000)
Turas
NAPOLEON
(74,000)
Puntowitz
St Hilaire
Austerlitz
R. Littawa
Krzenowitz
Kollowrath
(25,000)
Davout
(12,000)
Sokolnitz
Kienmayer
(20,400)
ALEXANDER
(85,000)
R. Schwarzawa
Raigern
Friant
Tellnitz
Augezd
0   1
SCALE OF MILE
Vienna
Menitz
Goldbach Brook
Satschen
Menitz Pond
Satschen Pond

Battle of Austerlitz 1805
Situation, 9 a.m., 2 December 1805

each other – Murat and Lannes, the thirty-six-year-old former dyer's apprentice – simply to prevent Bagration from intervening in the main battle. Distinguished by his tenacity in attack and defence alike, both Bagration and his opponent at Austerlitz, Lannes, were to be mortally wounded in battle; Bagration at Borodino, Lannes his leg carried away by a cannon-ball at Essling in 1809.

Bagration had started the day in a rage; he was receiving no detailed orders from Kutuzov or Weyrother, and Lichtenstein's cavalry who were supposed to be supporting him had strayed to the wrong end of the battlefield. Drawn by the noise of battle, it was on his initiative that the Imperial Guard retook Blasowitz. This in turn provoked Lannes to move his two infantry divisions forward, with the object of pushing Bagration away towards the north and widening the hole through which Murat's cavalry could then deploy. On the right was wooden-legged General Caffarelli's division, preceded at a steady jog-trot by the light cavalry of General Kellermann (son of the hero of Valmy), with the heavy cavalry of Nansouty and d'Hautpoul – Cuirassiers splendid in their red and gold tunics and armoured breastplates – in reserve at the rear. Prince John of Lichtenstein had in the meantime arrived, having had to make a detour round the Russian Guard to reach Bagration's left flank, and he promptly threw into the battle the first available cavalry units – the fearsome Uhlans of the Tsar's Imperial Guard.

So as to avoid being flung back on top of the advancing infantry, Kellermann cunningly withdrew his light horse, through the intervals between Caffarelli's battalions. The pursuing Uhlans

The Battle of Austerlitz, 10 a.m., by Siméon Fort. The Santon knoll is in the foreground, with
the Pratzen Heights behind, obscured by artillery and musketry smoke. The early morning fog has cleared.

were then caught on either flank by a withering musketry fire from the infantry squares – a
favourite tactic of Napoleon's, taking advantage of a typical Russian error. 'Our cavalry, like
the rest of our forces,' says Lieutenant-Colonel A. P. Ermolov (who was commanding a battery
of horse-artillery in Lichtenstein's column, where he admitted to having understood but little
of the Allied plan all day)

... acted largely on its own account, without any attempt at mutual support. And thus from one wing
to another, our forces came into action by detachments, and one after another they were put into
disorder...

In a space of three minutes, Caffarelli's squares brought down 400 men, including the commanding general, and many horses. Kellermann, reforming on a flank, now sliced into the Uhlans
before they could mount a second charge on the infantry. To help them out, Lichtenstein sent
in several squadrons of heavy dragoons, and a terrible, confused and steadily-escalating cavalry
battle now began. Back and forth the magnificent horsemen seethed, hacking and jabbing with
sabres, thrusting with swords, dismounting to fire their short carbines into the mêleé, and inflict-
ing hideous wounds on each other.

When Lichtenstein's cavalry dispersed, leaving the ground carpeted with dead and wounded,

Caffarelli's division was seen to be still advancing steadily. But in the interval Bagration had brought up forty cannon which cut great swathes in the French infantry – one volley alone sweeping away all the drummers of Caffarelli's leading regiment. Lannes then galloped up every gun at his disposal and personally placed them; hatless, his curly hair matted with powder and grime, he disregarded pleas from his men to take cover. He had only fifteen cannon in all, but, with the mobility in which the French artillery excelled, each piece fired one deadly round, then moved before the superior enemy guns could bear on it. A murderous fugue of cannon-ball and grape-shot now took over from the earlier cavalry contest. During this cannonade, General Valhubert had his thigh smashed, but when his men wanted to carry him off the field he ordered them: 'Remain at your post; I shall know how to die all alone; six men must not be taken away for the sake of one.'

At about 10.30 a.m., the opposing infantry moved forward again. On the northern extremity of the line, Bagration tried to turn Lannes' flank by a vigorous attack on the Santon. This being the cornerstone of Napoleon's position, he had ordered its defenders under the steadfast General Suchet to die rather than relinquish it. Bagration's men captured the hamlet of Bosenitz and advanced some 450 yards, but were then halted by a combination of French skirmishing tactics, light cavalry, and the dug-in Santon battery. At the other end of the sector, Lannes' infantry supported by Murat's heavy cavalry pushed back into Blasowitz in a bayonet charge which cost the life of its gallant commander, Colonel Casteix. As Caffarelli pressed forward beyond Blasowitz, Lichtenstein decided to launch an all-out cavalry attack to stop the French advance. Some 40 squadrons, nearly 6,000 men, thundered forwards. Three times Caffarelli's foot soldiers beat off their attack. Then Murat with his usual élan, though outnumbered at that moment by almost two to one, threw in d'Hautpoul's and Nansouty's Cuirassiers. In the heaviest cavalry engagement so far that day, the two sets of 'horsemen cased in iron' met with a clash that could be heard far across the field, above the din of battle. For an instant the two lines seemed to stand still, but after about five minutes of slaughter the Allied squadrons broke and turned about. One regiment of Cuirassiers, beyond its general's control, followed too far in pursuit and in turn was nearly engulfed by the Allied cavalry. Hordes of riderless horses milled anarchically back and forth across the battlefield.

By midday, Lannes and Murat had won a praiseworthy, though still limited, success on the northern sector. Four thousand casualties had been inflicted, and as many prisoners taken – together with a large amount of booty belonging to Bagration's force. Bagration had been virtu-ally excluded from joining the crucial battle in the centre; thus fulfilling Napoleon's instructions. However his main body was still intact and would continue effectively to bar the road to Olmütz, down which Napoleon intended to sweep in the final, annihilating phase of his plan. Typically, it was Murat who sent the first message claiming success to the Emperor: 'Tell him ... that my troops, together with those of Marshal Lannes, have succeeded in throwing Prince Bagration back towards Olmütz.' At the same time however, Bagration, still fuming at the absence of orders, was reporting to the Tsar: '... I have succeeded in keeping intact the whole of my army corps and we are only retreating foot by foot.'

At the other end of the front, the heavily outnumbered French were still fighting a critical and desperate defensive battle. But, good as his word, Davout was arriving with the main weight

Marshal Louis Nicolas Davout (1770–1823), later Duke of Auerstädt and Prince of Eckmühl, depicted in later life with all his justly-acquired honours. The nearest rival to Napoleon as a military commander, he saved the day at Austerlitz, Jena and Eylau.

of his superb III Corps, after an 87-mile forced march that was a staggering feat by any standard. For the soldiers it had been a nightmare, with officers having to kick to their feet men who had had only five hours rest out of the forty *en route*. Corporal Blaise[1] records:

We left the village where we were lodging at nine in the evening. We marched until two in the morning when we halted in a wood. Then we lit some fires and slept until five when we returned to the road. All day we marched and again camped in the woods; at 6 o'clock that evening we had not even had time to prepare our eagerly-awaited soup when we were informed that we should be leaving again at nine ... Then, leaving our position, we marched on until 5 a.m. when the regiment halted ... The colonel, whose interest in our welfare had never flagged from the opening of the campaign, now gave us an abundance of wine. This rallied our strength ...

Halting that night (1 December) at 7 p.m., Blaise's unit was allowed a good night's sleep. Up at dawn the next morning, there was another long approach march before the footsore soldiers were thrown into a counter-attack at Telnitz – without support of the artillery, which was still lagging behind. Approaching the line, Blaise heard:

... a most terrible fusillade which took place between the Russians and the 3rd Regiment of the Line, whose large number of wounded we came across. At that moment, we were made to double our step, which did not prevent me from eating the leg of a goose that I had on the top of my knapsack, well knowing I would scarcely have time during the battle. I was right; before ordering the charge, Marshal Davout, who did not leave us although the balls were beginning to bother us, reminded us of the Battle of Marianzelle.[2] General Heudelet placed himself at our head; we marched into battle very well until we were stopped near a ditch of such width that we could not cross it. General Heudelet ordered the Colonel to have us cross over a bridge to our left ...

In the confusion of crossing the Goldbach, Blaise and his fellows came under a devastating flank-fire from Kienmayer's Austrians, costing them many casualties. And so the battle raged back and forth; Telnitz was recaptured, but lost again by 9 a.m. General Friant, at fifty, one of the oldest veterans in the *Grande Armée*, was to have four horses killed under him before the day was done. At Sokolnitz the fighting was even more intense, with Langeron furiously flinging in every man and musket he could lay his hands on, from the Viborg, Perm, Kursk and 8th Jaeger Regiments. The ravaged village was defended largely by one French regiment, General Legrand's 26th Light, and it changed hands repeatedly. At one moment of close combat two French sergeant-majors were observed using the sanctified regimental Eagles like cudgels to defend themselves. But what most assisted the embattled French was the continued jamming of the Goldbach bridges by the mass of Allied troops, which prevented the arrival of the vast reinforcements available to the incompetent Buxhöwden. But still they were outnumbered by some 35,000 Allies to less than 8,000 infantry effectives and 2,800 cavalry, for most of the morning.

It was fortunate for Napoleon that Davout was on the spot. Aged only thirty-five, but prematurely bald, Louis Nicolas Davout (later Duke of Auerstädt and Prince of Eckmühl) was one of the few Napoleonic marshals to come from a noble though impoverished family, and had entered his father's old regiment; which initially slowed down his advancement. He was notably lacking in charm, and intolerant with civilians. Duchess Augusta of Saxe-Coburg-Saalfeld complained in 1809:

Marshal Davout's visit has been got over; it was a weary business trying to enliven him, for it is impossible to be more stolid and uncommunicative than was this thoroughly unpleasant man. His face betrays that he can be very harsh and brutal though not specially spiteful, or intellectual....

Very short-sighted, he wore special combat glasses fastening at the back of his head; because of the fog, however, myopia was a small disadvantage at Austerlitz that morning. But his men (even if not loving him) called him 'the Just', and they were invariably the best trained and most disciplined in the army. With a coldly-agile mind, Davout was probably the ablest of Napoleon's marshals and the only one for whom Napoleon felt a certain jealousy, as a possible rival. Renowned for its clock-work administration and attention to detail, Davout's III Corps was a model formation, probably the finest in the world at that time.

Back and forth along his battered line Davout ran, ordering and exhorting, and regaining a few yards here and there. But the odds looked like proving too much. With one nervous eye constantly on Davout's predicament, Napoleon shortly before 10 a.m. ordered General Oudinot's grenadiers from the reserve to move south and bolster up the line.

By that time, however, the news of Soult's success in the centre was beginning to have its impact on the attacking Allied left. Langeron recounts graphically:

Count Kamensky sent to tell me that the French had actually occupied the Pratzen Heights in strength, that he had made a right-about turn with his brigade, that he had reascended the ridge and that he had very strong forces in front of him.

It was difficult for me to understand what had happened and how the enemy came to be behind us...

The situation was little improved by Buxhöwden himself, apparently dead-drunk. Langeron thus left Sokolnitz and went to join Kamensky, on whose right he saw

... a few battalions who were faltering and appeared to be in retreat ... they were part of Kollowrath's Austrians who were withdrawing and were being pursued by the French.

It was eleven o'clock. ...

Up on the Pratzen the expected Allied ripostes had materialized, creating a series of crises for Soult's spearhead. Whereas Vandamme, sabre in hand, had born the brunt during the initial assault, it was now the turn of St Hilaire to his right. The slow start of Buxhöwden's infantry, caused by Lichtenstein's monumental error in the first phase, had in fact resulted in their being somewhat more enemy infantry left on the south-east slopes of the Pratzen than Napoleon had expected. St Hilaire thus found himself counter-attacked on three sides by the troops that Kutuzov was able to rally: on his right, by Kamensky's Russian brigade (from the tail of Langeron's column); to the front by Kollowrath's Austrians; and to the left by the Russian Imperial Guard. The main weight of the Allied effort descended on General Thiébault's brigade, on the bottom end of the French breakthrough and separated from its neighbour by Pratzen village. Having been told to expect no more than a chain of outposts, for nearly an hour Thiébault found his three regiments – the 14th, 36th and 10th Light – were subjected to perhaps the fiercest pressure of the whole day. The 10th Light was first overrun by Kamensky's Russians, after suffering heavy casualties. The 36th, exposed to a murderous musketry and grape-shot fire at not more than thirty paces' range, tottered when its commanding officer was shot down. A brave sergeant-major, Adjutant Labadie, seized the colours and advanced towards the enemy shouting: 'Soldiers, here is your line of battle!' The line steadied, but (says Thiers) the three regiments 'would soon have sunk under a mass of cross-fires, had the conflict been prolonged'.

As it was, the divisional commander, St Hilaire, was already consulting Thiébault as to whether they should withdraw, when Colonel Pouzet of the battered 10th Light interrupted with a roar of: 'General, let us advance with the bayonet, or we are undone!' 'You are right, forward!' agreed St Hilaire, and with a violent last effort Thiébault's infantry managed to push back the attackers. In the time gained by this spirited bayonet charge, Soult, who had been watching Thiébault's predicament with disquiet, was able to gallop forward six 12-pounder cannon, the whole of the corps reserve artillery available. Soult himself came up to lay the guns. Thiébault, nicknamed 'the Butcher', ordered the gunners 'to aim for the mens' belts and for the centre of the platoons, so that not a shot should be wasted ...'

Once his bayonet attack had expended itself, the guns '... abruptly unmasked right down the line, began one of the most destructive volleys ever made. ...' said Thiébault, describing the effect of Napoleon's *belles filles*:

... You can imagine how pleased I was when every discharge from my cannon opened great square holes in the enemy lines, and when their four regiments dispersed in mobs of fugitives.

Yet, in some of '... these terrible encounters, whole battalions of Russians got themselves killed without a single man leaving the ranks.'

Langeron himself now arrived to launch a fresh bayonet counter-attack in person against his countrymen. In the meantime however, Thiébault had received valuable reinforcements in two fresh regiments sent up by Soult. In the absence of any orders from the drunken Bux-höwden, Langeron then took the initiative to return to Sokolnitz in order to bring back a large contingent to the Pratzen Heights. This action would take the pressure off Davout, but would be too late to save the Allied centre.

Meanwhile, on Vandamme's front nothing of comparable seriousness had occurred. The florid Miloradovich had thrown nine battalions against Stari Vinobrady knoll, but these were flung back within half-an-hour. Two of his generals were wounded, one of them captured. Mounted on a fine English horse, Miloradovich rushed back and forth across the battlefield conspicuously but ineffectively, drawing from Czartoryski the acid aside: 'Have you noticed how he never goes out of the Tsar's sight?' A second half-hearted effort was then jointly mounted by Kollowrath's Austrians and Miloradovich's Russians. This too was dispersed before noon, with the virtual destruction of two Russian regiments. Miloradovich reported to Kutuzov:

...now the cumulative effect of the catastrophic situation, their own exhaustion, the lack of cartridges...and the enemy fire which came in from every side, all made them give way in disorder.

By midday, it was beginning to get bitterly cold – a reminder that the short winter's day was already more than halfway through. For the most of the combatants, all but a few square yards of the battlefield was obscured by the suffocating clouds of greyish-white smoke from the cannon, compounded by the dank mist undissipated in the still air. In isolated corners desperate episodes took place, invisible to the rest of the world; the cries of men drowned out by the terrible din of guns and musketry, thundering cavalry and the sinister whirr of cannon-balls flying overhead. Many participants seeing only the confused fringe of the fighting may well have wondered afterwards, like Stendhal's Fabrizio (in *The Charterhouse of Parma*) at Waterloo, 'was what he had seen a real battle?' Certainly only a privileged few could possess any idea of how the overall picture was developing. Yet, though the lines remained more or less static, and there was some savage fighting still ahead for Napoleon, a turning point in the battle had in fact been reached. Bagration had been neutralized in the north; the Allied counter-attacks had been repulsed in the centre, leaving most of the Pratzen firmly in Soult's hands; and on the French right flank Davout had managed (just) to hold out against the worst of the enemy encirclement thrust.

So far the battle had developed closely along the lines Napoleon had dictated; or, as he said with little modesty, '... as if both armies were performing manoeuvres under my direction.' Perhaps the most dangerous single moment had been when Thiébault's brigade wavered momentarily. If the Allied counter-attack here had been better co-ordinated and more forceful, Napoleon's gamble might have been thwarted. One French writer, Claude Manceron, considers that the true turning point at Austerlitz, that decisive 'one drop of water', had been Colonel Pouzet's plea to General St Hilaire to attack *à la baionnette*, instead of withdrawing.

Notes to chapter 11
1 See p. 106.
2 The more usual spelling is Mariazell.

12

'Many Fine Ladies will weep tomorrow'

2 December, 12 a.m. – evening

Strategy is the art of making use of time and space. I am less chary of the latter than of the former; space we can recover, time never ... I may lose a battle, but I shall never lose a minute.

Napoleon

BY 11.30 A.M. ON 2 December, Napoleon had moved his headquarters forward on to the Pratzen. Soon afterwards he estimated the time had come to launch the decisive phase of the battle. Accordingly he ordered Soult's corps to begin a quarter turn to right, bringing them to bear against the flank and rear of Buxhöwden's force. The gap created on the Pratzen was to be filled by Bernadotte's I Corps, withdrawn from its fight with Bagration and instructed to sweep the defenders remaining in the centre back towards Austerlitz. Simultaneously Davout was to go over to the offensive against Buxhöwden. There were, however, still no fresh orders for Lannes and Murat on the left.

In the centre, only one obstacle now stood between Napoleon and success; the superlative cavalry and foot soldiers of the Russian Imperial Guard, which had started the day ten thousand strong under Grand Duke Constantine. Younger brother of the Tsar, but lacking his grave good looks, Constantine is described as possessing 'a face all bumps, the hands of a gorilla, the gait of a peasant'. He was a Dostoevskian figure whose life apparently alternated between bouts of wild debauchery and religious atonement, and it was rumoured that he had strangled valets who displeased him. He revelled in the danger of battle, and the men he now led in one last desperate effort were hardly matched even by their French counterparts. All giants over six feet tall, magnificent in white and green uniforms, these were the men who guarded the Tsar (and occasionally deposed him) and they were brave to a fault.

It was on the division of the pugnacious Vandamme that Constantine's blow fell. At the time, Vandamme himself was sitting on an upturned cart, having his wounds dressed; his division had, so far, had a relatively easy time and had just dispersed Miloradovich's battalions. Over-eager, however, to get at the French after a morning of frustrating inaction, the Semenovsky and Preobrazhensky foot regiments started their bayonet charge at a distance of 300 paces, reaching the enemy line badly out of breath. Nevertheless, the tremendous Russian impetus overwhelmed the first ranks of Vandamme's 4th of the Line, and Constantine's foot guardsmen – their ranks cruelly thinned – withdrew in good order towards Krzenowitz. At this moment,

Vandamme received Napoleon's order and began to perform his right turn. This momentarily left the 4th and 24th out on a limb, because Bernadotte – who was certainly never one of Napoleon's fastest moving commanders, being usually more concerned with the integrity of his own corps than the fate of the rest of the army – was still lagging behind. (Ségur, sent by Napoleon to activate Bernadotte, found him 'disturbed and anxious. He had told his troops to be calm, but he was setting a pretty bad example.'[1]) The 4th had also apparently yielded to the temptation to pursue the retreating guardsmen, and suddenly Constantine, waiting with the impatiently snorting cavalry of the Guard, saw an opportunity that was not to be missed.

On the other side of the lines, Jean-Baptiste Bessières, commander of the French Imperial Guard and the last officer still wearing his hair powdered and in a queue in the old fashion, had also been chafing at the bit all day. Observing Vandamme's regiments in front of him with an expert eye, he remarked to his aide: 'Laville, we are going to have a cavalry engagement.' Asked later how he knew, the experienced Bessières replied: 'Because the retreating soldiers kept looking back. When infantry retires before infantry they never turn their heads.'[2]

His diagnosis proved correct. Six squadrons of heavy cavalry, led by Constantine himself, shouting 'For God, the Tsar and Russia', had charged into the open flank of Vandamme's isolated regiments. With ear-splitting Slav war-cries of 'Hurrah! Hurrah!', their sabres rising and falling, the Imperial Guard hit the 4th and 24th completely by surprise and with terrible force. At the same time, the retreating Russian foot guards had turned about and attacked the shaken French regiments again frontally. In the ensuing shambles, a colour-bearer of the 4th of the Line had been killed. Trying to save the eagle, a subaltern was killed in turn; an NCO had snatched it out of his dying grasp, but he too was struck down and the eagle was borne off triumphantly by the Russian Guard. With its commanding officer and ten other officers killed, and some two hundred men sabred, the battalion broke. According to Ségur, it 'got up to flee at full speed', and then

...almost passed ourselves and Napoleon himself – our attempts to arrest it being all in vain. The unfortunate fellows were quite distracted with fear and would listen to no one; in reply to our reproaches ... they shouted mechanically, '*Vive l'Empereur!*' while fleeing faster than ever.

At Napoleon's side, the ever-present Berthier – his vision perhaps distorted by earlier successes – misinterpreted the scene, and remarked to Napoleon: 'What a splendid crowd of prisoners they are bringing back for you!' The first reverse of this kind all day, it was fortunate for Napoleon that, coming so late in the battle, there were no longer any Allied reserves capable of exploiting it. Calmly, he gave Bessières the order he had been awaiting all too long: 'Take the cavalry of my Guard forward to support those brave fellows.'

Bessières, however, always economical with the lives of his valuable élite, at first sent in only two squadrons of *chasseurs-à-cheval* under Colonel Morland, renowned for his moustaches and for being one of the army's best horsemen. The Imperial entourage were shocked to watch the green-clad *chasseurs* beaten back by the Russian Horse Guards. Bessières next sent in three more squadrons of the legendary *grosses-bottes (grenadiers-à-cheval)*, their great red plumes tossing angrily as they trotted forward. They were supported by the horse artillery of the Guard, who

... dashed to the front at a gallop, unlimbered within 550 yards of the enemy, and proceeded to tear with extreme rapidity a hole in the opposing battle formation with case-shot.[3]

Meanwhile Bernadotte's line infantry were also at last reaching the scene, but still the Russian Imperial Guard fought back like madmen. Having seen enough of this slaughter, Napoleon now decided to administer the *coup de grace*. 'They are in disorder yonder; that must be set to rights' he told one of his aides, the Alsatian Brigadier-General Rapp, despatching him with two fresh squadrons of *chasseurs* and one of ferocious scimitar-wielding Mamelukes.

Disregarding the concentrated volleys of grape-shot, Rapp and his squadrons broke through the first line of the Russian Imperial Guard. Then Rapp discovered his impetus had carried him too far – an ever-present hazard in a cavalry engagement. Wounded twice by minor sword thrusts, he was surrounded by the Russian Horse Guards headed by their Colonel, Prince Repnin. But, with 500 men lying dead on the field, the magnificent Russian Imperial Guard had shot its bolt and the tide abruptly turned. In Rapp's graphic report:

The Russians fled the field and disbanded. The guns, baggage, and Prince Repnin were all in our hands. With my broken sabre and covered with blood, I went to give an account of the affair to the Emperor.

Riding with his Mamelukes, Napoleon's own Egyptian servant, Roustam, returned with a Russian standard and offered to bring back the Emperor Constantine's head as well; a suggestion for which he was harshly censured as being 'a ghastly savage'. Looking at the flower of the Russian aristocracy, which lay scattered across the Pratzen in bloodstained green and white heaps, Napoleon remarked: 'Many fine ladies will weep tomorrow in St Petersburg!' Losses of the French Guard in the ferocious mêlée had been comparatively light; they included, however, the gallant Colonel Morland, brought back mortally wounded.[4] The Allied centre had ceased to exist. Finding himself abandoned by the infantry regiment, to which his battery of guns was attached, Lieutenant-Colonel Ermolov describes how

I extricated one gun from the press of our own cavalry, but we were able to get off only a few rounds before the enemy captured the piece. My men were cut down in the process and I myself was taken prisoner.

Escaping back to his division that was 'milling about in disorder', he passed an all-but deserted Tsar, his features '... lined with deep sorrow, and his eyes were full of tears.'

Swiftly assessing the situation, Napoleon declared exultantly: 'It only remains to reap the reward of our plans.... Forward against the enemy left.'

It was shortly after 1.30 p.m. that Napoleon swung the weight of the *Grande Armée*, more than 25,000 men, southwards, off the Pratzen to trap and annihilate Buxhöwden. The battle now began to move at lightning speed. Within an hour Vandamme, now holding the left corner of the enveloping net, was at Augezd; thereby blocking any escape route eastwards, except across the more or less impassible bogs of the River Littawa. Next to him came St Hilaire, a sling supporting an arm broken in three places, thrusting down the east bank of the Goldbach. His men, sorely fatigued but still full of battle now that victory was in sight, were backed up by the grenadiers from Oudinot's division; a general whose favourite party game was shooting out candles, but who had been only briefly in action that day.[5] Beyond the Goldbach, Friant,

The Battle of Austerlitz, 4 p.m., by Siméon Fort. The last act. Napoleon, on the hill on the left, watches the broken Allies being driven towards the Satschen and Menitz Ponds.

whose stoical defence action throughout the morning had cost him over 300 dead and 1,700 wounded, was already recapturing Sokolnitz, where the 'corpses were heaped up on one another, and it was almost impossible to ride across the tangle of weapons and broken human bodies'.[6] Pinching the enemy up against St Hilaire, all along his sector the dependable Davout had switched over to the offensive (though with some bitterness as it was clear that, while his corps had had the dirtiest work to do that day, Soult was going to carry off the laurels). His instructions were simply, 'Let not one escape.' Thus, remorselessly, the French net closed in on three sides, pushing Buxhöwden back up against the Satschen and Menitz ponds on the fourth. In the mounting ferocity of the battles little quarter was given. General Thiébault, whose brigade had suffered so heavily earlier on, records:

Up to the last hour of the battle, we took no prisoners, it would not do to run any risk; one could stick at nothing, and thus not a single living enemy remained to our rear.

On the Allied side, the confusion inside the net was inimaginable. A savage exchange took place between Langeron and Buxhöwden. When Langeron asked angrily why he had not yet ordered his three columns to retreat out of the trap, the Russian commander mumbled:

'Are you forgetting that I have taken Telnitz and that I still hold it?'
'Telnitz, but that's ancient history!...We now have the French at our backs, do you hear? At our backs! We are being taken in the rear!'

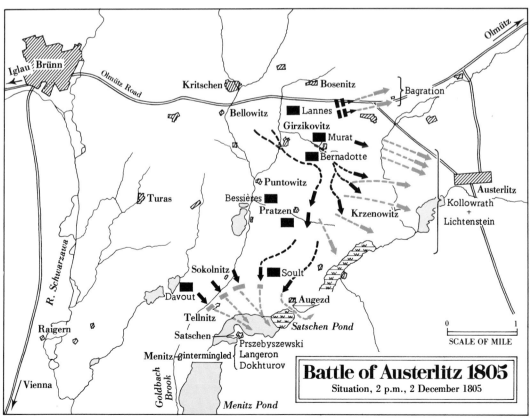

Iglau
Brünn
Olmütz Road
Kritschen
Bellowitz
Bosenitz
Lannes
Bagration
Olmütz
Girzikovitz
Murat
Bernadotte
Puntowitz
Turas
Bessières
Pratzen
Austerlitz
Kollowrath + Lichtenstein
Krzenowitz
R. Schwarzawa
Sokolnitz
Soult
Davout
Augezd
Raigern
Tellnitz
Satschen
Satschen Pond
Menitz
intermingled
Przebyszewski
Langeron
Dokhturov
Vienna
Goldbach Brook
Menitz Pond

0   1
SCALE OF MILE

Battle of Austerlitz 1805
Situation, 2 p.m., 2 December 1805

'*Mon cher ami*, you see nothing but enemies everywhere!'

'And you, *monsieur le comte*, are no longer in a state to see them anywhere!'

Before Buxhöwden could react to this deadly insult, a liaison officer from Kutuzov arrived bringing orders to withdraw. They had, apparently, been issued three hours earlier. As Langeron turned on his heel, he remarked to an Austrian officer: 'The rout has begun!'

From behind the pheasantry walls at Sokolnitz, Przebyszewski fought a desperate last stand, with the Russian gunners firing at such close range that they scorched the uniforms of the attacking French. Trapped, the gallant Przebyszewski later reported to the Tsar that, after eight hours in action:

One of my subordinate commanders had been killed, another wounded, and the rest were reduced to confusion by the vicious salvoes of canister which came in from three sides ... we had no hope of support. With all this, we fought on against the enemy to the limit of our strength, according to the loyalty we owe Your Imperial Highness.

Two French officers, General Lochet and Colonel Franceschi of the Hussars, raced each other to take the sword of 'the Pole with the unpronounceable name'. At the bottom of the net and with his back to the ponds, Dokhturov courageously formed his remaining 5,000 men into three lines – cavalry in front, artillery in the second line and infantry behind – and then counter-attacked while Cossacks hastily reconnoitred an escape route between the ponds.

Dokhturov's stubborn last-ditch effort sent Napoleon, who had moved up for the kill, into his first rage that day. He had just received word from the other end of the field that Murat and Lannes were, unaccountably, sitting still and doing nothing. A fine drizzle was falling and low clouds had brought nightfall closer. All of a sudden, victory seemed to be dwindling before his eyes. Peevishly he accused Soult's corps of being 'too slack': 'That's dreadfully slack! The dragoons weren't thrown in wholeheartedly! It's inconceivable to press home a decisive charge so feebly.' Soult protested that the Russian artillery was 'still impressive'. Further enraged, Napoleon berated a returning Dragoon colonel: '... Tell the general who commands you, on my behalf, that he is nothing but a coward!' Then, changing his mind, Napoleon despatched another of his aides, General Gardanne, to lead the chastened Dragoons back into battle himself, with the instructions: 'Clear all those Russian pieces within twenty minutes. And break those people's last squares for me.'

Collapsing before the renewed French onslaught, Dokhturov's and Langeron's survivors became the victims of a tragic and dreadful finale. Although Kienmayer, the survivor of Ulm, had managed to lead his Austrians back between the ponds in reasonably good order after a courageous fighting withdrawal, the Russian reconnaissance squadrons were unable to find a negotiable route. Thus, in their despair, some of the fugitives tried to set off across the ice itself. When it seemed that it would hold up under the weight of even a gun carriage, cavalry, infantry and artillery piled up in their hundreds, trying to get across the ponds. Napoleon promptly ordered 25 cannon to fire red-hot balls into the panic-stricken mass. As a result of the thaw of the preceding days, the ice was already treacherously weaker than it looked. The combined effect of the cannonballs and the Allied gun teams caused the ice to crack and break up in great slabs, cascading horses, guns, and infantrymen into the frozen waters. And still the murderous red-hot iron kept falling among them in the semi-darkness.

When the guns ceased firing, 2,000 half-naked Russian prisoners were fished out of the ponds. In his bulletin after the battle, Napoleon claimed that 20,000 men had been drowned in this final catastrophe, but he seems to have been wildly exaggerating. Later 38 guns and the corpses of 130 horses were recovered from the shallow water, and probably human deaths amounted to at most 2,000.[7] Nevertheless, it was a frightful humiliation to be inflicted on so mighty and once proud an army. Most of the Russian cannon that were not lost in the ponds became stuck up to their axles in the boggy ground, and abandoned. Only a few groups of dispirited stragglers managed to escape through holes in Napoleon's net. Among them was the defeated and befuddled Russian commander, Buxhöwden; hatless, his uniform in disarray, he declared that he had been 'abandoned' and 'sacrificed'. 'I had previously seen some lost battles,' commented Langeron; 'but I had no conception of such a defeat.'

The only part of the whole Allied array which had remained still relatively intact was Bagration's corps, on what seemed to have become the forgotten sector. Having effectively isolated Bagration from the main battle, shortly after midday, Murat, Lannes, and Bernadotte had remained curiously inactive. At one point the Russians had come close to overrunning Suchet's division, many of them young recruits, in front of the Santon, but by 3 p.m. Bagration, who had received a slight wound in the thigh, had set in motion an orderly withdrawal down the Olmütz highway. He was, in fact, covering the getaway of the two defeated Emperors and the forces remaining to them. Observing this, General Caffarelli, his uniform in shreds and begrimed with mud and powder strains, rode up to Lannes for further orders. But Lannes passed the buck: 'Go and see Murat ... You know very well I am under his orders.' By the time he reached Murat's headquarters, Caffarelli was in a seething rage, and demanded: 'Where the bloody hell is Murat?' It appeared that Murat had ridden out on reconnaissance, so Caffarelli was led to his chief-of-staff, General Belliard, to whom he shouted:

I have taken Krzenowitz, where the enemy left me three cannon! Our skirmishers have already crossed the stream and are spreading out to the rear of the hills.... Think of it! I might have laid hands on the Emperors' carriages....

Trying to calm down the enraged divisional commander, Belliard remarked that it was as well that Murat was absent, otherwise Caffarelli would probably have ended the battle in close arrest, then added bitterly: 'We have received one explicit order, just one since noon, for the Emperor has lost interest in us, it would seem ...' That order had been simply to preserve communications along the routes between Brünn and Olmütz. Yet, at the same time that Murat and Lannes were fretting for want of orders, Napoleon had worked himself into a fury at their passivity. Clearly it had been his original intention that, once Soult had broken through in the centre and the enveloping manoeuvre to the right was successfully under way, Murat was to perform a similar sweep round the rear of Bagration. But by 4.30 p.m. when the firing had begun to die down in the north and it was too dark to attempt such an ambitious cavalry action, Murat had still not moved; in any event, Bagration had pulled his hard-fighting corps back out of the trap, actually moving it unimpeded across the front of the sluggish Bernadotte's

I Corps, which was battered but still in good order. His withdrawal was to cheat Napoleon of the total victory he dreamed of.

What had gone wrong? There are various contributory explanations, but a certain mystery still remains. Lannes' infantry comprised a high proportion of inexperienced conscripts, which slowed down his advance; Bernadotte's supporting corps had also lagged, as already noted. Dispositions in the north had been somewhat thrown off balance by Napoleon's last-minute tilting of Soult's axis of attack southwards, and he had undoubtedly erred in not transmitting specific orders to Murat. But why? Had Napoleon allowed his attention to become so focussed on Soult's and Davout's operations that he had, as Lannes and Murat felt, 'lost interest' in them? It seems out of character. Or had he, in fact, decided to keep Murat's cavalry in hand to the last minute, just in case any unexpected reverse (like the riposte of the Russian Imperial Guard) should upset the fine balance of success on the primary battlefield? Or did he simply assume that the dashing Murat, so apt to act on his own initiative anyway, knew what to do without further interference? This might well be the most plausible explanation. At the same time, to account for Murat's own reluctance to move, one must remember that already twice in the campaign (once before Ulm and once at Vienna) he had received the most savage upbraidings of his career – for using his own initiative, and blundering. So, quite possibly, in this last phase of his terrifying brother-in-law's greatest triumph, Murat was simply playing safe. On the other hand, some modern historians (de Lombarès and Duffy[8]) hold that not nearly enough justice has been accorded to the *active* part played by Bagration's sturdy fight in spoiling the totality of Napoleon's victory, and here Tolstoy's fictionalized account is held in part culprit.

By 5 p.m. the guns were silent throughout the trampled, torn battlefield. Darkness and a flurry of snow blanketed the scenes of death and anguish. Napoleon had kept his promise of not exposing himself to danger that day, and had run about among his troops less than in any other battle he fought; he had not needed to, because – bar a few jarring setbacks – his battle plan, once set in motion, had proceeded so smoothly as to require little interference from on high. He had been able to stand there on his hill-top, coolly and detachedly pulling the strings. Throughout the battle, claimed a Prussian observer, Freiherr von Wolzogen,[9] 'the stormy calm of his face hardly altered a second'.

It was otherwise with the Russian Emperor. Shortly after the shock of Soult's men appearing on the Pratzeberg, Alexander had become separated from Kutuzov, and his own entourage had gradually dissipated, until he was apparently left with no one but his English physician, James Wylie, two aides and two Cossacks. Totally out of touch with the course of the battle that he had so much desired, he had however not left the danger zone until the end, and at one point was covered with earth from a cannonball falling directly in front of him. During the final débâcle, he was found by an astonished Russian staff officer, Major Toll, dismounted and apparently feeling unwell. When Toll tried to comfort the crestfallen young Tsar, seated under an apple tree, he burst into tears.[10] That night he spent as a refugee, collapsed on a pile of straw in a peasant's hut, several miles from the scene of defeat.

As so often, estimates of the casualties at Austerlitz differ. The French dead probably numbered at most 2,000, at lowest 1,300, with just under 7,000 wounded and 573 taken prisoner. But losses in individual units varied radically, according to their role that day. In St Hilaire's

RIGHT Napoleon's victorious proclamation after Austerlitz.

Soldats

Je suis content de vous ; vous avez à la journée d'Austerlitz, justifié tout ce que j'attendais de votre intrépidité ; vous avez décoré vos aigles d'une immortelle gloire. Une armée de cent mille hommes commandée par les Empereurs de Russie et d'Autriche, a été en moins de quatre heures, ou coupée ou dispersée ; ce qui a échappé à votre fer s'est noyé dans les lacs ; 40 drapeaux, les étendars de la Garde Impériale de Russie, 120 piéces de canon, 20 Généraux, plus de 30,000 prisonniers sont le résultat de cette journée à jamais célèbre. Cette infanterie tant vantée, et en nombre supérieur, n'a pu résister à votre choc ; et désormais vous n'avez plus de rivaux à redouter : ainsi en deux mois, cette troisième coalition a été vaincue et dissoute. La paix ne peut plus être éloignée ; mais, comme je l'ai promis à mon Peuple avant de passer le Rhin, je ne ferai qu'une paix qui me donne des garanties et assure des récompenses à nos alliés.

Soldats, lorsque le Peuple Français plaça sur ma tête la couronne impériale, je me confiai à vous pour la maintenir toujours dans ce haut éclat de gloire, qui seul pouvait lui donner du prix à mes yeux ; mais dans le même moment nos ennemis pensaient à la détruire et à l'avilir, et cette couronne de fer conquise par le sang de tant de français, ils voulaient m'obliger à la placer sur la tête de nos plus cruels ennemis : projets téméraires et insensés que, le jour même de l'anniversaire du couronnement de votre Empereur, vous avez anéantis et confondus. Vous leur avez appris qu'il est plus facile de nous braver et de nous menacer que de nous vaincre.

Soldats, lorsque tout ce qui est nécessaire pour assurer le bonheur et la prospérité de notre patrie, sera accompli, je vous ramenerai en France ; là vous serez l'objet de mes plus tendres sollicitudes ; mon Peuple vous reverra avec des transports de joye ; il vous suffira de dire : j'étois à la bataille d'Austerlitz, pour que l'on réponde : voilà un Brave.

Napoleon.

De notre Camp Impérial d'Austerlitz
le 12 Frimaire an 14

Par ordre de l'Empereur,
Le Major - Général
Mal BERTHIER.

division, Thiébault's 36th of the Line had lost the grim total of 220 grenadiers out of 230; with Friant, Corporal Blaise's unit alone had lost 4 captains, 2 lieutenants and 70 men killed, while two toes smashed by a spent ball had retired Blaise himself from the fray, and excused him from more of the marching he so detested. On the other hand, the Foot Guard 'cried with rage' (in the words of the official bulletin), because they had not been engaged at all that day, and had therefore suffered no casualties. By Thiers' reckoning, less than 45,000 troops could in fact be said to have fought that day, because of the inaction of the Foot Guard and Bernadotte's Corps. 'Thus 45,000 French had beaten 90,000 Austro-Russians.'

On the Allied side, losses seem to have numbered approximately 15,000 killed and wounded, of which 11,000 were Russians. Another 12,000 Allied troops were taken prisoner; making a total of 27,000, against fewer than 9,000 French. Thousands more of the defeated were, however, to succumb in a typhus epidemic that followed the battle. Among the vast booty captured, there were also 180 guns and 45 flags.

As Napoleon roamed the battlefield that evening, praising his men and administering brandy and encouragement to the wounded – the fate of the abandoned Russians, with many having their wounds left untended for forty-eight hours, being particularly atrocious – he was stopped short by the ranting of a wounded Russian major, hardly more than a boy, who called out:

'Sire, have me shot. I am not worthy to live, I lost all my artillery!'
'Calm yourself, young man,' replied Napoleon. 'One may be beaten by my army without dishonour.'

The following day he despatched a triumphant order to the *Grande Armée*:

Soldiers, I am pleased with you. You have, on the day of Austerlitz, fulfilled all I expected of your intrepidity; you have decorated your eagles with an immortal glory. An army of 100,000 men, commanded by the Emperors of Russia and Austria has, in less than four hours, either been cut up or dispersed. Those who escaped your steel have been drowned in the lakes. . . . Thus, in two months, this Third Coalition has been conquered and dissolved. Peace can no longer be far off.

. . . My people will greet you with joy, and it will be enough for you to say: '*J'étais à la bataille d'Auster-litz*,' for them to reply: '*Voilà un brave!*'

He closed his official bulletin with bitter words, showing he had still not forgotten that other enemy he had faced so menacingly little more than three months previously: '. . . May the cowardly oligarchs of London suffer the penalty of so many evils!'

To Josephine he wrote in rather less grandiloquent terms:

. . . . I have defeated the Russian and Austrian army commanded by the two Emperors. I am a little tired; I have been camping in the open for eight days and as many freezing nights. I shall rest tomorrow at the chateau of the Princes of Kaunitz where I count on sleeping for two or three hours. The Russian army is not only beaten, but destroyed. I embrace you. Napoleon.

The Empress appears, however, not to have been sufficiently impressed, for Napoleon was sending a somewhat acid follow-up two weeks later:

Mighty Empress, I have had not one single line from you since you left Strasbourg. You have passed through Baden, Stuttgart, and Munich, without writing me one word. That is not very nice, not very loving. . . . Deign from the height of your splendours to take a little notice of your slave . . .

LEFT The meeting between Napoleon and a crestfallen Austrian Emperor
following the victory at Austerlitz, a crayon drawing by Prud'hon.
Tsar Alexander was already well on his way back to Russia.

It seemed an incongruous tone to be adopted by the mogul who had just won one of history's most remarkable victories.

From the other side, the fugitive Emperor Francis wrote to his wife what must have been the understatement of the age: 'A battle was fought today which did not turn out very well.' For his part, Kutuzov's report somehow managed to make Austerlitz sound almost like a Russian victory.

Inevitably the defeat had created a coolness between the two Allied emperors. Tsar Alexander pulled out with the remnants of his army to avoid an undignified pursuit; leaving Francis to cover his retreat, negotiate with the enemy and defray the expenses of defeat. Abandoning stragglers and wounded, he would be in Hungary in four days, back in Russia in ten. On 3 December, Prince John of Lichtenstein was sent to Napoleon to request an interview for his Emperor, which – without being hurried – Napoleon agreed to the following day. With all the courtesy of an almost bygone age and wearing his first clean shirt in eight days, Napoleon received Francis in a humble dwelling, apologizing wryly:

'Such are the palaces which your Majesty has obliged me to inhabit for these three months.'
'The abode in them makes you so thriving, that you have no right to be angry with me for it,'

replied the Austrian. An armistice was swiftly concluded, and General Savary hastened after Alexander to bring him the news.

The Tsar admitted to Savary: 'Your master has shown himself very great. I acknowledge all the power of his genius, and, as for myself, I shall retire, since my ally is satisfied.' Savary then gave a discourse on the battle, explaining the reasons for the French victory and adding, rather patronizingly (says Thiers): '... that with experience Alexander, in his turn, would become a warrior, but that so difficult an art was not to be learned in a day.' On his return to Napoleon, Savary observed the defeated Russian Army streaming homewards: 'No more than 26,000 men passed by ... a great many were wounded, but they marched bravely in their ranks.' With them Alexander left Austrian soil, humiliated and his heart filled with the passion of revenge.

One of the last casualties of Austerlitz was Prime Minister William Pitt. His famous utterance, 'England has saved herself by her exertions and will, as I trust, save Europe by her example', had done little to encourage his distant allies on the eve of battle. With his health deteriorating, he had spent the autumn months grossly over-working, over-drinking or else lying listlessly on a couch at Bath. When the first rumours of Austerlitz reached London at the end of December, 'Prinnie' had assured his guests that 'all was over with the French and that they had been sent to the Devil'. A few minutes later the full details of the disaster were coming through, and doubtless the despair they induced hastened Pitt's end. The following month January, 1806, he, was making his remarkably accurate deathbed prophecy to his niece, Hester Stanhope, about rolling up the map of Europe: 'It will not be wanted these ten years.'

Austerlitz tempered the steel of the new *Grande Armée* into one of the finest weapons in military history. It was the victory of which Napoleon was proudest; justly so, for the results achieved, together with the risks they entailed, ensure its place as one of the greatest campaigns of all time. In twenty days the *Grande Armée* had marched from Boulogne to the Rhine; in two months, it had reached Vienna; within three it had shattered the potentially most powerful combination yet directed against France. The route was strewn with 'ifs': 'if' the Russians had reached Mack before he was encircled at Ulm; 'if' the Prussians had attacked Napoleon's long-extended flanks, in combination with the Austrian Archdukes'; 'if' Kutuzov had refused battle at Austerlitz, drawing Napoleon instead further into eastern Europe … Napoleon has been criticized for taking too many gambles in 1805, but he had several supreme advantages. So confident was he in his stars (and his army) that he rejected the thought of being anything but *totally* successful; secondly, much less was left to chance than appeared to be the case. As Napoleon himself frequently repeated: 'Nothing is attained in war except by calculation.' With his extraordinary insight, he calculated exactly how the enemy would react to his every move; and, as has been seen, his calculations were in general correct; though this did not mean that the battle had been without its moments of extreme anxiety for him. Austerlitz was also one of the last battles over which, tactically, he would be able to wield total personal control. Finally, doubtless as a direct result of all that intensive training at Boulogne, the *Grande Armée*'s numerical inferiority was counterbalanced by its supreme mobility. The key, wrote Savary:

… was that we moved about a good deal, and that individual divisions fought successive actions in different parts of the field. This is what multiplied our forces throughout the day, and this is what the art of war is all about. …

Napoleon was much assisted by the blunders of the Allies. Above all, they suffered from the divergent strategy of a coalition: 'Nothing is so important in war as undivided command,' declared Napoleon. Diversionary operations by the British and Swedes (not to mention the Prussians) could not be coordinated in time to affect the main battle, and the joint Austro-Russian councils of war always ended by adopting the worst, compromise decisions. The Allied commanders consistently failed to explore what Napoleon's own intentions might have been, and at Austerlitz erred fatally in allowing themselves to be drawn into battle on Napoleon's terms. Once the battle was joined, they proved tactically incapable of bringing all their forces to bear, largely on account of the over-crowding and jamming of Buxhöwden's massive force in the early phases.

Napoleon, too, had made his mistakes. Three of the gravest, as already noted, involved Murat: before Ulm, at Vienna, and – most seriously – in the pursuit of Bagration after Austerlitz. Some critics claim that the Eylau-Friedland campaigns of 1807 might have been avoided had Napoleon completely destroyed the Tsar's army at Austerlitz. But, with Russia's huge manpower reserves, the additional loss of Bagration's 10,000 men would have been a drop in the bucket. If anything, the fault lay – politically and psychologically – in Austerlitz being *too complete* a victory. As with Hitler in 1940, or, in more recent times, with the Israeli-Arab Six Day War of 1967, the defeated were *too* humiliated, the victor given *too* great a sense of superiority for the long term future to consolidate the victory. If Austerlitz raised Napoleon to the pinnacle of his success, it also turned his head and filled it with the delusion that no force, or combination of forces could now stop him conquering the world.

Summing up on the 'dazzling glory' of Austerlitz, Thiers was to write a generation later:

A campaign of three months, instead of a war of several years, as it had first been feared, the Continent disarmed, the French Empire extended to limits which it ought never to have passed, a dazzling glory added to our arms, public and private credit miraculously restored, new prospects of peace and prosperity opened to the nation.... For calm and reflective minds, if any such were left in presence of these events, there was but one subject for fear – the inconstancy of Fortune, and what is still more to be dreaded, the weakness of the human mind, which sometimes bears adversity without quailing and rarely prosperity without committing great faults.

Notes to Chapter 12

1 From Ségur, *Histories et Mémoires*, p. 468 (Paris 1837).

2 In his thought-provoking book, *The Face of Battle*, John Keegan appends a note on Waterloo that may well throw additional light on this particular episode at Austerlitz; it was, he claims, always the men at the *rear* of formations who broke and ran before those at the front – for the simple reason that the latter could not, trapped as they were between the attacking enemy and the ranks behind them.

3 A. F. Becke, *An Introduction to the History of Tactics* (London 1909).

4 Morland's death had a rather gruesome sequel; his viscera were buried ceremoniously in Brünn after the battle, the rest of his body being shipped back to the Invalides, embalmed by Larrey in a barrel of rum. When this was opened, it was discovered that Morland's famous moustaches continuing to grow, now reached down to his knees!

5 Already wounded in the campaign, Oudinot was to become Napoleon's most battered marshal, collecting thirty-four wounds in his service; nevertheless, he lived to the age of eighty.

6 From an account by Napoleon's aide, Lejeune.

7 The grossly inflated figure of 20,000 drowned was probably another example of Napoleon's use of terror-propaganda in his bulletins. The figure of 2,000 comes from Thiers and others; some authorities put it as low, while the official Austrian history claims that 'just two men and a few horses' were found when the ponds were subsequently drained. An instructive exercise in the unreliability of computing war casualities.

8 See bibliography.

9 *Memoiren des Königlichen Preussischen Generals der Infanterie Ludwig Freiherrn von Wolzogen*, p. 28 (Leipzig 1851).

10 A scene which Tolstoy, in *War and Peace*, has young Nikholai Rostov witness.

PART THREE

Astride the World

By 1807 a much diminished Johnny Bull
was indeed the only remaining obstacle
to Napoleonic ambition.

The Austerlitz Table, showing Napoleon and his marshals, was made at Sèvres between 1808 and 1810, and is currently displayed at Malmaison. It is of a garish vulgarity that would not disgrace the boutiques at Woburn Abbey.

13

'Roll up that Map'

1806

Napoleon did not, after all, vanquish his enemies so much by the battles of Ulm and Jena, however disastrous these were, as by his incredible marches.

Count Yorck von Wartenburg

IMMEDIATELY AFTER Austerlitz, Napoleon summoned Talleyrand to Brünn. He found it '...a horrible place – there are four thousand wounded here at present. There are a great many deaths every day. The smell yesterday was detestable ...' While Napoleon passed his time listening to Haydn and Cherubini in Schloss Austerlitz, his devious but far-sighted Foreign Minister constantly pressed him to conclude a magnanimous peace with prostrated Austria. Expanding on the arguments he had produced after Ulm, Talleyrand pleaded with him to strengthen, not weaken, the Habsburg monarchy because:

Such a power is necessarily weak, but she is an adequate bulwark against the barbarians – and a necessary one. Today, crushed and humiliated, she needs that her conqueror should extend a generous hand to her...

Talleyrand urged Napoleon to compensate Austria for the last Italian territories he intended taking away from her in the west, with the Russian provinces of Wallachia and Moldavia in the east. This, he astutely calculated, would make Austria an ally rather than an enemy, and alienate her from Russia; at the same time Russia, driven out of Europe, would inevitably come into conflict with Britain in the Orient. His statecraft was not unlike Bismarck's after Sadowa in 1866. But Napoleon, resembling more the triumphant Prussian generals of that era, would hear none of this. The wars with the First Coalition had lasted five years, the Second Coalition, two years, and now he had shattered the Third within three months. The prodigious successes of the *Grande Armée* led him to believe that no possible combination of enemies could defeat him, militarily. Accordingly he instructed Talleyrand on 4 December: '...Inform the Austrians that the battle has changed the face of affairs and that they must expect harder conditions...'

Talleyrand went to work in despair, and with foreboding. The resulting terms were extremely harsh. In addition to the Italian provinces, Emperor Francis was to forfeit the Tyrol (to Bavaria) and other territories containing over $2\frac{1}{2}$ million of his 24 million subjects, and producing one-sixth of his revenue. On top of this, he was to pay 40 million francs in war indemnity (enough to help balance Napoleon's precarious budgets, though initially he had demanded 100 million). On 27 December, the Austrians signed the Treaty of Pressburg – but with bitterness and lasting resentment. It meant that, henceforth, they would no longer be the first German power; instead, Napoleon would now fill the vacuum thus caused by creating his own satellite 'Confederation of the Rhine', comprising Bavaria, Württemberg, Baden and the lesser German principalities.

In Frankfurt's Roman Hall, Goethe recalled how as a child he had once noted that the line of portraits of the Holy Roman Emperors left only one space, which was filled by Francis II in 1792. It seemed an omen; having created himself Emperor of Austria in 1804, so as not to be upstaged by Napoleon, in August 1806 the dispossessed Emperor finally doffed the thousand-year-old crown of the Holy Roman Empire (which, for a long time already, had neither been Roman nor particularly holy). Despite all this humiliation, Napoleon accused Talleyrand of being 'soft' on the Austrians. However, for Talleyrand, it marked the beginning of his all-out opposition to Napoleon which culminated in betrayal. He refused ever to visit the principality of Benevento with which he was rewarded after Austerlitz, and when, in 1812, Napoleon planned to erect a monument to the Peace of Pressburg, Talleyrand refused to be associated with it. Beyond the ephemeral glories offered by the New Year of 1806, Talleyrand could see more bloodshed and disaster ahead.

When Napoleon returned, triumphant, to Paris on 26 January, the mood of the city was very different to that of the autumn. If Austerlitz had removed an imperial crown from Francis's head, it had secured that on Napoleon's. Said the sober Cambacérès: 'The joy of the people resembled intoxication.' A popular cartoon of the time shows a street crier pointing to a sketch of a galloping Napoleon, holding out a letter in his hand, with the caption:

PEACE – THANKS TO . . . THE IMMORTAL NAPOLEON
It is I, *Messieurs les Français*, who offer you
the best New Year's presents.

Mementoes of almost Woburn-like bad taste, such as the famous Austerlitz table currently displayed at Malmaison, were run up to celebrate the famous victory. On a grander scale, the grateful Senate decreed the erection of a triumphal monument to Napoleon-the-Great; modelled on Trajan's Column, it would be set up in the Place Vendôme[1] with bronze reliefs depicting the glorious feats of 1805, and cast from melted-down enemy cannon seized at Austerlitz. Accompanying it was a triumphal arch, the Arc d'Austerlitz (now the Carrousel), but facing it on a hill two miles away up the Champs Elysées was projected a far more grandiose structure that would commemorate all Napoleon's victories.

To his followers, Napoleon handed out the spoils of victory with largesse: out of the reparations milked from Austria, two million gold francs for his senior officers; an extra fifteen days' pay for each member of the Guard; liberal pensions for widows of the fallen. Battle orphans were formally adopted by Napoleon himself, and permitted to add 'Napoleon' to their christian names. On his family and intimates he also showered kingdoms and dukedoms as if creating so many corporals, causing Talleyrand to remark acidly that: 'Since he had become an Emperor, he no longer wished there to be any more republics.' In March 1806, Murat was proclaimed Grand-Duke of Berg and Cleves (a territory with which Prussia had tried to buy Napoleon's friendship), and, three years later, he became King of Naples. Joseph Bonaparte was made King of Naples (later, King of Spain); his sister, Pauline Borghese, became Duchess of Guastalla (which deeply disappointed her, when it turned out to be a mere village). Louis Bonaparte became King of Holland; Talleyrand, Prince of Benevento; Berthier, Prince of Neuchâtel; and Bernadotte (for no very clear reason), Prince of Ponte-Corvo.

With peace once more in his grasp, Napoleon's fertile mind now set anew to contemplating all manner of vast civil engineering projects – such as tunnels under the Alps. The Sorbonne (suppressed under the Revolution) was reopened, the Panthéon restored briefly to Catholicism, the desecrated cathedral of Saint-Denis restored. While David and the new court painters busied themselves with vast canvasses of *la gloire d'Austerlitz*, one of the last – and greatest – of the old school died quietly: J.-H. Fragonard. Napoleon also set to work extensively reorganizing the Treasury, but it was here that he was forced to face, or rather to re-face, the less agreeable realities on the reverse side of the medallion of military triumph.

During the campaign, France's rickety finances had gone from bad to worse in the incompetent hands of brother Joseph, left behind as Regent. Several banks had collapsed; the Minister of the Treasury himself was under suspicion of embezzlement, and the country faced bankruptcy. The British naval blockade was biting. With an ingenuity worthy of Hitler's *Ersatz* scientists, saltpetre for gunpowder was being produced synthetically, indigo dye had been made from a plant found near Strasbourg, substitutes for silk and cotton were being pursued, while efforts to obtain sugar from seaweed would lead (five years later) to the introduction of the sugar-beet as a major crop. Yet, for all this resourcefulness, the severance of France's foreign commerce was adding a further weighty burden on the already extreme debility of her economy. Unemployment was acute, and Napoleon sought to occupy the unemployed with such Rooseveltian projects as the excavation of the new Ourcq Canal, while prison sentences were freely meted out to workers who dared strike. The Emperor's presence was also badly needed in Paris to carry on with the work on the various half-completed Codes.

So, from the time of his victorious return in March 1806, Napoleon yearned once again for a period of peace in which to set his own house in order. But within a brief term of six months he would already be off to the wars again, the great industrial exhibition planned to celebrate Austerlitz – at the same time as it distracted minds from economic realities – somewhat eclipsed by the new campaign.

Following Austerlitz and the death of Pitt, none of Napoleon's adversaries looked more ready for peace than England. The collapse of Pitt's short-lived Third Coalition had left an expeditionary force of 25,000 of her scant army marooned on the freezing Elbe, at the mercy of the unpredictable Prussians, her Swedish Allies having decamped back across the Baltic. Troops were alerted to deal with riots in London, and it seemed no exaggeration (nor unprophetic) when Captain Thomas Fremantle declared in May: 'If England gets out of the many difficulties that now press on her, she will be the greatest nation in the world.'

On the death of Pitt even his rival and antithesis in all things, Charles James Fox, groaned that it felt 'as if something was missing in the world'. Impetuous to the point (so it was said) of putting the shot into his gun before the powder when out shooting, he was regarded – not entirely without affection – by Sydney Smith as '... one of the most luminous eloquent blunderers with which any people was ever afflicted'. Dedicated equally to gambling and the championing of 'generous causes' (which included marrying his mistress in middle age), Fox had always stood for two great ideals – abolition of the slave trade, and peace with France. Now, as Foreign Secretary and the real power under Pitt's successor Grenville (in what was unkindly dubbed the 'Ministry of All the Talents'), Fox hastened the pursuit of an accommodation. But Napoleon proved elusive, and greedy, while – stricken with dropsy – Fox was to follow Pitt to the grave less than nine months later. 'The giant race is extinct,' mourned a supporter, 'and we are left in the hands of little ones.'

For England, the next three years would be (says Winston Churchill[2]) 'uncheered by fortune', with only two small rays of sunshine illuminating the glum year of 1806. The first, in the shape of the return home from India of a brilliant young general, Arthur Wellesley, was however to remain imperceptible for some time yet. The second was the success in July of a British amphibious operation at Maida, on the toe of Italy. With little more than 5,000 men, Major-General Sir John Stuart, acting on his own brief, routed the over-confident French defenders by their disciplined fire-power.

'Such a thing has not been seen since the Revolution!' confessed one French officer. Admittedly on a very small scale, Maida dispelled the myth of the invincibility of the French line; more important it was one of the first fruits born of the seed of Trafalgar, while it proved as demonstratively as anything else could that at least England's seapower made her free of the terrors of invasion. Once Fox was gone, however, any serious prospect of peace with Napoleon was as remote as ever. In June, Napoleon suddenly offered to return Hanover to George III; but, at a time when many Englishmen would have preferred to return both King George and his frivolous, obese heir to Hanover, it was a hollow gesture. The only impact it had was to incense Prussia, and goad her finally into a suicidal war against France.

A month before Austerlitz, Frederick William III of Prussia and his vivacious Queen, Louise, had held a macabre tryst with Tsar Alexander. Inside the torchlit tomb of Frederick the Great, his successor – having wavered all year about supporting the Third Coalition – finally and solemnly pledged to join in the war against Napoleon. In effect, a kiss imprinted on the sarcophagus to seal the bargain dug the grave of the Prussian Army. Bearing what amounted to a declaration of war, Prussia's unenthusiastic envoy, Count Haugwitz, was dispatched to Vienna but dallied so on the way that he was only to reach Napoleon after the Allies had already lost the day at Austerlitz. In some confusion, Haugwitz modified his missive to sound like an obsequious message of congratulations. Napoleon, always well-informed about Prussian intentions, was not deceived. Treating Haugwitz – and, through him, his ruler – with contempt, the conqueror imposed the most degrading terms on Prussia. All of this the once proud soldier-nation was forced, in her isolation, to accept without having fired a single shot in her defence. Never had her reputation been so besmirched, and the humiliation rankled intolerably. As a result, a war party emerged in Berlin, headed by the spirited Queen and the nationalist Foreign Minister, Hardenberg. To them, compounded by all the slights that Prussia had suffered at Napoleon's hands beginning with the violation of Ansbach's territory on the march to Ulm the previous year, the proposed transfer of Hanover to England came as the last straw. In August 1806 the weak Frederick William finally mobilized for war against France.

RIGHT King Frederick William III of Prussia (1770–1840). His queen, Louise, was very much the better half; a fact which, combined with his humiliation at Napoleon's hands, may have contributed to the look of gloom in this portrait by Wilhelm Herbig.

BELOW Field-Marshal Gebhard Leverecht von Blücher (1742–1819), a detail of a portrait by Lawrence. At Jena, he was one of the most competent of the Prussian generals, though already sixty-four years old. After a brief aberration when he believed himself to be pregnant by an elephant, the ponderous Blücher survived to help administer the *coup de grace* to Napoleon at Waterloo. Poorly-educated and frequently drunk, Blücher once admitted that 'something could have been made of me if only I had had the sense to study'. However he was a general who would never admit defeat.

ABOVE Birds ready for the plucking. A crude French cartoon at the time of Jena. The sword-bearing goose is the Duke of Brunswick, who would not survive the battle.

BELOW 'The precipitate march of the flying Russian Army to the rescue of the Prussians.' A French cartoon of the 1806 campaign; once again, the savage humour is not ill-founded. On the left, Frederick William is already being carried off by the Napoleonic eagle before the 'flying' Russian steam-roller can arrive.

To have done so twelve months previously might have made sense, when there were powerful allies in the field, but now it was insensate folly. Says Thiers: 'Nothing short of the most fatal infatuation could account for the conduct of Prussia; but such is party-spirit, such are its incurable illusions ...' Such also, he might have added, are the consequences of a mortally-wounded pride which Napoleon had grossly underestimated. The Prussian 'hawks' based their miscalculation on precisely the same error that had brought Austria low at Ulm – that the plodding Russians would reach them before Napoleon. But, even more, they placed their faith mystically in the military inheritance of Frederick the Great. That, too, was utterly mistaken; for virtually nothing had changed (for the better) in the Prussian Army since the great victories at Rossbach and Leuthen half a century earlier. The King's senior military advisor, Field Marshal von Möllendorf, was a veteran of Leuthen and eighty-two years old, while the principal commander, the Duke of Brunswick, was seventy-one and had learnt little since his defeat at Valmy back in 1792. Even the most capable of the more junior generals, Blücher, was already sixty-four. (Pugnacious to a fault – the Duke of Wellington later said of him that whenever there was a fight he was 'always ready and eager – if anything too eager' – Blücher was also a ponderous mover; during a mental breakdown in 1811, he believed that he was pregnant by an elephant!)

During the last years of Frederick the Great, the military art had already ossified and by 1806 (says General Fuller[3]): 'Tactically the Prussian Army was a museum specimen.' In no way short on courage, its men were educated to fight like automatons in tight, rigidly-disciplined linear formations, equipped with the worst muskets in Europe, dating back to 1754. They moved even more heavily encumbered than the Austrians, and when war came in 1806 the army was just in the process of being reorganized along divisional lines – the system abandoned by Napoleon back in 1800. Commanders were totally inexperienced in handling the new organization. Worst of all, at the top the leadership was hopelessly divided.

In Paris, Napoleon hesitated a month before persuading himself that the Prussians really meant business. On 10 September, he was writing to Talleyrand: 'The idea that Prussia could take the field against me by herself seems to me so ridiculous that it does not merit discussion.' What particularly surprised him was that the Prussian Army appeared to be concentrating *west* of the mighty Elbe, with the formidable river barrier at their backs. Were they planning to strike at the communications of the *Grande Armée*, extended as it now was all the way from the Danube to Holland? Or would they actually dare to repeat the operations of 1792, and thrust westwards across the Rhine? Nothing was clear. Still hoping to avoid a new war which he in no way wanted (for all that he had provoked Prussia into it), Napoleon wrote to Berthier at *Grande Armée* headquarters in Bavaria: '... If the news continues to indicate that the Prussians have lost their heads, I shall go straight to Würzburg or to Bamberg.'

On 18 September, Napoleon learned that the Prussian Army had moved south-westwards into Saxony, bullying her reluctant neighbour to join cause with her. This news meant that the Prussians had indeed 'lost their heads', and war was unavoidable. Napoleon now moved with his usual speed and decisiveness. On the night of 24/25 September, accompanied by Talleyrand and (this time) Josephine, he left Paris for Mayence, arriving there on 28 September. (In the meantime a messenger had set out from Berlin bearing an impossible ultimatum to Napoleon: withdraw all French troops behind the Rhine.) Still without knowing exactly what

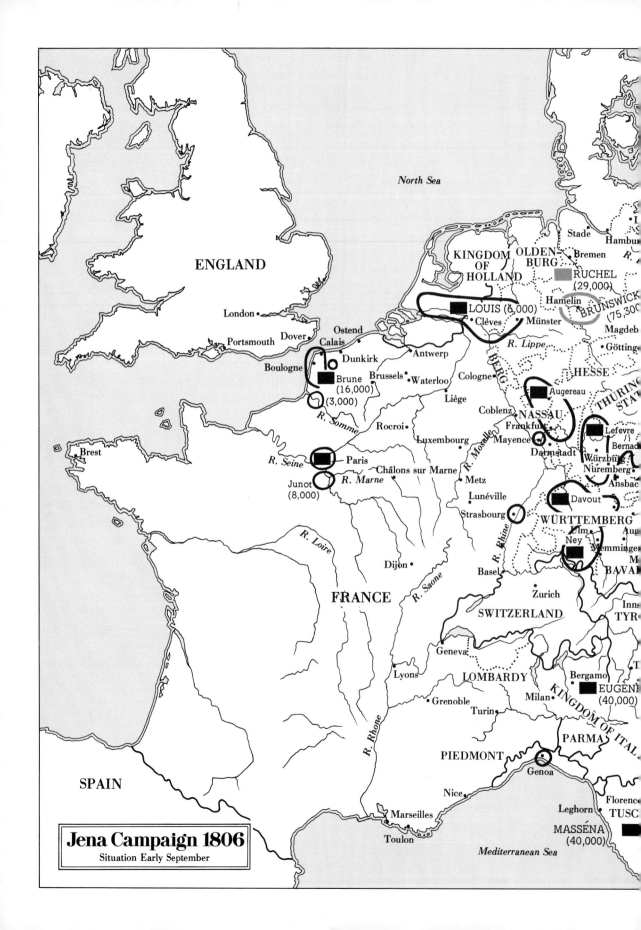

North Sea

ENGLAND

KINGDOM OF HOLLAND

OLDEN-BURG

Stade   Hambu
Bremen

RUCHEL
(29,000)

London

Dover

Ostend
Calais

Antwerp

Hamelin

BRUNSWICK
(75,30

Portsmouth

Boulogne

Dunkirk

Brussels

Waterloo

LOUIS (8,000)
Clèves   Münster

R. Lippe

Magdeb

Götting

Brune
(16,000)
(3,000)

Cologne

Liège

HESSE

Augereau

THURIN
STA

R. Somme

Rocroi

R. Seine   Paris

Junot
(8,000)

R. Marne

Châlons sur Marne

Luxembourg

Coblenz
NASSAU
Frankfur

Mayence

Darmstadt

Metz

Lefevre

Bernad
Würzbur
Nürember
Ansbac

Lunéville

Strasbourg

Davout

WÜRTTEMBERG

Brest

Dijon

Basel

R. Loire

R. Saone

R. Rhone

FRANCE

SPAIN

Geneva

Lyons

Grenoble

Zurich

SWITZERLAND

LOMBARDY

Milan

Turin

Ulm
Ney
Memminger

BAVA

Inns
TYR

Bergamo

EUGENI
(40,000)

KINGDOM OF ITAL

PIEDMONT

PARMA

Nice

Genoa

Marseilles

Toulon

Leghorn

Florenc
TUSC

MASSÉNA
(40,000)

Mediterranean Sea

Jena Campaign 1806
Situation Early September

SWEDEN

Copenhagen

R. Niemen

Königsberg
Tilsit

Lauenbourg
Eylau
Friedland

PRUSSIA

alsund

POMERANIA
Allenstein
Grodno

Berlin
Stettin
Bialystok

R. Narew

LESTOCQ
(25,000)
Thorn

R. Oder

R. Spree
Posen
Pultusk
Warsaw

RUSSIA

Brest-Litovsk

SAXON Y
R. Vistula

eipzig
HOHENLOHE
(42,000)

Dresden
SILESIA
R. Vistula

R. Bug

Krakow
GALICIA

BOHEMIA
Lemberg

Olmütz

R. Moldau
MORAVIA

Austerlitz

AUSTRIA

Soult
Wagram
Pressburg

Linz
Vienna

Aspern
Essling

Salzburg

Bruck
Buda Pest

Leoben
HUNGARY

Neumarkt

ARINTHIA
TRANSYLVANIA

ETIA

Trieste

nice
ISTRIA

R. Drave

R. Danube

Adriatic Sea

MARMONT
(13,500)
OTTOMAN EMPIRE

DALMATIA

PAPAL
STATES

0   20 40 60 80 100 120 140

SCALE OF MILES

the Prussian strategy was, Napoleon formulated his own. First of all he eschewed the notion of a straight thrust eastwards across the flat North German plain, over all those awkward rivers, like the route the victorious Anglo-Americans were to follow in 1945. Instead without waiting to be attacked, he would seek out the main Prussian force, get between it and the approaching Russians, and destroy it in detail. In simplest terms, it would be a repeat of the Ulm manoeuvre.

Meanwhile, on the Prussian side mobilization had proceeded with sluggish inefficiency. Forces in East Prussia were not called in, perhaps partly out of traditional mistrust of the Russian ally. From an imposing potential of over 200,000 men little more than half reached the concentration area in Saxony. Towards the end of September endless inconclusive councils of war took place between the Prussian commanders, Hohenlohe and Brunswick, with the King shuttling between the two. By 7 October, a clear-sighted officer called Scharnhorst, chief-of-staff to Brunswick, was writing in despair: 'What we ought to do I know right well, what we *shall* do only the gods know.' What the Prussians *should* have done, (says General Fuller)[4] was to have retired behind the broad Elbe and 'to have disputed its passage until joined by the Russians'. Instead, Hohenlohe, with no general strategy agreed upon, decided on his own initiative to push part of his army south-westwards from Jena towards the River Saale. Brunswick and Rüchel remained stationary on the northern slopes of the Thuringian Forest. Thus, already, the Prussians were moving eccentrically, and dispersing their main forces over a sixty-mile front.

Napoleon, on the other hand, was concentrating his forces. On 30 September he revealed his plan in a long dispatch to his brother Louis, who was commanding the forces in Holland. He would denude the entire area between the Rhine and Bavaria to bring all his might to bear on the extreme right. Only Louis' army of some 30,000 men would stand between the Prussians and a possible frontal attack across the Rhine. Louis for his part was to make aggressive noises to 'deceive' the Prussians into looking due westwards, while in fact Napoleon and an army twice as large as that which he had taken to Austerlitz was moving onto the Würzburg-Bamberg line, thence to strike obliquely north-eastwards into the heart of Saxony and Prussia. He would only count on Louis' forces, he told his brother '... as a means of diversion to amuse the enemy up to 12 October, which is the date on which my plans will be unmasked ...' The remarkable accuracy of this projected date would indicate to what extent, once again, Napoleon was making the enemy dance to *his* tune. At the same time, he did not omit the element of caution:

... in case of a serious event, such as the loss of a great battle, while I make good my retreat to the Danube, you can defend Wesel and Mayence ... and ... hinder the enemy from crossing the Rhine and pillaging my estates ...

By the beginning of October, Napoleon had made his mind up that the key to his plan lay in the Leipzig-Dresden area of Saxony. There he would seek his battle of destruction – manoeuvring 'in a *bataillon carré* of 200,000 men',[5] Napoleon wrote Soult (on 5 October) in one of his most instructive letters of the whole campaign. 'However, all that demands a little skill and some luck,' he admitted, while assuring Soult that:

With this immense superiority of force united in so narrow a space, you will feel that I am determined to leave nothing to chance, and can attack the enemy wherever he chooses to stand with nearly double his force ...

He stressed to Soult, as to his other corps commanders, how imperative it was to keep in *closest contact* with him, for the success of his plan. What Napoleon meant by his '*bataillon carré*' – a somewhat curious term for so vast a mass – was a disposition that would enable him to fix the enemy with part of his army, while a second part was free to wheel against one of the enemy flanks or rear, and a third remained in reserve. Capable of operating against a force coming from any side, it was ideal for the opportunist 'encounter' battle likely to occur in the continuing uncertainty about Frederick William's thoroughly illogical intentions.

While the Prussian dithered, Napoleon's forces – greatly aided by Germany's excellent pavé roads – had mustered with great speed. For once the Guard had clattered part of the way in requisitioned post chaises, covering 340 miles in just over a week. There were, of course, the usual signs of improvization. At Strasbourg, the main replacement depot for the Austerlitz campaign, only 3,000 uniforms could be found for 15,000 new conscripts, while many troops marched eastwards without overcoats for an autumn and winter in the field. Reviewing one of Augereau's regiments in Würzburg, Napoleon complimented the soldiers on being '... the best marchers in the Army; one never sees anyone left behind, particularly when approaching the enemy'. Then, observing the ducks and geese sticking out of his soldiers' haversacks, he added, laughing: 'But to render you complete justice I must tell you that you are also the worst grumblers and the worst pilferers in the Army!' Austerlitz having cost 12,000 muskets, weapons were also in short supply; but these would soon be made up from amply-stocked Prussian depots.

At dawn on 8 October, Napoleon began moving north-eastwards, disappearing through the dense Thuringian Forest into Saxony. A manoeuvre with similarities to Hitler's unanticipated thrust through the Ardennes to Sedan in 1940, it enabled the *Grande Armée* to pass unseen across the left flank of the Prussian forces. By routing his army along three parallel defiles, two corps to each, he saved himself several valuable days. The *Bataillon Carré* was so disposed that it could rally on any one of its component corps within forty-eight hours. As in 1805, it marched preceded and masked by Murat's screen of light cavalry. Bursting out of the forest, on 10 October, Lannes' V Corps struck the advance guard of Hohenlohe's army at Saalfeld on the River Saale. Commanded by the fiery nephew of the King, Prince Louis Ferdinand, who had been a leader of the Prussian 'war party', it consisted of only 8,300 men and so was outnumbered two-to-one by Lannes' crack formation. Nevertheless, the Prince pressed the attack in a fierce, but uneven action which lasted four hours. Leading a last desperate cavalry charge, Louis was hacked down in hand-to-hand combat by Quarter-Master Sergeant Guindet of the Hussars. At a total cost of less than 200 casualties, Lannes wiped out nearly half the Prussian force, capturing 33 guns and 1,800 prisoners.

This local defeat was to have greatly magnified consequences. The effect on morale was disastrous, with Saxon troops at Jena panicking hopelessly two days later and fighting with their Prussian allies for supplies and firewood. When the news reached Prussian headquarters, all thoughts of further advance were promptly put into reverse. Brunswick gave the order to reconcentrate on Weimar, while both he and Hohenlohe prepared to fall back towards the Elbe – a course they ought to have adopted in the first place. Meanwhile, the engagement at Saalfeld had given a surprised Napoleon a first clue as to the location of the enemy army, and an idea of what its line of retreat might now be. Accordingly he ordered Davout to hasten to Naumburg lower down the Saale, astride the main route to Leipzig, and to hold the bridge-head there. After one of his characteristically long-legged marches, Davout was in position with his 26,000-strong III Corps by the evening of 12 October, thereby sealing the Prussians from the rear in much the same way as the bulk of the *Grande Armée* had trapped Mack at Ulm. In view of what was to follow, it was indeed fortunate for Napoleon that he had selected his best marshal as the cork in the bottle. To the other leading corps commanders, his orders were: '... The game today is to attack everything we encounter, in order to beat the enemy in detail while he is uniting his forces.'

Realizing that the entire enemy force was on the far side of the River Saale, Napoleon now performed – with the flexibility and order for which the *Grande Armée* was famous – a 90° left wheel with his whole vast mass of men. This brought Lannes' V Corps onto the heights overlooking the small town of Jena on the River Saale. At 9 a.m. on 13 October, Napoleon received various pieces of intelligence which persuaded him that, in the first place, the Prussians were preparing to retire *due northwards* on Magdeburg, and secondly that Hohenlohe and the main weight of Frederick William's forces were massed within a few miles of Jena and Lannes' single corps. With all probability, Napoleon deduced, they would launch a spoiling attack on Lannes, so as to ensure their unimpeded withdrawal. 'At last the veil is torn aside,' he declared in a letter to Murat – but, in fact, he was about to commit one of his greatest miscalculations. At about 4 p.m. that afternoon he reached the Landgrafenberg Heights occupied by Lannes; looking down he could see some 30,000 of Hohenlohe's men encamped, and took them, erroneously, to comprise the whole Prussian Army, thereby confirming his earlier assessment. With utmost dispatch, Napoleon now ordered up Soult, Ney and Augereau, plus the Guard, to reinforce Lannes at Jena – in other words, the bulk of the *Grande Armée*. Davout, already at Naumburg, was to cross the Saale and head southwest towards Apolda, so as to take the enemy in its left rear, cutting its (supposed) line of retreat on Magdeburg. Bernadotte, on his way to back up Davout at Naumburg, was instructed to turn back to Dornburg, little more than seven miles downstream from Jena, in readiness to strike into the Prussian left flank. Napoleon himself resolved to attack the following dawn: 'There are moments in war when no consideration should override the advantage of anticipating the enemy and striking first.'

On the other side of the Saale, however, the situation was rather different. Morale was low. The Saxons, who had received almost no food for four days, were mutinous and threatening to leave the Prussians; even some of the Prussian battalions were down to half-strength as a result of straggling and desertion. In this sorry state, a council of war decided that Brunswick and the main army should withdraw immediately up the west bank of the Saale, taking the shortest route towards the Elbe – and Berlin; this meant adopting an axis closer to Leipzig than Magdeburg, which, in turn, would bring Brunswick into head-on collision with Davout. Meanwhile, Hohenlohe would act as a mere rearguard to cover the withdrawal, with Rüchel's 15,000 men hovering uselessly in the wings at Weimar. Thus, as the day of battle approached, Brunswick and 63,000 men were pushing down a single road towards Davout's corps of 26,000 men; while, at Jena, Hohenlohe and a force of 38,000 faced Napoleon with 55,000 troops already in hand and a further 40,000 that could reach him by noon on 4 October. It produced an intriguingly unbalanced picture.

At Jena, the night before the battle, there was confusion as Lannes' approach route was blocked when one of his cannon became wedged on a narrow trail; but Napoleon himself was on hand, calmly untangling the traffic snarl. As the attack went in at dawn, confusion was compounded by fog – thicker than at Austerlitz, and far less welcome. The first objective was for Lannes to seize, by straight frontal attack, the Dornburg plateau, so as to provide elbow room for the other three corps. With some disorder (Augereau getting his entire corps jammed into a ravine on the left flank), this succeeded by 11 a.m. Matters on the left were not helped by the impatient Ney, who, chafing at the bit for orders, plunged into battle in a foggy gap between Lannes and Augereau. This led him straight into the mouth of a powerful Prussian battery. Suffering terrible casualties, Ney overran the guns but this impetus then carried him so far that he found himself cut off, and had to be rescued by the personal intervention of a displeased Emperor with the only available cavalry reserve.

More orderly was Soult's advance on the right, led by St Hilaire's men who had acquitted themselves so superbly on the Pratzen the previous year. Towards midday, Hohenlohe led a concerted counter-attack on the centre of the line. His troops went in bravely with bands playing and colours flying, aligned as if on parade ground. When they reached the village of Vierzehn-heiligen, his 20,000 infantrymen were picked off for two hours by French marksmen firing from under cover of garden walls and broken masonry, with minimal losses to themselves.

By 2.30 p.m., Hohenlohe's army was reduced to fragments. But as he gave the order to retreat, Rüchel came marching onto the lost battlefield at last, with his 13,000 men from Weimar in a tight wedge formation. At first his attack shook the French, but after they had rallied Rüchel found himself exposed to fire from nearly the whole of Napoleon's four corps. Despite extraordinary bravery by some of the Prussian grenadiers, they broke, and retreat became a rout, with the French cavalry sabring and trampling the wretched fugitives in a six-mile pursuit. By 6 p.m., Murat was riding into the streets of Weimar contemptuously brandishing a whip instead of a sabre. It was how Austerlitz should have ended, but did not.

When the casualties were counted, French losses at Jena amounted to approximately 5,000; the Prussians lost 25,000 men, 200 cannon and 30 flags. Clausewitz was to write savagely of his nation's performance:[6]

When the Prussian generals ... threw themselves into the open jaws of destruction in the oblique order of Frederick the Great, and managed to ruin Hohenlohe's army in a way that no other army has ever been ruined on the actual field of battle – all this was due not merely to a manner which had outlived its day, but to the most downright stupidity to which methodism has ever led.

But, ultimately, sheer weight of numbers would have defeated Hohenlohe at Jena anyway. Far from being one of Napoleon's tidiest battles, it was one of encounter and accident; much of his initial plan had fallen apart, partly because events had occurred so rapidly as to prevent formulation of a careful plan, such as had won the day at Austerlitz. Comparing him to General Grant at Chattanooga fifty-seven years later, two American military historians, Esposito and Elting,[7] also claim that he '... seems to have at times lost control of the battle ... Had the whole Prussian-Saxon army faced him, the struggle would have been desperate ...'

Because of the intensity of the cannonade, sounds of a fierce battle some thirteen miles to

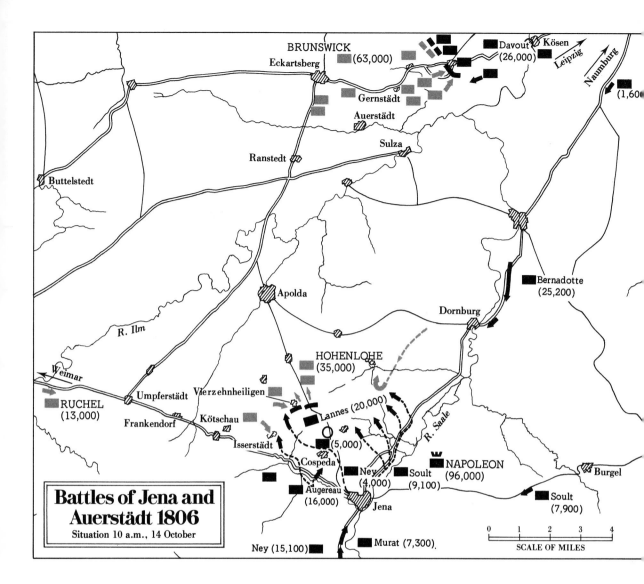

BRUNSWICK
(63,000)
Eckartsberg
Gernstädt
Auerstädt
Davout (26,000)
Kösen
Leipzig
Naumburg
(1,60...

Sulza
Ranstedt
Buttelstedt
Bernadotte (25,200)
Apolda
Dornburg
R. Ilm
HOHENLOHE
(35,000)
Weimar
Vierzehnheiligen
Umpferstädt
RUCHEL
(13,000)
Frankendorf
Kötschau
Lannes (20,000)
R. Saale
Isserstädt
(5,000)
Cospeda
NAPOLEON
(96,000)
Burgel
Augereau
(16,000)
Ney (4,000)
Soult (9,100)
Soult (7,900)
Jena
Ney (15,100)
Murat (7,300)

Battles of Jena and Auerstädt 1806
Situation 10 a.m., 14 October

0   1   2   3   4
SCALE OF MILES

the north had all but escaped Napoleon's attention. Thus, at the end of the day, he was surprised and aggravated to receive a staff captain sent by Davout who reported that the marshal had won a great victory, defeating the main body of the Prussian Army near Auerstädt. Perhaps thinking of Davout's notorious short-sightedness, he snapped 'Your marshal must be seeing double!' but was soon retracting his words.

In compliance with Napoleon's orders, Davout had begun moving his three divisions (one commanded by General Friant, the hero of the bitter defensive fight at Sokolnitz-Telnitz the previous year) towards Apolda at dawn. Reaching the heights of the key Kösen Pass, through which Frederick William intended to pass his entire army, Gudin's lead division ran into Blücher's cavalry in thick fog. Four times Blücher charged, but, with the speed at which Davout's superbly-trained corps excelled, the infantry formed squares, repulsing all the Prussian attacks. By mid-morning, Friant's division arrived at the double and went into the attack directly in

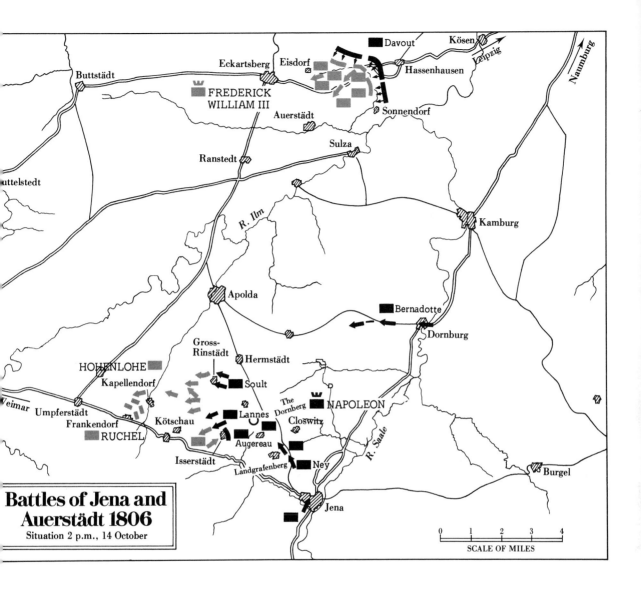

SCALE OF MILES

battalion column on the right flank. Blücher had his horse shot from under him and was sent reeling back toward Auerstädt. More serious was the threat to Davout's left flank, where at one point vastly superior forces under Schmettau and Wartensleben nearly enveloped Morand's division. Appearing personally to be at almost every critical point on the front at once, Davout brilliantly sited Friant's and Morand's guns[8] so as to decimate Schmettau's infantry with interlocking fire. In the course of the battle, Schmettau was mortally wounded; the Duke of Brunswick, the army commander, was himself shot through both eyes, and died later; and the King's ancient advisor, Marshal von Möllendorf, was taken prisoner. With its command virtually wiped out, Frederick William's army lost its will to fight at around midday. Had the Prussians but known it, however, Davout by then had had to throw into the battle even his specialist (and preciously few) sappers, leaving himself with barely a battalion in reserve.

Nevertheless, realizing that the enemy were hesitating, Davout now thrust forward 'in a

The Battle of Auerstädt by Calle. The dying Duke of Brunswick is
carried from the field. His death preceded the Prussian defeat
at the hands of Davout's heavily-outnumbered forces.

menacing crescent-shaped formation, horns pushed aggressively forward'.[9] For a while the
Prussians fought back stoically, in murderous close-in fighting. Davout wrote in his *Journal*:

We were within pistol range, and the cannonade tore gaps in their ranks which immediately closed
up. Each move of the 61st Regiment was indicated on the ground by the brave men they left there.

Suddenly the defence broke, with demoralized units of Brunswick's army reeling back through
Auerstädt on top of the fugitives streaming northwards away from Jena. Roads were blocked
with abandoned waggons; hungry troops looted as they went. Having fought his most brilliant
battle against far greater odds than even at Austerlitz, Davout had inflicted 13,000 casualties
in six savage hours. But he had also suffered painful losses: 6,794 men and 258 officers – approximately one-quarter of his effectives. Many senior officers had fallen, and most of the rest had
either been grazed by bullets or had at least one horse killed under them. One division (Gudin's,
which had taken Blücher's first shock) had lost 41 per cent of its men – one of the heaviest
losses on a victorious side ever to have been recorded.

Undoubtedly Davout's losses would have been a good deal less severe had he been supported by Bernadotte's 20,000-strong I Corps. But where was 'Sergent Belle-Jambe' during the battle? He had reached Naumburg at 2 p.m. on 13 October, complaining that his troops were fatigued. Despite then receiving Napoleon's instruction of that morning, which ordered him back to Dornburg, Bernadotte dossed down for the night. At 3 a.m. Davout had received his final battle-order from Berthier, obviously drafted under extreme pressure, and adding a somewhat less than precise postscript for Bernadotte: 'If Bernadotte is with you, you can march together, but the Emperor hopes that he will be in the position assigned him, at Dornburg ...' Davout immediately passed this note to Bernadotte. But Bernadotte, apparently in a high sulk and professionally piqued at receiving orders via someone he considered his junior, refused Davout's repeated entreaties to move with him. Instead he insisted on carrying out to the letter the first order he had received. Behaving much as he had at Austerlitz, the Prince de Ponte-Corvo sauntered at an almost leisurely pace to Dornburg – away from Davout. Though all the time he could hear Davout's guns behind him, he turned a firmly deaf ear on them. He spent the rest of the day uselessly at Dornburg, making no attempt to join in the fight, either at Jena or Auerstädt. At 4 p.m., when it was all over, Bernadotte headed towards Apolda, and had the nerve to claim that his arrival there had saved Davout!

Bernadotte's deplorable conduct could well have caused Davout's defeat at Auerstädt, and the mind boggles at what the outcome might have been had the roles of the two marshals been switched, with Bernadotte confronting Brunswick unsupported. Defenders of 'Belle-Jambe' blame Napoleon for sending out inadequate orders – comparable to those which Murat and Lannes had (or had not) received when facing Bagration at Austerlitz. Indeed, one major failing of the whole Napoleonic command system was that few of his generals would act on their own initiative (save Davout, and Murat who often got it wrong); on the other hand if there was one axiom bred into all of them it was always to 'march towards the guns'.

At the end of the day, while Napoleon lavished praise on Davout for his victory – subsequently giving him the well-earned title of Duc D'Auerstädt – his rage nearly cost Bernadotte his head. On St Helena Napoleon revealed he had actually signed a court martial order, but tore it up; no doubt influenced by the fact that Bernadotte was married to his early love, Desirée Clary. The uncharitable, however, might well consider that a firing squad in 1806 would have saved Napoleon trouble seven years later, when 'Belle-Jambe' was to betray him totally.

On 15 October there began one of the most famous pursuits in military history. On the previous night Murat had already gone on to capture the citadel of Erfurt, taking another 10,000 Prussians without a fight. Supported by Ney, he was now ordered to pursue what remained of Frederick William's forces, 'his sword point at their kidneys', while Soult and Bernadotte moved along parallel routes sweeping north-eastwards into the heart of Prussia. Napoleon, with Davout and the rest of the army, moved on Berlin. By 28 October, Murat was mopping up the last remnants of Hohenlohe's army twenty-five miles short of Stettin on the mouth of the River Oder, having covered two hundred miles as the crow flies in the two weeks since Jena. Swinging westwards, he then joined up with Soult and Bernadotte in pursuit of Blücher, who, with characteristic pugnacity, fought back much of the way. By 5 November, Blücher

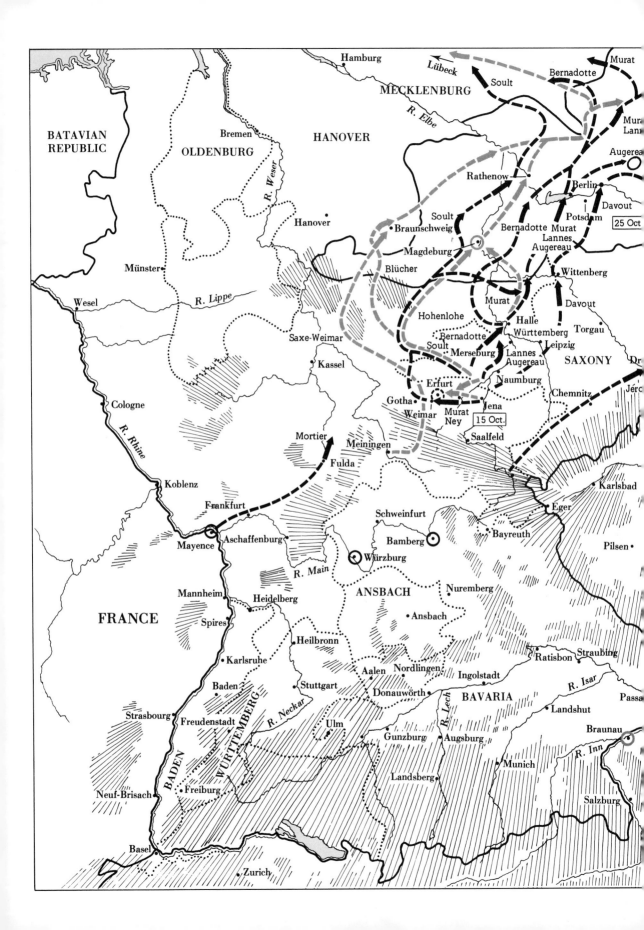

BATAVIAN
REPUBLIC

OLDENBURG

HANOVER

MECKLENBURG

Hamburg

Lübeck

Soult

Bernadotte

Murat

R. Elbe

Murat
Lan

Augerea

Bremen

Hanover

Rathenow

Berlin

Davout

25 Oct

Münster

Soult
Braunschweig

Magdeburg

Blücher

Bernadotte Murat
Lannes
Augereau

Potsdam

Wittenberg

R. Weser

R. Lippe

Wesel

Murat

Davout

Cologne

Saxe-Weimar

Kassel

Hohenlohe

Bernadotte
Soult

Halle

Württemberg

Torgau

Merseburg

Leipzig

Lannes
Augereau

SAXONY

R. Rhine

Naumburg

Chemnitz

Dr

Erfurt

Gotha
Weimar

Jena

Murat
Ney

15 Oct.

Saalfeld

Jer

Koblenz

Mortier

Meiningen

Frankfurt

Fulda

Mayence
Aschaffenburg

Schweinfurt

Bamberg

Bayreuth

Karlsbad

Eger

Pilsen

R. Main

Würzburg

Mannheim

Heidelberg

ANSBACH

Nuremberg

FRANCE

Spires

Ansbach

Heilbronn

Karlsruhe

Ratisbon

Straubing

Baden

Stuttgart

Aalen

Nordlingen

Ingolstadt

BAVARIA

R. Isar

Strasbourg

Freudenstadt

R. Neckar

Donauwörth

R. Lech

Landshut

Passa

WÜRTTEMBERG

Ulm

Gunzburg

Augsburg

Braunau

R. Inn

BADEN

Neuf-Brisach

Freiburg

Munich

Landsberg

Salzburg

Basel

Zurich

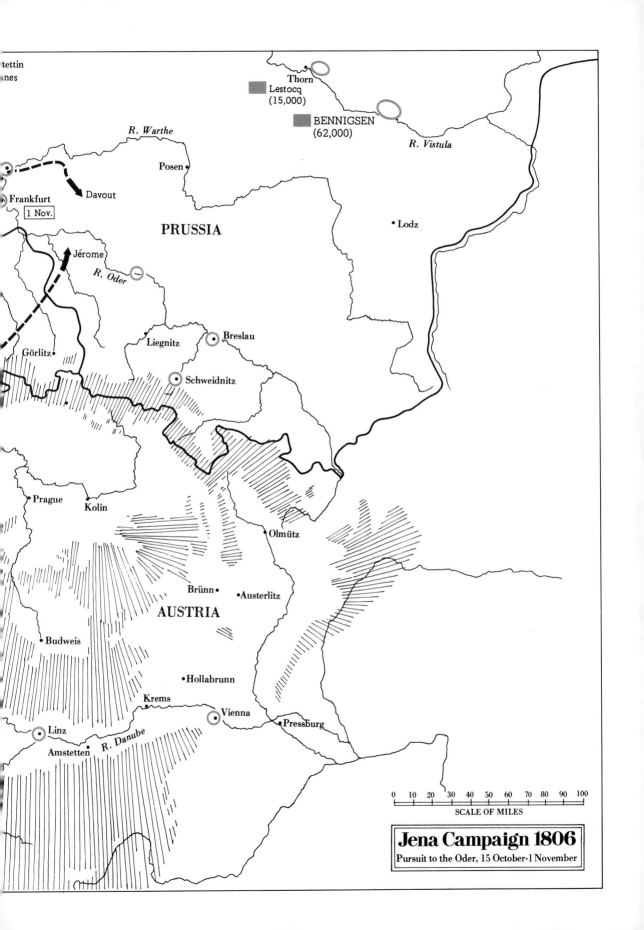

tettin
nes

R. Warthe

Thorn

Lestocq
(15,000)

BENNIGSEN
(62,000)

R. Vistula

Posen •

• Lodz

Frankfurt
1 Nov.

Davout

PRUSSIA

Jérome

R. Oder

Görlitz •

Liegnitz •

Breslau

Schweidnitz

Prague •

Kolin •

Olmütz

Brünn •

• Austerlitz

AUSTRIA

• Budweis

• Hollabrunn

Krems

Vienna

Linz

Pressburg

Amstetten

R. Danube

0   10   20   30   40   50   60   70   80   90   100

SCALE OF MILES

Jena Campaign 1806
Pursuit to the Oder, 15 October-1 November

was cornered in the neutral Hanseatic port of Lübeck, where he had hoped to find his Swedish allies; but most had already re-embarked. The next day the French stormed Lübeck, ruthlessly sacking it and committing grievous atrocities against its civilians. Although this was perhaps his principal contribution to the campaign, Bernadotte nevertheless managed to ingratiate himself with the Swedish prisoners there, thereby – ultimately – taking out an assurance policy for a comfortable old age. Having captured Blücher, Murat now reported laconically to the Emperor: 'Sire, the combat ends for lack of combatants!'

Meanwhile, on 24 October, Napoleon himself had reached Frederick the Great's capital at Potsdam, on the outskirts of Berlin. Respectfully, he went to pay homage at the tomb of the

warlord he had most admired. Inside the tomb, according to Ségur, '... he remained nearly ten minutes, motionless and silent'. Nevertheless he could not quite resist the temptation to 'liberate' as trophies Frederick's sword, belt and Order of the Black Eagle, declaring: 'What a capital present for the Invalides ...!' To Josephine he reported: 'I'm wonderfully well ... I found *Sans Soucis* very agreeable.'

For their distinction at Auerstädt, the honour of entering Berlin first was granted to Davout's III Corps; having completed another staggering march of 166 miles in fourteen days, as well as winning one of the Empire's toughest battles. On 27 October, Napoleon made his own triumphal entry, escorted by the Foot Guard (who had grumbled all the way from Jena, because they had not been permitted to fire a single shot there) up to the Brandenburger Tor, where he received the keys of the fallen city. Among his resplendent marshals, Napoleon seemed, 'with his penny cockade, the most poorly-dressed man in the army', while one observer expressed surprise that such 'lively, impudent, mean-looking little fellows' could have thrashed the best troops of Prussia.

It was a glorious (perhaps *too* glorious) finale to one of the most remarkable campaigns in history; a true *Blitzkrieg* in which, over twenty-four days, the entire military potential of both Prussia and Saxony had been utterly destroyed. In addition to those killed at Jena and Auerstädt, 140,000 prisoners were taken, together with an immense booty totalling 4,000 cannon and 100,000 muskets in Berlin alone. For speed it would beat even Hitler's mechanized triumph over France in 1940.[10] In England, Wordsworth wrote in total gloom:

> *...another deadly blow!*
> *Another mighty Empire overthrown!*
> *And we are left, or shall be left, alone;*

Yet, still, it did not bring peace for Napoleon; nor would Fortune send him any more such easy victories.

Notes to chapter 13

1 Only to be felled by Courbet and the anti-Imperialists of the Paris Commune of 1871 (see Alistair Horne, *The Fall of Paris* and *The Terrible Year*).
2 *A History of the English-Speaking Peoples*, Vol. III, p. 251.
3 *Decisive Battles of the Western World*, Vol. II, p. 418.
4 Fuller, op. cit, p. 421.
5 The actual total forces Napoleon would be able to bring to bear would be 180,000, compared to 171,000 Prussians, thus reversing the numerical ratios of Austerlitz and giving himself an even greater advantage over a less impressive enemy. (On the other hand, the Prussians would be able to field well over twice as many cannon as the French.)
6 In *On War*, p. 91 (New York 1943).
7 See bibliography.
8 Davout's maximum artillery potential was only 40, against 230 for Brunswick.
9 David Chandler, *The Campaigns of Napoleon*, p. 494.
10 See Alistair Horne, *To Lose a Battle – France 1940*.

14

'Another Deadly Blow'

1807

So war was no longer that noble and universal impulse of souls devoted to glory
that he had figured it to be from Napoleon's proclamations!...

Fabrizio, *The Charterhouse of Parma* by Stendhal

FOR ALL THE BRILLIANCE of Napoleon's victory over Prussia, news of it was greeted
with markedly less enthusiasm in Paris than that of Austerlitz. 'So great was the
public desire for peace,' wrote the French historian, Louis Madelin,[1] 'that it even
surpassed the gratification of pride ...' A deputation was sent by the Senate to
Berlin, more to persuade Napoleon to make peace than to offer congratulations. Her economic
problems still unresolved, France was wearying of war and wondering nervously – where next?
    Although his army had been destroyed, his capital and most of his country occupied, and
he himself was a fugitive at Königsberg in faraway East Prussia, Frederick William was still
obstinately refusing to accept peace terms. His resolve had been hardened by the Tsar's promise
to come to his aid (belatedly) with 140,000 men. Further disquieting reports reached Napoleon
that the conquered Austrians, too, were re-arming at his rear. The danger of Russian intervention
(backed, as usual, by English gold) was a very real one; so, to begin with, he found himself
forced to secure the line of the River Oder; then, to take preventive action across it. Next,
the pursuit of the elusive Russians would lead him to the Vistula; and finally across that river
and onto the Niemen, at the very gates of Holy Russia herself. Thus, instead of peace, another
eight months of the grimmest campaigning Napoleon had yet experienced lay ahead of him.
Such are the laws that govern military conquest.
    First, on 21 November, to strike what he intended would be a mortal blow against that
implacable English paymaster before yet another Coalition could be mounted against him,
Napoleon issued the famous 'Berlin Decrees' ordering the closure of all continental ports to
British trade. All commerce was to be seized, even letters 'written in the English language'.
To his brother, King Louis of Holland, he explained that he was 'going to reconquer the
colonies by means of the land'. The beginning of the much vaunted 'Continental System',
this signified land blockade of sea-power – but as such it was to backfire. Immediately there
proved to be numerous 'black market' loopholes, where vast profits were to be made and in
which King Louis himself was one of the worst offenders. In order to provide the *Grande
Armée* with the overcoats it would need for the coming winter, the Minister in Hamburg was
forced to buy the necessary cloth by wheeling-and-dealing on the English market! Meanwhile,

says Winston Churchill,[2] the British blockage wrapped Napoleon's Europe '... in a clammy shroud. No trade, no coffee, no sugar, no contact with the East or with the Americans!' The greatest sufferers were the neutral mercantile nations; particularly the United States.

Pressed on by the logic of his own actions, Napoleon now moved into Prussian Poland to approach England's one remaining ally, Russia, and compel her too to accede to the Continental System. He also had a political motive. Over the previous thirty-five years, the proud but geographically ill-placed Poles had been partitioned three times by their greedy neighbours, Russia, Prussia and Austria – all Napoleon's enemies. Traditionally the Catholic Poles looked – and would long continue to do so – to France as a distant friend, and Napoleon now saw an opportunity to create a new ally in the East between his enemies by reconstituting Poland. More immediately he reckoned it could provide him with 50,000 superbly brave soldiers.

News was received that a powerful Russian army (the one which had materialized too late to help Frederick William) was concentrating there. Following the disgrace of Kutuzov and Buxhöwden at Austerlitz, it was commanded by sixty-one-year-old Count Bennigsen, a Hanoverian who had preferred to choose the Tsar's services and was as yet unblooded in battle against Napoleon. He had been implicated in the murder of Tsar Paul I, and was described as 'a pale, withered personage of high stature and cold appearance, with a scar across his face'. Not lacking in courage, he was however a clumsy tactician. Bennigsen was also supported by some 15,000 Prussians under General Lestocq – all that was left of Frederick William's army, plus elements of Buxhöwden's army moving down from the Niemen. Contemptuously, Napoleon told his troops at Potsdam: '.... The Russians boast of marching on us, but they will find only another Austerlitz...' For the first time, however, he also found himself up against a new and far more dangerous enemy – 'General Winter.'

In sharp contrast to the excellent German highways along which the *Grande Armée* had rattled to the Danube and the Oder, the unmetalled Polish roads had been turned into bottomless morasses of mud by the October deluges. Then savage November frosts changed them into deep frozen ruts; followed by worse mud after an unseasonable thaw in December. Even with quadruple horse teams, cannons sometimes completely disappeared in the mud. The most the infantry could march was $1\frac{1}{4}$ miles in an hour, and their sufferings were appalling; even for the favoured Guard. Wrote Sergeant Coignet of the Grenadiers:[3]

We sunk down up to our knees. We were obliged to take ropes, and tie our shoes around our ankles. ... Sometimes we would have to take hold of one leg, and pull it out as you would a carrot, carrying it forward, and then go back for the other. .... Discontent began to spring up among the old soldiers; some of them committed suicide...

Hospitals filled with the sick; according to Intendant-General Daru, out of every 196 hospital cases during the 1807 campaign, only 47 were wounded. The vast Polish plain west of the Vistula being one of the least fertile areas of Europe, it was no longer possible to 'live off the land', and food became acutely short. Napoleon's ramshackle logistics all but broke down, forcing him to revert to the discarded depot system; all of this slowed down the army's movement. Morale plummeted, with General Rapp noting in December.[4]

Our soldiers were less satisfied; they showed a lively distaste to crossing the Vistula. Misery, the winter, the bad weather, had inspired them with an extreme aversion for this country.

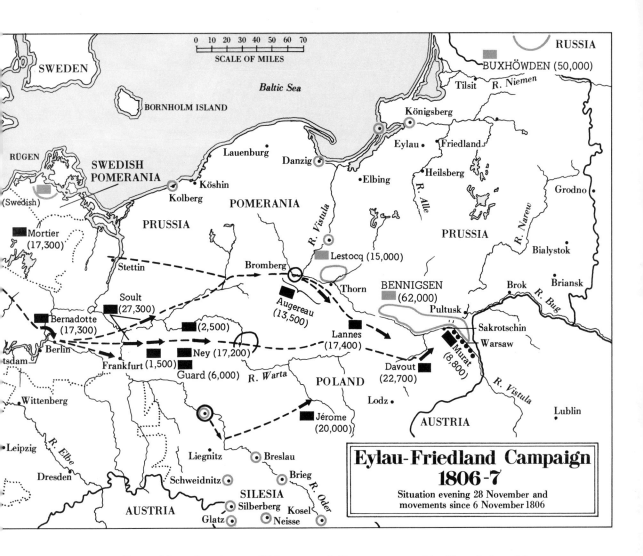

It was supposedly at this point that an ill-humoured Emperor gave his Guard the nickname of *grognards* (grumblers). 'General Winter' was also no respecter of persons; the coach carrying General Duroc overturned, breaking his collarbone, and even Napoleon was forced to ride on horseback into Warsaw, his carriages having been left bogged down on the road.

True to form, the Russians had withdrawn across the Vistula, abandoning Warsaw without a fight. Murat occupied it on 28 November, with Napoleon arriving a few weeks later. Having crossed the broad Vistula, Napoleon now marched – or rather floundered – towards Pultusk on the River Narew, where he hoped to trap a reported Russian concentration. The attack began with Davout surprising Bennigsen in a brilliant night crossing of the River Wkra; something difficult enough to achieve with all the technical innovations of the Second World War, but in 1807 – and in the appalling conditions that prevailed – it showed the sheer genius of Davout and his corps. Despite this first success, however, 26 December saw only two inconclusive battles at Pultusk and Golymin. If there was a victor, it was the mud which had prevented Napoleon from concentrating his forces. Little damaged, Bennigsen returned north-eastwards, towards the

East Prussian capital of Königsberg. Thoroughly disconsolate, Napoleon returned to Warsaw
to reorganize his logistics.

By way of compensation, there now occurred an interlude that was, for Napoleon, to be almost
as important as a campaign, but rather more enduring. Its opening phases are graphically
depicted in his own letters. On entering Poland, he had written to Josephine from Posen on
2 December:

This is the anniversary of Austerlitz. I have been to a ball; it is raining; I am well. I love you and
desire you. . . . All those Polish women are French. There is only one woman for me. Do you know
her? I could draw her portrait; but I should have to make it too flattering if you were to recognize
yourself; however, to tell the truth, my heart would only have agreeable things to say to you.

These nights here are long, all alone . . .

The cryptic references to 'all those Polish women' reveal how profoundly Napoleon's and
Josephine's relationship had altered in the ten years since 1797, when, agonized with jealousy,
he had written from Verona: '. . . You are a wretch. . . . You never write to me at all, you do
not love your husband. . . . Who can this wonderful new lover be who takes up your every
moment . . .?' How the tables had turned! Now aged forty-four, six years older than the husband
for whom she was unable to produce an heir, the Empress was sitting miserably in the boring
provincial German town of Mainz with no one to distract her, bombarding Napoleon with jealous
notes and begging to be allowed to join him. From Warsaw on 20 December, still complaining
about the wet weather, Napoleon wrote: 'I hope, within five or six days, to be able to send
for you.' On New Year's Eve he was writing from Pultusk, after the battles: 'I laughed heartily
on receiving your last letters. You create an image of the Polish beauties that they do not
deserve . . .'

The next day he was eating his words. On his way back to Warsaw he had met Countess
Walewska and been immediately stricken. With his customary despatch, Napoleon wrote to
her the following day: 'I saw only you, I admired only you, I desire only you. A quick answer
will calm the impatient ardour of N.' The next day the enamoured male chauvinist was writing
again to Josephine in a cooler note:

. . . Your pain touches me; but one must submit to events. . . . I have a lot to deal with here. I am
inclined to think you should return to Paris, where you are needed. I am keeping well. The weather
is bad . . .'

Blonde with an exquisitely white skin, intelligent but also soft and yielding, Marie Walewska
gazes disturbingly out of the famous portrait by Lefevre with passionate blue eyes. In this young
wife of an ancient nobleman, virtue vied with patriotism. For nine days she held out, until
Napoleon struck her Polish Achilles heel, imploring: 'Oh come! come! All your wishes shall
be complied with. Your country will become more dear to me if you take compassion on my
poor heart. N.' Meanwhile he was repeatedly telling Josephine (not without truth) that the
roads were impassable, that he could not have her exposed 'to so much fatigue and danger',
that she should return to Paris for the winter, and finally he was urging her to 'be gay and
show some character'. On 1 February, he wrote berating her for her tears and adding,
outrageously: '. . . the trouble is that you have no religion!' It was not long before details of

A portrait of the Countess Marie Walewska, after Lefevre. Patriotic, beautiful and more shapely than her great portrayer, Greta Garbo, she was eternally loyal to Napoleon. How could an Emperor resist!

Napoleon's new love were reaching Josephine. In February she recognized defeat, and crept back miserably to Paris. On 21 February the heartless husband wrote expressing his pleasure that she had been seen at the *Opéra*. Recovering, Josephine began to exact a woman's revenge, provoking angry letters from Poland containing instructions to stop gossiping.

The beautiful, and now adoring, Countess moved into Napoleon's headquarters for the remainder of the campaign. She bore him his first son (who half-a-century later was to become Foreign Secretary to his ill-starred nephew, Louis-Napoleon), and remained loyal to him to the end – even after he had abandoned her to marry an Austrian princess for dynastic reasons. Finally visiting him secretly in exile on Elba, she was, apart from Josephine, probably his only real love. But was Napoleon honourable in his intentions towards the cause for which Walewska had originally given herself? Constantly badgering him to make it a sovereign state, Talleyrand was probably a truer friend to Poland, while Napoleon seems to have had no genuine thought beyond creating a rump duchy or principality dependent upon himself, leaving half the Poles still under foreign domination. 'They have allowed themselves to be partitioned. They are no longer a nation – they have no public spirit,' he once declared contemptuously.

In the middle of his Polish winter idyll, Napoleon was suddenly roused by the disturbing news that Bennigsen had launched a surprise attack on his extended left flank, driving back Ney and Bernadotte towards the west. It was the third week of January. By the end of the month Napoleon had regained his balance, and realized that the Russians, in thrusting westwards, had exposed their southern flank to him. He saw an opportunity to perform one of his favourite manoeuvres – to get in behind the enemy to the east and cut him off from his base at Königsberg. But Fortune continued to play him false; at least on the battlefield. An inexperienced, newly-commissioned staff officer sent with detailed orders to Bernadotte got lost and fell into the hands of Cossacks. On 1 February Bennigsen knew the full plan of Napoleon's envelopment manoeuvre. Exploiting the traditional Russian expertise for winter movement, he slipped out of the trap, withdrawing northwards on Königsberg. Napoleon stumbled after him, once again failing to allow for the state of the roads, now made worse by several feet of snow. On 7 February, Bennigsen turned and stood, like a cornered bear, at the small town of Eylau, only twenty miles south of Königsberg.

On the afternoon of 7 February, Murat and Soult in the van of the army fought a bloody but inconclusive action around the Eylau cemetery. Each side lost about 4,000 men when Bennigsen pulled back to the ridge east of the town. It was clear to Napoleon that he faced a major action the next day. That night the *Grande Armée* experienced its most miserable night since

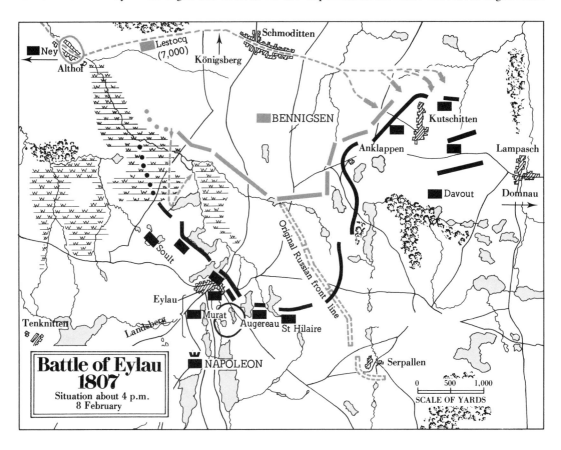

The eve of the Battle of Eylau.
Napoleon cadges potatoes and
firewood off his hungry Guard.

marching out of Boulogne, huddled together in 30 degrees of frost. The Russians had pillaged
all the food in the area; according to Baron Marbot[5], a young captain on Augereau's staff, one
of his regiments had received no rations for eight days and now had to make do with potatoes
and water. Even Napoleon is described as begging a log and a potato from each squad of his
Grenadiers, then squatting by the fire with them. The next morning the half-starved French
attacked, into blinding snowstorms blowing from the east. Such was the chaos of his communications that, out of some 300,000 effectives in Prussia and Poland, Napoleon could immediately
count on only about 45,000 men to face 67,000 Russians, with both totals rising to roughly
75,000 in the course of the day. But, as so often was the case, the Russians had more than
twice the number of guns. Many of the famous names of Austerlitz were once again to the
fore. Murat, Soult with St Hilaire and Legrand; on the other side, Dokhturov and Kamensky
with Bagration in the wings. Notably absent was Lannes, who was seriously ill, while Augereau
– on whom the main weight of the day was to fall – was so sick he could hardly ride. Neither
Ney nor Bernadotte were to take part in the battle[6] for reasons for which, this time, Napoleon
seems to have been to blame. Napoleon's deployment also bore a passing resemblance to Austerlitz: a thrust through the Russian centre (by Augereau's VII Corps), leading to a double
envelopment, with Davout moving up from the south to strike the Russian left flank. But nothing
was to happen according to plan.

Early in the battle, the redoubtable Soult on Napoleon's left flank was severely mauled. A
far worse fate befell the men of the sick but gallant Augereau. The son of a fruit vendor who
at fifty was Napoleon's oldest combat marshal, Augereau permitted his corps to stray fatally
to the left in the blizzard, presenting its flank to a powerful concentration of 72 Russian cannon.
With the snow blowing from behind them, Bennigsen's gunners could see the advancing

OVERLEAF *The Battle of Eylau*, 8 February 1807, by Siméon Fort. Napoleon throws in Murat's cavalry and the
Guard to assist Augereau, badly mauled by the Russians after his Corps had lost its way in the blizzard. On
the left, the disputed cemetery and the church belfry used by Napoleon as an observation post, and where he
narrowly escaped capture by the Russians.

French, but not vice versa, and they raked them with a merciless hail of shot at almost point-blank range. Worse still, their straying brought Augereau's men under the fire of their own artillery, which was maintaining a blind bombardment into the obscurity. By 10.30 a.m. VII Corps had virtually ceased to exist (the first time that such a disaster had ever overtaken Napoleon); Marbot, who was later severely wounded, claims that the corps now numbered no more than two to three thousand. The French position was extremely precarious, and at one point Napoleon – up in Eylau's church tower – came perilously close to being engulfed himself by the advancing Russians. At 11.30 a.m., he called on Murat and his cavalry reserve to fill the vacuum in the shattered French centre. Now re-equipped with superb horses taken from the Prussians, Murat found his moment of true glory, sweeping forward into the massed Russians in one of the greatest cavalry charges in history. Behind followed the Horse Grenadiers of the Guard, the élite 'big heels,' their colonel, Lepic, shouting 'Heads up, by God!' when they ducked the bursting shells: 'Those are bullets – not turds!'

After Eylau, Murat's action established the French heavy cavalry as 'the dread of Europe and the pride of France'; more immediately it had saved the day for Napoleon. In the respite provided, Davout's newly-arrived corps bit into Bennigsen's left flank, bending his whole line back 'like a hairpin'.[7] By mid-afternoon it looked as if the Russians might break; then, in the nick of time, Lestocq arrived with his 7,000 Prussians and in turn took Davout on his exposed (right) flank. According to one of his officers, Pasquier, even Davout was about to sound the retreat as dusk fell, when:

... Putting his ear to the ground he recognized the distinct sounds of cavalry and guns on the move, and as the noise was receding ... he no longer doubted that the enemy was in full retreat.

There was no question of any pursuit. Like Jellicoe at Jutland, Napoleon was left in possession of the field but he had suffered (again for the first time) far higher losses than the enemy. Before the battle he was boasting to Cambacérès 'I am going to throw it [the Russian army] the other side of the Niemen'; afterwards, his letters reveal an unusual humility. To Talleyrand, he was revealing that the day had been 'pretty risky'; to Josephine, 'I have lost a lot of people'; while he made a rare admission that his 'soul was oppressed to see so many victims'. But Napoleon's own figure of 1,000 killed and 4,000 wounded was cast ridiculously low; David Chandler puts the overall total possibly as high as 25,000, compared to 15,000 for the Russians (and Prussians). No less than 23 French generals were also among the casualties. The suffering of the wounded exposed on the frozen battlefield was unimaginable; it was not much better once they had been removed to the barns in the neighbourhood that had been converted into temporary hospitals, because the thatch from the roofs had been removed to feed the cavalry horses. Of those lucky enough to have been evacuated, many died on the long jolting journey back to base hospitals in Prussia. But, as always, the suffering was that much worse on the Russian side where medical provisions were virtually non-existent.

When Napoleon visited his troops the following day, more surly cries of '*Vive la paix!*' and '*Du pain et de la paix!*' greeted him than the usual shouts of '*Vive l'Empereur!*', while Ney made one lapidary remark on surveying the battlefield: '*Quel massacre! Et sans résultat!*' If Eylau had any results, they were all unfavourable to Napoleon. It was the first time since Egypt, eight years previously, that he had experienced such a reverse on land. After Eylau, something of the terrifying mystique of the *Grande Armée* had evaporated; for the first time also; it had been fought to a standstill, and was proven to be invincible no longer. The effect this would have on Napoleon's enemies in the long run was to be considerable. Unfortunately for France, five years later Napoleon would have forgotten the lessons of this bitter winter battle.

He now withdrew to reorganize his forces for a spring campaign, made inevitable by the drawn results of Eylau, and found solace whenever he could in the arms of his fair Pole. Reaching down deep into the barrel, Napoleon called up part of the class of 1808, eighteen months ahead of schedule, thereby raising a new army 100,000 strong, plus two new Polish divisions. But already it was not the same in quality as the First *Grande Armée* that had set off so zestfully from Boulogne eighteen months previously. On the other side, encouraged by Eylau which Allied propaganda had converted into something resembling a major victory, a new 'Coalition' all but got off the ground. Under the Convention of Bartenstein on 26 April, Russia and Prussia bound themselves to drive Napoleon out of Germany, with Britain undertaking to subsidize Prussia with yet another one million pounds. But a month later the fortified port of Danzig surrendered, after an old-fashioned siege lasting three months; this released another 20,000 French troops to join in the pursuit of Bennigsen.

By the beginning of June, Napoleon was on the move again; squeezing the Russians once more towards Königsberg. The roads had dried out to a dusty hardness. A rashly-conceived attack by Bennigsen was broken, leaving the Russian commander off balance. Napoleon now slid northwards along the west bank of the tortuous River Alle, dangerously threatening Bennigsen's links with Königsberg. On 13 June, Murat and Soult were sent directly against the city from the south, thereby forcing a disagreeable choice on Bennigsen. He would either have to withdraw to the east, abandoning Königsberg and with it the rest of East Prussia and Poland, or else remain on the west bank of the Alle to fight and defend the city. Napoleon guessed correctly that Bennigsen would adopt the latter course; but where? At dawn the next day, Lannes came up against Bennigsen's main army holding the small town of Friedland, its back to the Alle. With only 26,000 men facing at least 45,000 Russians, Lannes realized at once that it was his duty to pin Bennigsen down until Napoleon and the rest of the army could arrive. This he achieved for some nine hard hours, by shifting his effectives skilfully from one end of the front to the other. On seeing the situation, Napoleon at once realized that he had Bennigsen at an impossible disadvantage; crushed into a small space on the wrong side of an unfordable river, and connected to the rear by only three hastily-prepared pontoon bridges, Bennigsen's front was also bisected laterally by the *Mühlen Fluss* (or mill stream), with Bagration to the south of it and Gorchakov to the north.

Napoleon's staff urged caution: wait another day until Murat and Davout could bring the army up to overwhelming strength. But Napoleon was adamant: 'We can't hope to surprise the enemy making the same mistake twice.' By 4 p.m. he had 80,000 French opposing 60,000 Russians. Baron Marbot, sent by Lannes to report developments, found the Emperor 'radiating joy'. Smiling, he asked Marbot if he knew what anniversary it was:

'That of Marengo.' 'Yes, yes ... and I am going to beat the Russians just as I beat the Austrians!'

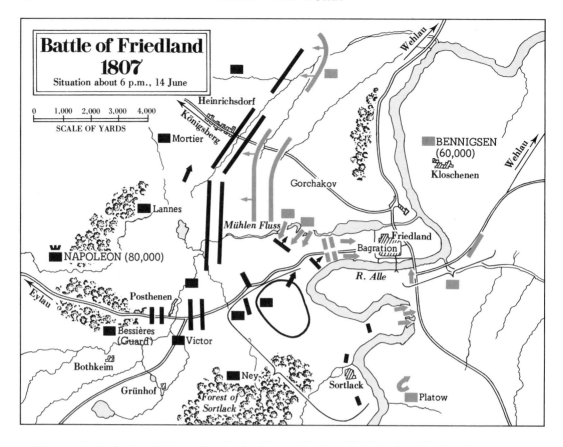

**Battle of Friedland
1807**
Situation about 6 p.m., 14 June

Ney – who had missed Austerlitz (he had been clearing the Tyrol) and played only a minor role at both Jena and Eylau – was selected to lead the attack, against Bagration on the Russian left flank. It was evidently just in time as Bennigsen, realizing his plight, was giving orders to withdraw across the Alle; where once again his army would have escaped destruction. Initially Bagration's cannon, massed across the river, inflicted heavy losses on Ney's infantry. Then Napoleon threw in I Corps, which he had been holding in reserve, now commanded by Victor. A new star among Napoleon's commanders, Victor (his real name was Claude-Victor Perrin) had started life as a bandsman in Louis XVI's army, and served as Chief-of-Staff to Lannes in 1806. In marked contrast to his predecessor Bernadotte (who had retired with a head wound from a spent musket ball) he was a combat officer full of thrust. Deploying his cannon in much the same way as Rommel was to use his anti-tank guns in the Western Desert, Victor wheeled thirty of them forward in a series of bounds; first to 600 yards from the Russians, then 300, then 150. At each bound the guns poured a devastating salvo into Bagration's densely-massed men. Finally the guns halted at 60 yards, almost point-blank range, reducing whole companies to a shambles with canister-shot. Inside of twenty-five minutes, 4,000 Russian infantrymen had been bowled over, while cavalry trying to silence the deadly guns suffered a similar fate. At the same time the combined efforts of the French artillery set on fire Bennigsen's pontoon bridges. Trapped in Friedland, the Russians formed one vast and largely unprotected target.

Eylau redeemed. Napoleon victorious after his crushing defeat of Bennigsen on the ill-chosen
field of Friedland. The end of the campaigns that began with Ulm and Austerlitz in 1805, and left
Napoleon undisputed master of continental Europe. Painting by Horace Vernet.

As his final effort, Bennigsen sent in the Russian Imperial Guard. Ney's infantry fell with
bayonets on these 'northern giants ... the last and redoubtable hope of the great enemy army'.
It was, wrote a participant,[8] 'a victory of pygmies over giants ...'

Discovering a ford north of Friedland, Bennigsen managed to evacuate the ruins of his army
across the Alle under cover of darkness, but leaving behind 11,000 dead and 7,000 wounded
– a third of his effectives. Eighty guns, but few prisoners were taken, and over the next days
the local inhabitants – revenging themselves for months of brutal mistreatment and pillaging
– mercilessly hunted down Russian stragglers. Bennigsen was a broken man. For a total French
loss of less than 10,000, Napoleon had at last won the decisive victory that had eluded him
over the previous six months' campaigning. To Josephine he reported:

My children have worthily celebrated the anniversary of Marengo. The battle of Friedland will
be just as famous and as glorious for my people. . . . It is a worthy sister of Marengo, Austerlitz and
Jena. . . . Goodbye, dear friend, I am just getting into the saddle,

he added ambiguously.

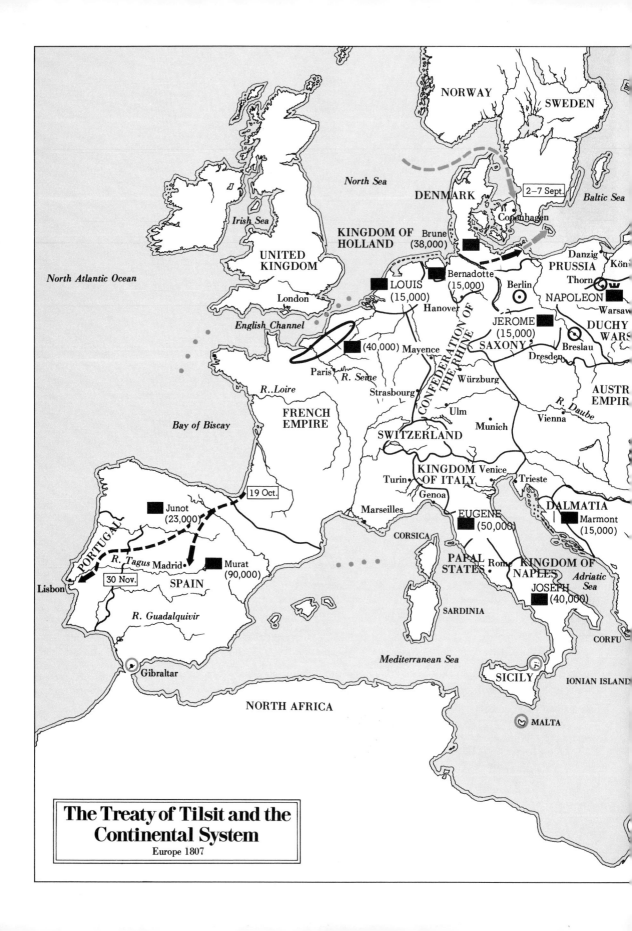

NORWAY

SWEDEN

North Sea

DENMARK

2–7 Sept.

Baltic Sea

Irish Sea

Copenhagen

KINGDOM OF
HOLLAND

Brune
(38,000)

Danzig

Kön

PRUSSIA

Thorn

UNITED
KINGDOM

Bernadotte
(15,000)

Berlin

NAPOLEON

North Atlantic Ocean

LOUIS
(15,000)

Hanover

Warsaw

London

JEROME
(15,000)

DUCHY
WARS

English Channel

(40,000) Mayence

SAXONY

Breslau

Dresden

AUSTR
EMPIR

Paris

R. Seine

Würzburg

R. Daube

R..Loire

Strasbourg

Ulm

Vienna

FRENCH
EMPIRE

Bay of Biscay

SWITZERLAND

Munich

KINGDOM
OF ITALY

Venice

Trieste

Turin

Genoa

DALMATIA

Marmont
(15,000)

Marseilles

CORSICA

EUGENE
(50,000)

19 Oct.

Junot
(23,000)

PAPAL
STATES

Rome

KINGDOM OF
NAPLES

Adriatic
Sea

PORTUGAL

R. Tagus Madrid

30 Nov.

SPAIN

Murat
(90,000)

JOSEPH
(40,000)

CORFU

Lisbon

R. Guadalquivir

SARDINIA

Mediterranean Sea

SICILY

IONIAN ISLAND

Gibraltar

NORTH AFRICA

MALTA

The Treaty of Tilsit and the
Continental System

Europe 1807

St. Petersburg

Moscow

R. Niemen

(100,000)

RUSSIA

R. Dnieper

R. Dniester

R. Donets

R. Volga

MOLDAVIA

(50,000)

R. Don

CRIMEA

WALLACHIA

R. Danube

Black Sea

Caspian Sea

Constantinople

OTTOMAN EMPIRE

ANELLES

Acre

Alexandria

Cairo

| 0 | 100 | 200 | 300 | 400 | 500 |

SCALE OF MILES

Next to Austerlitz, Friedland was probably Napoleon's most distinguished victory; but it had been a hard fought one, and his manoeuvring beforehand had certainly not been as impressive as that which preceded Ulm or Jena.

On 19 June, Murat's cavalry reached the River Niemen near Tilsit, over one thousand miles from Paris. There they were met by the Tsar's envoys, sent to request an armistice. Internal pressures inside a hungry and disoriented Russia had become too great for him to continue the war. In the less than two years since he had paced the cliffs at Boulogne in deepest frustration, Napoleon had won Ulm, Austerlitz, Jena and Friedland. They added up to:

... the longest, the most daring expedition, not through defenceless Persia or India, like the army of Alexander, but through Europe, swarming with soldiers as well-disciplined as brave ... unparalleled in the history of the ages...

wrote Thiers.[9] No unqualified admirer of the victor, he added, however; 'Everyone will ask himself how it was possible to display so much prudence in war, so little in politics.' Yet none of this was immediately apparent when, the following week, Napoleon, at the peak of his power, received the Tsar aboard his raft on the Niemen. At that sublime moment of glory, 'he dominated all Europe' (says Winston Churchill[10]):

The Emperor of Austria was a cowed and obsequious satellite. The King of Prussia and his handsome queen were beggars, and almost captives in his train. Napoleon's brothers reigned as Kings at The Hague, at Naples, and in Westphalia...

The treaties with both the Tsar and Frederick William were signed by 9 July, and that same evening Napoleon set off on the long journey back to Paris, bringing with him – so it seemed – prosperity and peace in his time. He was eager to resume the business that had been rudely interrupted by the Prussians the previous summer. To his Minister of the Interior he wrote menacingly: '*Monsieur le Ministre*, peace has been made with the foreigners; now I am going to make war on your offices ...' Orders were dispatched to remove the last of the ancient houses perched on the Seine bridges because they spoiled the view down the river; a new bridge was to be built, the Pont d'Iéna, named after the victory of the previous year.[11] The Imperial Court assumed a new brilliance, with Napoleon spending much of his time hunting and shooting, attending parades and court entertainments. At the end of November, the Imperial Guard marched into Paris in full regimentals, the bands playing 'What Better than to be Home with your Family?' All Paris went mad; the military fête lasted a month, with the theatres giving free performances specially for the heroes of the Guard. But already there were shadows...

Almost immediately after Tilsit, France was surprised by the unexpected resignation of Talleyrand as Foreign Minister. Talleyrand had disapproved of the humiliating terms Napoleon had insisted on exacting after each of his recent triumphs, and Tilsit was the last straw. From now on began Talleyrand's active opposition to his Emperor; an opposition which ended in treason. He was convinced now that Napoleon could only bring more, and endless, war to France. To the Tsar, Talleyrand would soon be appealing:

Sire, it is in your power to save Europe, and you will only do so by refusing to give way to Napoleon. The French people are civilized, their sovereign is not. The sovereign of Russia is civilized and his people are not: the sovereign of Russia should therefore be the ally of the French people.

The SPANISH - BULL - FIGHT. _ or _ the CORSICAN-MATADOR in Danger _

But still no lasting peace for Napoleon. In 1808, the 'Spanish ulcer' erupts, eventually destined to bring him down. Note the unfortunate plight of brother Joseph, 'King of Spain', which the other royal *afficionados* of Europe look on and applaud. Cartoon by Gillray.

Talleyrand's defection marked the turning-point in Napoleon's fortunes. Already the month before the Guard arrived back in Paris, a new expedition under General Junot was on its way, westwards now across the Pyrenees and into Spain and Portugal. It looked like the old, familiar tale all over again – but this time a terrible novelty in modern warfare was introduced. In the summer of 1808, the Spanish people rose in violent, savage revolt against the harsh French occupation and called upon England to intervene. 'The opportunity,' says Arthur Bryant, 'for which Pitt had sought so long, and of which his successors had grown to despair, had come at last.' England now had her 'second front' on the Continent. In the nearly six long years of grinding attrition that lay ahead, by Napoleon's own admission it was 'the Spanish ulcer' which was eventually to bring about his destruction.

In England the truly remarkable fact was that, far from urging her to seek an accommodation, every successive continental disaster up to Tilsit only seemed to rouse her to greater heights of patriotic fervour and to stir her resolve. Afterwards, the general attitude was summed up by Tom Campbell[12]: 'If Bonaparte has beat the Russians, he has not yet beaten English freemen on their own soil!' Within a month, Britain showed what mastery of the seas could do to the land-locked 'Continental System' by launching a ruthless pre-emptive blow against the neutral Danish fleet at Copenhagen, to prevent it falling into Napoleon's hands. From now on, in effect, the Continental System – and Napoleon – would be on the defensive. Following Tilsit, France herself undoubtedly experienced an illusory period of unprecedented economic prosperity. But – as with Hitler's Reich in the halcyon years of 1940–2 – it was largely at the cost of her subjugated neighbours, and as such was to build up a massive reservoir of resentment against Napoleon, which in due course would play its due role in his downfall. Also, the Continental System never really worked; as late as 1810, embattled Britain would still somehow be receiving over 80 per cent of her wheat imports from France or her allies, while in the long run its failure would turn out to be perhaps fatal for France herself.

British experience with the Napoleonic Blockade was, a century later, to have a most important influence in the shaping of grand strategy in both world wars. Indeed, in the Second World War the timetable for Britain shows a curious similarity to what happened during the Napoleonic Wars:

1 Defeat of the First Coalition. (1939–40)
2 Banishment of Britain from Europe. (Dunkirk)
3 Failure of invasion from Europe and triumph of sea power. (1940–1)
4 Formation of new coalitions but continuing enemy land triumphs. (1941–2)
5 Backbone of enemy broken in Russia. (1942–4)

The parallel ends there; in 1815, with Napoleon defeated and the rest of Europe exhausted by war and blockade, the field was left clear for Britain 'to become the workshop and the banker of the world, the very thing Napoleon had sought to prevent'[13]; in 1945, it was Britain that emerged devitalized.

Once the spirit of Tilsit had begun to wear thin, more than any other factor it was the Continental System and its consequences that led Napoleon on the fell road to Moscow in 1812; just as it was, still, the English dynamo and treasury that would continue to sustain his enemies. 'Russia was the last resource of England,' Napoleon admitted on St. Helena, 'The peace of the world rested with Russia. Alas! English gold proved more powerful than my plans.' But, by 1815, England herself would at last provide Wellington with a land force capable of meeting, and beating, the *Grande Armée*.

For the *Grande Armée*, Tilsit was a kind of watershed, after which it never seemed quite the same again. First of all, with longed-for peace at hand it would prove difficult to keep up the old revolutionary fervour, let alone the standard of training with which it had marched out of the Camp of Boulogne in 1805. While recruitment grew increasingly inefficient, losses had left their mark, particularly those suffered at Eylau, and particularly among the *cadres*. Goering-like, some of the marshals began to wax fat on the fruits (and loots) of peace. They took to quarrelling with each other and disobeying orders. As a result of all this, after 1807 units of the *Grande Armée* were less capable of performing the complex manoeuvres that had brought victory at Austerlitz and Auerstädt, and they indulged more in costly mass tactics. Meanwhile, enemy armies were at last studying and emulating the Napoleonic technique; for instance, after 1807 it was discovered that Napoleon's valuable shock weapon, his shield of skirmishers, could no longer shake a prepared enemy line. He would also find himself fighting in countries where, for the first time, the inhabitants would prove virulently hostile. Finally, with each succeeding battle, the forces present grew steadily larger, and this had a disastrous effect on Napoleon's highly personal style of command. He had but one great victory of the old kind left in his quiver: the Battle of Wagram in 1809, fought against the Austrians unsupported, but resulting in an unprecedentedly high casualty ratio of 32,000 French to 40,000 Austrians. For as the armies grew larger, so did the casualty lists, until, at grim Leipzig in 1812, a terrible battle of attrition cost Napoleon 73,000 men (or eight times the losses at Austerlitz) to 54,000 of the enemy.[14] The *Grande Armée* never recovered.

The lessons to be derived from Napoleon's amazing run of victories in 1805–7 are those that have been learned (or not learned) by military adventurers through the ages, from Xerxes to Hitler – there is seldom is such a thing as a *limited* victory. One conquest only leads on, ineluctably, to another, to protect what has already been won. Napoleon's wars on the Continent had gained him no real friends (Talleyrand understood this), only crushed enemies; 'Prussia vanquished but fuming, Austria secretly implacable', in the words of Thiers. Resurgent already in 1809, only to be knocked down again at Wagram, Austria would be at Napoleon's throat once more in the Leipzig campaign of 1812. As far as the Russian colossus was concerned, although Napoleon had left Tilsit persuaded that he had effectively seduced the Tsar – 'estranged from England by the paltry support he had received' (Churchill[15]) – it was clearly a seduction requiring constant attention and refurbishment. For it was upon Russia's continuing benevolence that Napoleon's grandiose future schemes depended; unlike Austria and Prussia, she alone had not been invaded and subjugated on her own territory; her armies had been defeated in a series of great battles, but all of them on somebody else's soil; and, in terms of manpower she still remained the world's most powerful land force. Defeated in 1805 and 1807, invaded and desperately mauled in 1812, in 1814 the Tsar's armies would be in Paris, forcing Napoleon to abdicate.

There remained the role of Prussia, in 1806 more deplorably humiliated than all the rest of his enemies. ('Don't beat so loud – he's only a king!', the drummers of Napoleon's Guard had been contemptuously ordered when Frederick William arrived at Tilsit). Despite Talleyrand's warning, Napoleon committed his gravest error at Tilsit in imposing the harsh terms which, *inter alia*, deprived Prussia of half its territories and subjected it to a degrading occupation. At Jena he had destroyed a feudal army, as well as the feudal nation to which it belonged. But he would be responsbile for the *national* army which, out of the ashes, would arise to destroy him at Leipzig, in the War of the Nations. Although Napoleon had defeated every professional army in Europe, it was the sheer numerical weight of the resurgent peoples that finally ground him down. As he himself once confessed: 'Against greatly superior forces, it is possible to win a battle, but hardly a war.' In the long run (as Hitler was to discover), military brilliance is not enough; numbers are what count.

In the wider historical context, Jena was perhaps to produce the most dire political

Napoleon watching Moscow burn in 1812. Eylau should have forewarned him. Detail of a painting by an unknown French artist of the nineteenth century. (Some believe it could have been Géricault.)

consequences for successive generations of Napoleon's countrymen; and, indeed, all Europe. His attempts to sweep away the medieval structure of the German states and 're-order' it – much as he had done in North Italy – would unwittingly pave the way for German unification. Out of it would emerge a new super-state east of the Rhine: the Prussian-led German Reich. Sixty-five years after Austerlitz, it would inflict upon Napoleon's own nephew as shattering a defeat as any he had ever dealt out.

Perhaps the superb irony of Napoleon's culminating years of glory, 1805–7, lies in what he did to the ethos of the French Revolution, the impetus of which had so materially aided him in his conquering sweep to the Niemen. While at home, in France, he had put into reverse many of its principles, he carried those same principles in the baggage-train of the *Grande Armée* to the nations it conquered. Born and bred in Paris, ideals of liberty, egalitarianism and nationalism had been unleashed among all the European peoples, and – long after Napoleon's conquests were forgotten – these would clash resoundingly with the Old Order.

Notes to chapter 14

1 *Le Consulat et l'Empire*, Chapter I, p. 307.

2 *A History of the English-Speaking Peoples*, Vol. III, p. 254.

3 *The Narrative of Captain Coignet*, ed. Loredan Larchey, p. 138 (New York 1890).

4 *Mémoires*, p. 118 (Paris 1823).

5 *Mémoires*, (Paris 1891).

6 Ney's arrival late in the afternoon did, however, influence Bennigsen's decision to withdraw from the disputed battlefield.

7 David Chandler, *The Campaigns of Napoleon*, p. 545.

8 J. de Norvins, *Souvenirs d'une Histoire de Napoléon*, pp. 204–5 (Paris 1897).

9 *The Consulate and Empire*, Vol. VII, p. 362.

10 Op. cit., Vol. III, p. 254.

11 In 1815, Blücher was for having it destroyed, to erase a national affront; Wellington intervened to save it.

12 Arthur Bryant, *Years of Victory*, p. 221.

13 Major General J. F. C. Fuller, *The Decisive Battles of the Western World*, Vol. II, p. 441 (London 1954–56).

14 David Chandler's figures (op. cit. p. 1120), which however include some 30,000 prisoners on the French side.

15 Op. cit., Vol. III, p. 252.

Notes on Source Material

Even a 'select biography' covering this period of Napoleon's life would fill many pages, so only those sources actually consulted or referred to have been listed. Certain primary material (for example, Napoleon's Correspondence) has been used throughout, and among the secondary accounts similarly exploited are A. Thiers' and the (more recent) study by David Chandler, which contrives remarkably to contain in one volume far more than just the military aspects of *The Campaigns of Napoleon*. Also used throughout have been the West Point publications by J. Esposito and J. R. Elting, and A. S. Britt III, for details of Napoleon's strategic and tactical movements, as well as J. F. C. Fuller's more compressed account in his *The Decisive Battles of the Western World*. For the Ulm–Austerlitz campaign, I have drawn extensively on Christopher Duffy's recent study, which is particularly good on the Allied side of the hill, and also the (somewhat more flamboyant and French-orientated) account by Claude Manceron. For details of warfare techniques, both of Napoleon and his enemies, I found G. E. Rothenberg's concise book valuable. Among many sources used in the wider background of both Revolutionary and Napoleonic France, George Rudé's *Revolutionary Europe 1783–1815* and J. C. Herold's *The Age of Napoleon* seemed particularly useful. But on the English backdrop to the Napoleonic Wars, I am particularly indebted to Arthur Bryant's *The Years of Victory*; though written under the influence of the threat of Hitler, it still stands up astonishingly well to the passage of time, conveying a picture of contemporary Britain that is hard to better.

SELECT BIBLIOGRAPHY

Anderson, J. H. *The Napoleonic Campaign of 1805* London 1912

Baldet, Marcel *La Vie Quotidienne dans les Armées de Napoléon* Paris 1964

Barnett, Corelli *Bonaparte* London 1978

Bidou, Henry *Paris* London 1939

Bonal, H. *La Manoeuvre de Iéna* Paris 1855

Bourienne, M. de *Memoirs of Napoleon Bonaparte* London 1836

Bowle, John *Napoleon* London 1973

Britt III, A. S. *Campaign Atlas to Wars of Napoleon* New York 1972
The Wars of Napoleon New York 1977

Bryant, A. *The Years of Endurance* London 1942
The Years of Victory London 1944

Burton, Lt. Col. R. G. *From Boulogne to Austerlitz* London 1912

Caulaincourt, Gen. A. A. L. de *Memoirs* London 1950

Chandler, D. G. *The Campaigns of Napoleon* London 1967

Christian, R. F. *Tolstoy's War and Peace. A Study* London 1962

Churchill, W. S. *A History of the English Speaking Peoples*, III London 1957

Clausewitz, Gen. C. von *On War* London 1962

Clunn, Harold *The Face of Paris* London 1933

Coignet, Capt. J. R. *The Notebooks of Captain Coignet* London 1929

Colin, Comdt. J. *La Campagne de 1805 en Allemagne, Revue Historique de l'Armée* Paris 1905–7

Cooper, Duff *Talleyrand* London 1932

Crankshaw, Edward *The Habsburgs* London 1971

Creevey *The Creevey Papers (ed. Sir H. Maxwell)* London 1903–5

Czartoryski, Prince A. *Memoirs* London 1888

Davout, Marshal *Opérations du 3ᵉ Corps 1806–1807: Rapport du Maréchal Davout, Duc d'Auerstädt* Paris 1904

Dixon, Pierson *Pauline: Napoleon's Favourite Sister* London 1964

Duffy, Christopher *Austerlitz, 1805* London 1977

Ermolov, A.P. *Zapiski [Memoirs]* Moscow 1865

Esposito, Brig. Gen. Vincent J. and Elting, Col. John Robert *A Military History and Atlas of the Napoleonic Wars* New York 1963

Fairon, E. and Heusse, H. *Lettres des Grognards* Paris 1936

Fraser, Antonia *Love Letters* London 1976

Fuller, Maj. Gen. J.F.C. *The Decisive Battles of the Western World*, Vol II London 1957

Goltz, Gen. C. von *Jena to Eylau: The Disgrace and Redemption of the Old Prussian Army* New York 1913

Harvey, P. and Heseltine, J.E. *The Oxford Companion to French Literature* Oxford 1959

Herold, J.C. *The Age of Napoleon* London 1963 (ed.) *The Mind of Napoleon* London 1955

Janetschek, C. *Die Schlacht bei Austerlitz* Brünn 1898

Jarrett, Derek *Pitt the Younger* London 1974

Jomini, Gen. Baron Antoine H. *The Art of War* Philadelphia 1875 *Life of Napoleon* Kansas City 1897

Keegan, John *The Face of Battle* London 1976

Lachouque, Comdt. Henry *Napoléon à Austerlitz* Paris 1960

Lachouque, Henry and Brown, Anne S.K. *The Anatomy of Glory: Napoleon and his Guard* London 1961

Las Cases, Comte E.P.D. *Mémorial de Ste Hélène* Paris 1823

Laver, James *The Age of Illusion* London 1972

Lejeune, Col. L.F. *Souvenirs d'un Officer sous l'Empire* Paris n.d.

Lewis, Gwynne *Life in Revolutionary France* London 1972

Lombarès, M. *Devant Austerlitz. Sur les Traces de la Pensée de l'Empereur, Revue Historique de l'Armée* Paris 1947

Madelin, L. *Le Consultat et l'Empire* Paris 1932

Mahan, Admiral A.T. *Influence of Sea Power upon the French Revolution and Empire* London 1892

Manceron, Claude *Austerlitz* London 1966

Marbot, Baron M. de *Mémoires* Paris 1891

Masson, F. *Napoléon et les Femmes* Paris 1894

Maurois, A. *Chateaubriand* London 1938

Méneval, Baron C.F. *Mémoires* Paris 1894

Mikhailovsky-Danilevsky, Lt.-Gen. *Opisanie Pervoi Voiny Imperatora Aleksandra s Napoleonom v 1805-m Godu* 1844

Montgomery, Field Marshal *A History of Warfare* London 1968

Montholon and Gourgaud *Memoirs of Napoleon*, Vols I and II London 1823

Morison, S.E. *The Oxford History of the American Peoples* New York 1965

Napoleon I *La Correspondance de Napoléon 1ᵉʳ*, Vols XI–XV Paris 1862, *Maximes* Paris 1874

Norvins, J. de *Souvenirs d'un histoire de Napoléon* Paris 1897

Oman, Carola *Nelson* London 1947 *Napoleon at the Channel* New York 1942

Parquin, Capt. D.C. *Napoleon's Army* Camden, Conn. 1969

Pocock, Tom *Remember Nelson* London 1977

Quennevat, J.-C. *Atlas de la Grande Armée* Paris 1966

Rapp, Gen. Count J. *Mémoires* Paris 1821

Rémusat, Mme. C. de *Mémoires* Paris 1893

Rogers, Col. H.C.B. *Napoleon's Army* London 1974

Rothenberg, G.E. *The Art of Warfare in the Age of Napoleon* London 1977

Rudé, George *Revolutionary Europe 1783–1815* London 1967

Savary, Gen. A.J.R. *Mémoire sur l'Empire* Paris 1828

Ségur, Gen. P. Comte de *Histoire et Mémoires* Paris 1837

Stendhal, H.B. *The Charterhouse of Parma* London 1962

Stutterheim, Major-Gen. *A Detailed Account of the Battle of Austerlitz* London 1807

Thiébault, Gen. A.C. *Memoirs* London 1896

Thiers, A. *History of the Consulate and Empire*, Books XIX–XXIV, Vols. VI and VII London 1845

Tolstoy, Leo *War and Peace* London 1869

Trevelyan, G.M. *English Social History* London 1944

Weber, Eugene *Peasants into Frenchmen. The Modernisation of Rural France, 1870–1914* London 1977

Wilson, Major Gen. Sir R. *Brief Remarks on the Character and Composition of the Russian Army* London 1810 *Narrative of Events during the Invasion of Russia* London 1860

Yorck von Wartenburg, Gen. *Napoleon as a General* London 1902

Young, Peter *Napoleon's Marshals* London 1973

Acknowledgments

The author and publisher would like to thank the following museums, collections and private individuals by whose kind permission the illustrations are reproduced. The page numbers of those pictures reproduced in colour are italicized.

By gracious permission of Her Majesty the Queen 183 (left)
Bibliothèque Nationale, Paris 73 (below)
Bildarchiv der Osterreichische Nationalbibliothek, Vienna 44
Bobrinskoy Collection 220
British Museum 48
Jean-Loup Charmet 2
Department of the Environment 59
René Dazy 39
Francoise Foliot 91
John Freeman 15, 184 (below), 177, 199
Giraudon endpapers left-hand page left, left-hand page right, 8, 12, 19, 37, 194
Samuel S. Kress Collection endpapers right-hand page centre
Mansell Collection 49, *51*, 83, 159
Paul Martin 95
National Maritime Museum 115
Ogonyok, Moscow 135 (above left)
Photo Bulloz endpapers left-hand page centre, right-hand page left, right-hand page right, 16 (above), 18, 24–5, *33 (above)*, *34*, 43, *52*, 54, 56, 64–5, 68, 76–7, 87, 90, 100, 103, 110 (below), 113 (below), 114, 119, 122, 133, 135 (below), *141, 142–3, 144 (above)*, *144 (below)*, 151, 153, 155, 166–7, 171, 172, 184 (above), 198–9, 205, 207, 208–9, 217
Réunion des musées nationaux, Paris 16 (below), 31, 38, 104, 122–3, 139, 147, 157, 213
Snark International *33 (below)*
Studio Laverton 29 (below), 178
Victoria and Albert Museum 26 (above), 41, 42, 183 (right)
Rogert Viollet 79
Weidenfeld and Nicolson Archives 135 (above right)

The author and publisher would also like to thank the Department of History, United States Military Academy for their permission to base the maps in the text on maps from the following books:
A Military History and Atlas of the Napoleonic Wars by Vincent J. Esposito and John Robert Elting, the maps on pages 108, 109, 110, 113, 126–7, 149, 156, 167, 192, 193, 196–7, 214–15.

Campaign Atlas to Wars of Napoleon by A. S. Britt III, the maps on pages 72–73, 80–1, 186–7, 203, 206, 212.

The author and publisher are grateful to David Chandler for his permission to adapt the diagrams which appear on pages 92–3, 96, 97, and 152, which are based on those in *The Campaigns of Napoleon.*

Index

13

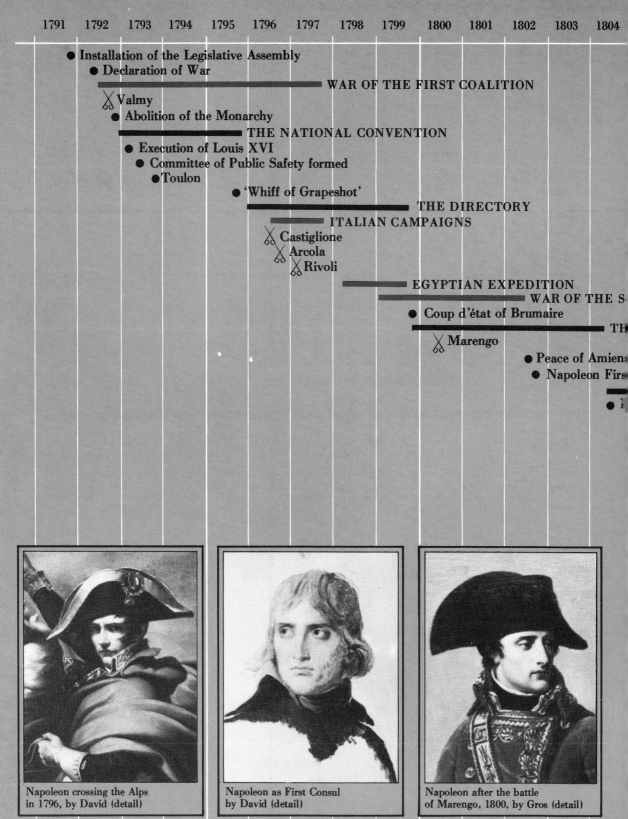

| 1791 | 1792 | 1793 | 1794 | 1795 | 1796 | 1797 | 1798 | 1799 | 1800 | 1801 | 1802 | 1803 | 1804 |

● Installation of the Legislative Assembly
   ● Declaration of War

━━━━━━━━━━━━━━━ WAR OF THE FIRST COALITION

⚔ Valmy
   ● Abolition of the Monarchy

━━━━━━━━━━━━━━━ THE NATIONAL CONVENTION

  ● Execution of Louis XVI
    ● Committee of Public Safety formed
     ●Toulon

      ● 'Whiff of Grapeshot'

━━━━━━━━ THE DIRECTORY

━━━━━ ITALIAN CAMPAIGNS

⚔ Castiglione
⚔ Arcola
⚔ Rivoli

━━━━━ EGYPTIAN EXPEDITION

━━━━━━ WAR OF THE S

● Coup d'état of Brumaire

      TH

⚔ Marengo

● Peace of Amien

● Napoleon Firs

● l

Napoleon crossing the Alps
in 1796, by David (detail)

Napoleon as First Consul
by David (detail)

Napoleon after the battle
of Marengo, 1800, by Gros (detail)

| 1791 | 1792 | 1793 | 1794 | 1795 | 1796 | 1797 | 1798 | 1799 | 1800 | 1801 | 1802 | 1803 | 1804 |